I Became Him

Kent Hermoso

I Became Him
Chesapeake, Virginia

Copyright 2022 Kent Hermoso
ISBN 979-8-9907464-0-4 (paperbook)
ISBN 979-8-9907464-1-1 (hardback)
ISBN 979-8-9907464-2-8 (epub)

No part of this book can be transmitted or reproduced in any form, including print, electronic, photocopying, scanning, mechanical or recording, without prior written permission from the author.

Kenny Hermoso takes no charge of the opinion that any of the third-party or unrelated individuals have. If the content inculcated in the publication becomes obsolete because of technical reasons or other changes, Kenny Hermoso or the publication house are entitled to no fault.

All the events stated in the book result from personal experience of the person(s) involved in formulating the book and bringing it into the form it is in today.

All the content used in this book belongs solely to the author.

This book provides information only up to the publishing date. Therefore, this book should be used as a guide and not as the ultimate source.

Dedicated to the beautiful
Kathleen Joan Roche

Contents

Prologue 9
Childhood Sneaking 11
The Filipino Alpha 13
My Trip to the Motherland 15
The Maternal Hook 18
Cavite City to US Navy 19
His Origin 20
Mother's Cuisine 23
The Japanese Occupation 25
The Massive Plane 27
Lola's Visit 29
The Mother's Strength 32
The Disturbing Truth 37
The Early Departure 39
The Unique Letter 41
Living Alone 43
Dad's Trip Back 45
Unspoken Lessons 46
The Japan Connection 48
The Toilet Repair 52
Imelda 53
Welcome to the Philippines 55
The Small Restaurant 60
Uncle's Residence 62
Grocery Shopping 68
The Lavish Dine In 70
Auntie Wen's Residence 71

House in Aniban	74
Uncle's Truck	77
Ending First Day	78
The Unique Fishing	80
The Family Tree	82
Family Mausoleum	83
Dad's Illness	86
Dad's Surgery	90
The First Movement	93
Natural Disasters	95
The Will to Survive	98
The Extended Relations	102
The Grandson Visit	104
Things We Left	107
The Worst Movie Night	109
Family Visit at Sangley Point	111
Extended Visit	113
Alfonso Trip	116
Fishpond Fun	125
Naval Base	133
Local Festivities	140
SM Mall	144
Sunday Mass	147
Aguinaldo Shrine	148
Waterpark	152
Games	154
Ternate	156
Corregidor Island	158
Birthday Party	161

Pacquiao Fight	164
Karaoke Night	167
Terrace Sleep Over	170
The Visit to The City	172
The Hotel	175
Mall of Asia	179
Casino	189
Persistent Filipina	191
Mesmerizing Bohol	194
Manila Bay	209
Meet-Up with Imelda	212
The Holiday Girl	221
First Encounter	224
The Reunion	226
Journey to Bicol	228
Bicol	230
My Fishing Credentials	234
Imelda's Family	237
Mayon Volcano	242
Back To Cavite	245
Became Him	251
United States	253
Reflection	255
About the Author	257

Prologue

Growing up in the United States was different for my siblings and me versus your ordinary American family, as our father raised us in his traditional Filipino culture. We were not privy to many things as children. We had a difficult time understanding this during our adolescence.

It wasn't until I visited his hometown that I realized why he raised us in such a manner. Dad rarely showed emotion and worked very hard to support his family as a typical Filipino male. I would come to understand him and never felt closer to him than I did when I walked in his footsteps in the Philippines.

I became him.

Childhood Sneaking

Dad rarely showed any emotion in front of us. When you look up the definition of "father," it says, "A man in relation to his natural child or children." It does not define how to, or why, or when.

It was a hot steamy summer night in Washington, DC, and the year was 1972. My two older brothers and I were on the prowl to catch night crawlers for the next day's fishing excursion on the filthy Potomac River. The mosquitoes were out in full force. It had to be about nine-thirty p.m., way past our curfew, but my older brothers had talked me into going, anyway. As we walked around the mud mounds at the infamous Devils Hill, we shined flashlights on the ground to see night crawlers all over the place. This was where everyone in the neighborhood went to catch night crawlers because there were so many. You had to be quick with your hands to catch them; when the light hit the worms, they would retreat to the hole.

Devils Hill got its name from being a steep hill that curves at the bottom; many of us kids, using our bicycles, tried to make that downhill turn but had crashed into the playground's fence at the very bottom. Living on-base housing, the cars had no problem as the speed limit was only fifteen miles per hour. We had lots of made-up names for places we explored as kids. I knew one place as the Land of the Giants. It was across the interstate from the housing complex. We would have to crawl through a concrete drainage pipe underneath the freeway to get there. Land of the Giants was actually an abandoned firefighter training facility. The only reason we could get in was because of the drainage pipe. Eventually, the authorities would find out that there had been trespassers on-site and barred the drainage entrance.

The military housing complex was constructed back in 1941, and they built each unit exactly the same: two bedrooms and three bedrooms all throughout the complex. There were 600 units built in all and served as housing for enlisted men and women and their families. The houses had been built in a circle facing a field in the middle, or what the military called "Greens." The Greens were all different sizes, with the roads being located in the back of the greens. All the houses had concrete porches with thick steel bars as rails. The shingles on the side of the houses were all painted white with green shutters. These were very sturdy fortresses that could withstand just about anything. They built the entire neighborhood as if it were a giant maze with no real direction. A small shopping center with a dry cleaner's, a pizza parlor, a laundry mat, and a grocery store were in the main area. Our church was right next to the store. Between Bolling AFB and the Naval Research lab, with the Washington sanitation plant right down the street, on a hot and humid night, you had the suffocating combination of air from the smell of both low tide and the plant.

As we filled our coffee can with worms, my eldest brother heard a familiar sound. He told us to turn off the flashlight and be quiet so he could hear better. We all stopped and waited to see if we could hear it again. It was Dad, using his traditional Filipino call. The call was a long "Ssssssssssssssstttttttt." My heart stopped because that only meant one thing. We would be in big trouble if he was out looking for us. I looked at my brothers and told them we were in deep shit now with Dad. Dad had been patrolling the neighborhood, looking for us in his car. We shined the light on over to the car, and he immediately saw us. He shouted, "Get your asses over here right now!" When we reached the car, a 1968 AMC Rambler station wagon with wood panels, we tried to open the doors, but they were locked. Dad rolled down the window and told us we were walking back. So, we had about a good fifteen to twenty-minute walk to think about how Dad would punish us. We could hear Dad curse us in his native tongue on the way home. One by one we blamed each other, with none of us taking the blame. We were doomed, and for sure, Dad would introduce the belt to us.

The Filipino Alpha

Our father was born and raised in the Philippines and had a powerful accent. Sometimes he would get so pissed with us we could not understand him because he would not finish the sentence but continue in English and Tagalog, mixing it up. He would also curse us in Tagalog. Later, we found this amusing, but we would never let our father know, never.

Dad was the typical strict Filipino father. Dad snatched all of our hearts very early and maintained his alpha role, even when we became teenagers. He laid down his law to us and made sure we all knew that there were consequences if we dared to break them. Dad was not the overpowering type of man, he was maybe 5'7", with a dark complexion and black hair and a signature Filipino mole. He had a very mean look also when he was mad.

Mom and our sisters were sitting on the porch as we reached the house. Our mother knew we were in big trouble. When the streetlights came on, that was our signal to get home. We all knew of this rule and knew that the night crawlers only came out at night. My eldest brother tried to explain, but Mom did not have it. It was now around ten pm. Mom's last words to us were, "I can't help you."

Of course, there was protocol when we all had to get our asses whipped simultaneously. First the eldest, then the second, and last, my turn. I was the youngest brother of three, and the middle child of five. I had two younger sisters. So, if Dad were not already primed, he would be in full swing by the time he got to me. I always thought that was not fair. Dad would give each of us three good lashes with his belt, and then it was off to bed for us.

As we lay there in our beds, we talked about the fishing trip to the river in the morning. We could still go, as the subject never came up during our ass whipping. While we tried to fall asleep, we would laugh out loud at some joke, and we could hear dad with his Filipino call again, meaning for us to be quiet. Still, nobody took the blame.

My Trip to the Motherland

The night before my flight to the Philippines was a series of checks, ensuring I had everything I needed to survive for two weeks away from home. I had probably over-packed and from the weight and size of my luggage, I could probably survive an entire month. I brought medicines I was told were unavailable in the Philippines. I also had picked up some hometown souvenirs or pasalubong for the family members and wanted to make sure that I had packed them.

Since everyone knew I was going to the Philippines, I had so many instructions on what not to do, what not to wear, and what not to eat or drink. I was even being told not to carry any money in my wallet but to carry it in a money clip in my front pocket in case I get robbed. If I were to get robbed, they would check all my pockets if they found no money in my wallet. Come on now, a foreigner with no money? I was told a few myths from older Filipinos, do not stare in the eyes or they could cast a spell on you, or do not hold their hand so long because you could catch something. I started thinking to myself, am I going to be meeting some kind of witch doctors there? I was also taught how to greet my elders. In the states, it was always a handshake or a kiss on the cheek, but in the Philippines, it was called a bless, where you would take the hand of the elder and bring to your forehead as you bowed to them. They did this out of respect and was very traditional.

Since it was still cold here in the states and such a long flight, I dressed for comfort, not style. I wore some roomy sweatpants and a hoody to match. I took the early flight out of Norfolk, thinking I would be well-rested and arrive in Detroit, my connection, with plenty of time to go from one terminal to the next. There was so much excitement that I did not sleep the night before. As I waited for my flight, I could not help but notice an older Filipino couple sitting there waiting for the flight as I was. I assumed they would be flying to the Philippines but did not have the nerve to ask. I became heavy-hearted as I remembered how my late parents would interact. Despite being split up for months on end because of the military, they were always showing their affection to each other. I kept thinking, do not become so emotional on this trip. It will be a long trip, and I have too much to cover while I am there. My mission was to see where my father had grown up and learn about his culture and why he raised us the way he did. I wanted to walk, breathe, and live where he once did.

Being in sales, I traveled all over the country and found it easier to get the TSA precheck to bypass the long lines going through security. Probably one of the smartest investments I have ever made. As a frequent flyer, I could get on board a lot faster than your regular passengers.

The gate agent scanned my ticket and said, "Congratulations, you have been upgraded to first-class."

I thought, This is going to be a great trip. I hope I can get an upgrade on the long flight from Detroit to Japan. I took my upgrade and sat in the first seat on the plane with no leg space. No one wanted to sit here. That's why I ended up with the upgrade.

The flight attendant immediately approached me and asked if I would like a drink. I said coffee would be great, but I wouldn't get that until the plane had reached its flying altitude.

As the rest of the passengers continued to board the plane, I wondered why I was closer to my father than my mother? Oddly, I felt this way because growing up as a kid, my father was the biggest pain in my ass. I could not do anything right in his eyes, but I was always called upon when he needed something done. My mother would always take up for me when she thought I was mistreated if she felt it was not deserved. There was no problem rearing your children the way you thought best as a parent back in my younger days. If we grew up in the '90s, my dad would be in jail for beating us. I laugh about it now because it is amusing that he got away with this back then. I always remembered my dad coming home from work late at night, around 11:00 p.m., and waking us up if we had been bad during the day. My mother would undoubtedly give him a report. We had to stand there next to him while he ate his dinner, waiting for our punishment. The anticipation was just as bad.

When he finally finished, he drilled us as to why we had done something wrong; we always had the same answer, "I don't know." He would then rake his forefinger across our temple. That was the worst. I would have rather taken a punch because my father had these short, fat fingers and big biceps, so it was like a board raking across your temple. It used to leave welts for a few hours. Years later, when we were grown, me and my brothers would joke about those types of incidents. I laughed out loud when I realized the passengers were still boarding. I quickly turned to stare out of the window.

I had asked the flight attendant for some extra cookies because of my long flight coming up. She told me that once she served first class, I could take all I wanted that was leftover. Those Biscoff cookies are excellent with the coffee they serve. I probably grabbed about ten packs of those cookies and stuffed them in my bag.

The Maternal Hook

My mother died at the early age of fifty-seven because of heart conditions. I mentioned earlier that I was not as close to her as to my father for some crazy reason. I remember my mother telling me at a young age that I would always be okay because of my hard work ethic. As a kid of only ten years, I always cut some neighbor's grass or raking leaves to make money. I even had my paper route. Having a paper route was cool because nobody bothered you as it was all done very early in the morning. When I got paid, I would usually buy groceries for the family or what I liked we were out of. This is the thing my mother was most proud of me for. It was not much, maybe a loaf of bread or two and milk, but enough for Mom to notice that I was doing good.

My studies were never on point, so I fell off as the favorite. I found that my brothers and sisters were always a lot smarter in books than I ever was. I was certainly the family's black sheep; being the middle child, I would fit the part. Always in trouble in school, getting into fights, talking back to teachers etc. My lack of interest was the biggest reason. When I started to play sports, I had to motivate myself to do the work. I was not a stupid kid or anything like that, just lazy. Throughout my schooling, I was never the one to brag about when it came to your child's success. When I was graduating high school, I had to call my twelfth grade English teacher the morning of graduation to see if I had passed.

Cavite City to US Navy

My father was in the US Navy, he was gone frequently, so my mother became the center of our lives. Dad joined the Navy from his hometown province of Cavite, Sangley Point in Cavite City. He enlisted at the ripe age of eighteen. Back in those days, because of an agreement between the US and Philippine governments, only 1000 Filipinos could be recruited into the US Navy per year. They recruited the Filipinos as stewards. So, it was a big deal for a Filipino if you could be one of the lucky recruits. That meant a steady job, benefits, and the opportunity to come to America.

Back in the early 1950s, the economy in the Philippines was not so stable, so there were not a whole lot of jobs to be had. Being a third-world country, any type of job outside of the province was a great deal to the families of the recruits. Sangley Point was used early as a US Naval operation base, mainly for seaplanes. They also used it during the Vietnam War for Naval patrol squadrons forward deployed. It would later be turned over to the Philippine government and used by the Navy and Air Force.

As we took off, I tried to think back. The only time I met Uncle Ren was at my father's seventieth surprise birthday party. That was the very first time I had met him. Although we had some family chat rooms via Yahoo back in the day, I never got to know him. Most of the chats were in their native tongue, so following was complicated. Dad never took the time to teach us Tagalog, so we only knew the bad words he would use when we were in trouble. He used them so frequently.

His Origin

Uncle Ren and I spoke very little as it had been a long time since Dad had seen his brothers. It was probably ten years since the last time they were all together in the Philippines. Uncle Ren had flown in from the Philippines just for this occasion. Uncle Ren was one of eight siblings of my father. Both he and one of my aunts never had the desire to leave the Philippines for the states. I will explain that later. Dad asked me to drive for him while everyone was in town. I had spent an entire weekend driving my father and his brothers around town. From the hotel to the store, church, and back to the hotel. My father had many siblings, a typical Filipino family. He was the eldest of all, with two dying early. As I found out, the culture of my father's race was a hell of a lot different from the US. The oldest of all the siblings was treated with respect, and all other siblings looked up at him.

Dad's party guests were mainly family friends, a few of his workmates and some of his bowling buddies. We had hidden his brothers in the backroom and waited for his arrival. This was a surprise birthday party my siblings and I had put together for his seventieth birthday. As he walked through the doors, all the guests had yelled surprise and caught him off guard. I thought he would lose it, but he did not. After all the warm birthday wishes were given, the DJ announced we will eat dinner soon and everyone should take their seats.

As everyone took their seats, the DJ announced a special surprise for Dad that had choked up all the guests. His brothers were escorted by all his children to a special table up front and seated. We had saved Uncle Ren for last as he traveled the furthest. When Dad finally realized that all his brothers were in attendance, he became emotionally overwhelmed. Everyone comforted him until he was okay to hold a conversation. The brothers, five in all, had traveled from New York, California, and the Philippines. I spent little time talking with them as it had been many years that all the brothers were together, so I thought it would be more appropriate to give him his space until he needed me. I think the uncle that we were closest to was the youngest, Uncle Gus. We used to visit him in New York because he was the closest in proximity. As for my father's other siblings, I would visit them on the west coast when my work would take me there. Out of all my siblings, I was able to see my uncles and aunties more because of my travels, so I was a little closer to them than they were.

After the party, Dad asked me to hang out with them just as a driver and to fetch whatever they needed. It was like they were all back home in the Philippines; it is very common to have the youngest boy be the gopher for the group. We pulled up to the hotel and as they all got out of the car; I asked what room they were going to because I would stay outside and smoke first. They gave me the room number and proceeded into the elevator. It was not two minutes before they all came back to the car laughing. I asked what had happened, and they said they were at the wrong hotel. They went to the room and realized the key card was not working. So, they went to the front desk, where the night attendant asked them for some ID. The attendant then said that they were not registered guests at this hotel. He would find out they were staying in another hotel with the same name a few blocks down. The guests in the room, which they thought was theirs, must have been scared shitless.

I had to laugh at the situation. We arrived at the correct hotel a few minutes later, and they would all still be laughing about it. That is the role I took for their entire visit. As they sat all together and conversed, I watched to see if they would summon me for drinks, food, or cigarettes. I turned on the TV and waited; they would speak in Tagalog after all, and I did not understand the language. I knew Dad was pleased to have them all together; the last time he saw most of them was at my mother's funeral. That was ten years ago, and not all the siblings attended. Because it was so sudden, Uncle Ren and Auntie Wen could not get Visa's quickly enough to travel to the states from the Philippines.

I had never been on a flight this long, other than flying to England, but that was only six hours. This was a total of twenty hours. It will originate in Virginia, a two-hour flight to Detroit, then a thirteen-hour flight to Japan, and the last leg was a five-hour flight into Manila. Including the layovers, the total trip would take twenty-four hours. Before the trip, I contacted Uncle Ren to let him know I was coming there and asked if he could pick me up at the airport. He said do not worry; he will be there. Uncle Ren had told me when we first met that I could stay at his place if I ever visited the Philippines. So, I have kept in contact with him since our meeting years ago.

My Detroit flight landed about fifteen minutes early, so I went to grab something to eat at McDonald's, right across from my connecting gate to Japan. I grabbed a coffee and a breakfast sandwich and proceeded to my gate. I thought it would be a long two weeks before I could have authentic American food.

Mother's Cuisine

I always loved to eat Filipino foods and could not wait to taste them in the motherland. Over the years, my father had taught my mother how to cook Filipino food, and she became very good at it. My favorite is Pork Adobo, and I used to love it when mom would prepare this for dinner. I did not care about a handful of dishes, and when Mom would cook those dishes, you either did not eat dinner that night or you went to a friend's house to eat. Those dishes usually included fish. I grew up in a household where we cooked pretty much all the food inside the home. When my dad had his friends over for dinner, he would cook an enormous pot of rice and a couple of fish plates. He would fry the entire fish, including the head, and serve it to his friends. They would sit around the table with no utensils, just their hands. They would grab a piece of fish, dip it into a sauce that dad had mixed, mix it with rice, and down the hatch. They would eat that all night as they sat around the table. The only other food that were brought around were bananas and pork rinds. The cooked fish smell would linger in the house for days, no matter how much mom tried to get rid of it. It used to make me sick to continue to smell it. As I grew older, I started disliking fish more and more, to the point if something smelled fishy, it would make me sick to my stomach.

As I sat at the gate, eating my last American breakfast sandwich, I overheard many of the passengers speaking in the native tongue of Tagalog. In the Philippines, just about every province speaks its own dialect. It is hard to imagine that they can all still communicate, no matter which region they are from. I had studied a little about the Philippines so that when I arrived, I was not totally ignorant of their culture. It surprised me to find out that there are approximately 187 dialects in the Philippines, with Tagalog being the national language; Dad did not speak about the history of his home country a whole lot. I learned that there are three major regions of the Philippines: Luzon, the northern part, Visayas, the central part, and Mindanao, the southern part.

Approximately 7600 islands make up the 120,000 square miles, all in an archipelago in the Pacific Ocean, where one island is more beautiful than the next.

I remember when Dad would tell us a few stories of how he grew up in the Philippines. Even as a kid, I always took an interest in his stories. I would later find out why my father was the way he was as a father in life. The most interesting story he told was the Japanese invasion of the Philippines. Japan invaded the Philippines on December 8th, 1941, only a few hours after the Pearl Harbor attack, and occupied the Philippines until September 2nd, 1945, when Japan finally surrendered to the United States. My father was only six years old at that time of the invasion but had been the eldest male in the family. Being the eldest, my Lolo (Grandfather) hid him rather than have the Japanese enslave him. Many children were used to working in the rice and sugar fields for the Imperial Army. They also used many male children as servants, while the female children as young as ten were raped and sent to camps for the Japanese soldiers. As disgusting as it was, I would later hear that there are many more horrific things the Japanese did to the Filipinos and the American forces that had been captured. We have all heard about the Bataan Death March. I just wanted to lay some background.

The Japanese Occupation

My *Lolo*, the grandfather in Tagalog, had taken my father to a town called Alfonso, a small province in the mountains of Cavite where the family owned some farmland. I would soon discover that the farmland is an actual jungle these days. My father spoke of surviving on fresh fruits and whatever he could catch as far as meat. Small lizards and monkeys were in abundance, so if he could catch one, that would make for a tasty meal. Dad made it home inside bamboo clumps, approximately two kilometers from the main road. One story that I remember from this era was when Dad was walking in the jungle and just happened to look up into the sky and see paratroopers from the 11th Airborne Division. Not knowing what they were, it literally scared the shit out of him. He took a shit in his pants as he was running away. Later that evening, his father had explained to him that the flying men in the sky were the Americans landing on Corregidor Island.

My father told me another story about my Lolo being a guerilla fighter for the Province of Cavite, better known as the Adevoso's Hunters. The guerillas got that name from a cadet that did not want to give up his country. As an ROTC cadet himself, Terry Adevoso, took over as the leader once the Japanese caught the officers. Terry continued to recruit cadets as the occupation grew longer and created havoc for the Japanese soldiers. The "Adevoso" became a legend in Philippine history. Dad mentioned Japanese soldiers set up checkpoints in certain areas at the beginning of the invasion. One evening Dad was sent to the grocery store to pick up some stocks for the family. As Dad came upon the checkpoint, the Japanese soldiers had taken what little pesos he had and beat him. When dad returned home, Lolo asked where the stocks (groceries) were. Dad told them what had happened at the checkpoint and later that evening, the Hunters went into action. Without telling us what had happened to those two unfortunate soldiers at the checkpoint, Lolo had told my father he would never have to worry about those soldiers again. This caused significant problems in the future as the Japanese beat and tortured Filipinos trying to find out what had happened, another reason my father went into hiding.

The Massive Plane

After I finished my breakfast sandwich, I took a quick stroll to the duty-free store and thought I would pick up some little extra gifts for the family. I bought some expensive chocolates that were probably half the cost outside the airport. I also picked up a carton of smokes. Being a smoker, I was dreading the long flight. I would connect in Tokyo the next day. I was trying to imagine how I would feel traveling for twenty-four hours, leaving on a Friday morning and arriving on a Saturday night. It would be like I just lost a whole day of news and events.

While waiting to board, I peeked at the plane that we would fly on. It was a massive sucker with a two-story first class, and the Pilots were also located upstairs. I think it was a Boeing 777. I have never seen or flown on a plane that large before. I wondered, how in the hell is this big thing going to take off. They called them Jumbo jets or wide bodies because of the amount and size of cargo they could handle. I booked a seat all the way in the back, where there were only two seats in the row, and at the time, no one had booked the other seat. I wanted to have some privacy and be close to the bathrooms for this 13.5-hour flight. This big sucker could hold up to almost 400 passengers. As we boarded, I walked through the first-class cabin and thought, this must be nice. The price tag was about $4000 more dollars than I was willing to spend.

I took my seat and waited to see if the seat next to me was still open. After thirty minutes, I was a happy camper. It remained empty. I got situated and even pulled my backpack down from the overhead since the seat would be empty. This flight would include two full meals along with a snack in between. As the flight attendants were preparing the cabin for takeoff, I noticed that the announcements were not only in English but also in Tagalog and Japanese. So, it took three times as long for them to get through the safety announcements. I took the seat next to the window and watched as the baggage handlers loaded massive crates into the plane.

Lola's Visit

I remember asking Dad to take a trip with me to the Philippines, but he said he could not make that long trip again. By that time, Dad was pushing seventy-four years of age. I even offered to pay. I wished we could have made a trip back together; that would be special. My father left the Philippines back in the late fifties and would not return until our grandmother was sick, some thirty years later. Since then, I think he went back three more times, one to see his mother buried, to see his father buried, and one more time after my mother died. I know the flights were very expensive, so when Dad went back home, he always went by himself. When our grandmother passed, my siblings and I all chipped in for his flight and expenses. He did not even have to ask for it. My mother was very grateful that this had happened. The first time I met my *Lola* was when she visited us from the Philippines. It had been approximately twenty-five years since my dad had seen his mother. Before her visit, Dad had given all his children instructions on what to do when she arrived. The main thing he told us to do was that if she cooked something, no matter what, we had to eat it, or she would get insulted.

The days before her arrival were all about preparation. Dad even took me with him to an Asian grocery store to pick up some essentials that we never had at the house. His children made sure the house was spotless and that the yard had been in tip-top shape. I figured Dad wanted to let his mother know that things were fine here in Virginia. I can still picture her walking down the airport terminal all by herself. A small old lady stood maybe 4'9" and probably less than 100 lbs. She was very dark-skinned, with graying hair. I could never forget this moment because this was the only time I had seen my father crying. We all stayed back while he approached her at the gate entrance. She had started to cry as soon as she realized it was him. At that point, we were all crying. It was a very emotional moment. They hugged what seemed like an hour before he turned and waved us to come. He was speaking to her in Tagalog, which I thought was very special. We gathered her luggage and made our way back to the car. Dad was trying to explain the last twenty-five years to Lola on the way back home. We could not understand them, but they both seemed thrilled. We just sat and watched them reunite. It was good to see Dad in such good spirits. That night we gave dad and Lola their space as they had a lot to catch up on. Dad had us construct a makeshift bedroom in our living room because he did not want our Lola to climb the stairs every day. The very next morning, Lola was already cooking breakfast for everyone. She made fried rice, sunny side-up eggs, and *longanisa*, a Filipino sausage that Dad and I had picked up at the Asian grocery store. This was a typical Filipino breakfast. Once Lola made this dish called *Dinuguan*, it is a stew of pork offal simmered in pigs' blood. Dad didn't make this dish, but I heard about it. I was the only one who came to lunch that afternoon because my siblings said they had something to do, right? I sat at the table with an enormous glass of water and started eating the *Dinuguan* and washing it down with water. I was so happy that I finished my plate so fast. My Lola saw this and put another portion on my plate. I thought I would die, but the look on her face made it all worth it. She really thought I was enjoying this. Lola did not sit still for a minute, and Dad explained she was keeping herself busy so she would not miss home. After her visit here in Virginia, Lola would spend another month in California with the rest of Dad's siblings. One day Lola cut down this huge ten-foot bush next to the window because she said she could not see out of it. She was always so full of energy when she woke up. If Lola started doing the dishes, Dad would say let her finish and not bother her. I can remember Lola calling me to the door and showing me a duck that had landed out front. She spoke very little English, so it was hard for me to understand. When I gave her the universal, I do not know sign; she went into the kitchen and pulled out one of Dad's large machetes and pointed to me than the duck.

    That's when I realized what Lola wanted me to do. She wanted me to kill the duck and bring it to her to cook for dinner. I held in my laughter so hard that I farted right in front of her. She looked at me like I was crazy. I tried to explain to her we could not kill the duck for dinner. I gave her the Filipino hand signal for no, which was holding up your open hand

and turning it from right to left. We would all crack up when I told Mom and Dad the story later that evening.

As our plane was pushed back from the gate, the flight attendant offered headphones, so I grabbed them. I would add them to my collection of goodies from the airline. I had slippers, blindfolds, a blanket, and a pillow. Make that two sets of everything, since no one was sitting next to me. I took my shoes off and put the slippers on. I had placed my backpack under the seat next to me, so I had leg room. I realized I had a tv as well. So, I figured out how to plug the earphones in and turned on the tv and started browsing for movies. I could feel our massive plane move forward slowly. After we taxied to the runway, I felt the plane getting faster and louder. I looked out of the window to see our progress down the runway. It was one of the smoothest takeoffs I had ever been involved in. The giant airplane was airborne. As I looked out of the window, I could see the landscape getting smaller and smaller. The sun started blaring in each window as we pierced through the clouds. Every window-seated passenger almost simultaneously pulled the shades down. I studied the flight path of our route and noticed that we would fly north through Canada, the Northwest Territories thru Alaska, and across the Pacific Ocean to Japan. We would fly over 6500 miles at a speed of 590 mph. It also showed our arrival time, and I cringed as I looked at it.

Being a big *Lord of the Rings* fan, I watched the *Fellowship of the Ring*. I knew it was a long movie, so I would not have to do anything for three hours. I pulled out a pack of the cookies that I received on my first flight along with bottled water and started to watch the movie. About a half-hour into the movie, the flight attendants started handing out hot towels. I gladly took one and wiped my face and hands. That meant that the first meal would soon be served. I had asked for a coffee and water. About a half-hour later, the first meal was served. I chose the chicken. Since the seat next to me had been open, I had plenty of room for the food tray and drinks. I must have been hungry because I ate everything! After the food was served, the second wave of drinks came by and I asked for another coffee. If you are wondering, coffee does not affect me like other people. I can drink it all day and still be able to sleep. According to my watch, it was probably about five in the late afternoon.

The Mother's Strength

I wondered how I would react to see my father's sister since we never met. I have only seen her in pictures and knew little about her, much about any of the family there. I tried to remember any of Dad's stories, if it included his sisters, but there weren't any, other than my sisters being named after his sisters.

When we were younger, we wrote letters to our cousins, but that was forty-five years ago. It took about a month to mail a letter to the Philippines back in those days. But only a few cousins would write back; the others were not even born yet. Dad came from a typical Filipino family, with six brothers and three sisters. A brother and a sister would perish at a very young age for reasons I did not know. My dad was the eldest out of all his siblings, so they would all look up to him growing up. When Dad joined the US Navy, he had left them at a very young age. He arrived in the states in the late 50s, where he then met my mother. Mom was a few years younger than Dad. Going into the Navy, Dad was an E1, and in those days' Filipinos were used as stewards because of their cleanliness, congeniality and ability to cook amazing dishes. Dad hit it off right away with some admirals, so they stationed him in Bethesda, MD. He would often cook meals for the admiral's parties and then tend bar afterward. Mom was working in my grandmother's restaurant in Washington, DC. It was a small diner that seated maybe 50 customers. As the story goes, it was love at first sight. Grandma, or Lola, as we would call her, introduced them back in 1959. They were married a year later and the following year had their first child, my eldest brother. A year later, they would have their second son, and another year later, on their anniversary, they had me. After three sons, Mom and Dad wanted a girl. Dad was eventually transferred to San Diego aboard one of the ships and would be deployed for six months. We all followed Dad there. Mom had taken us across the country on a train. I could not remember that ride, but as it goes, my mother had three young boys, two still in diapers and the eldest being just four years of age, and to our surprise, one on the way. I cannot even imagine how she made it across the country, but Mom was a very strong-willed woman. Mom would tell the story later about how a young lady on the train had helped her throughout the trip. She was indeed an angel in my mother's eyes. While Dad was deployed, Mom gave birth to their first daughter. So, we were now four siblings, all born within five years. It did not end there; we had another sister born when Dad received orders back to Bethesda. Now there were five of us born within six years of each other. My sister, born in San Diego, quickly became my dad's favorite because she was the first girl, but the only child not born in Bethesda Naval Hospital. As we all grew older, it became very apparent that there was not anything this girl could do wrong and if she did, we all got blamed for it.

So, Dad had five kids in six years and was still an E1, so as you can imagine, we were a lower-class family trying to make ends meet early on. We were all very close growing up, and Mom made sure that we were brought up in the Catholic church. None of us were bad kids. I was probably the only child that got into trouble. I was getting my ass beat every other day for doing stupid shit. Although I did not think it was stupid.

Being a low-income family, we wasted little, so if you spilled a full glass of milk by accident, that was considered a waste. I can remember eating oatmeal for breakfast, lunch, and dinner for weeks. Dad always took a second job at some officers' club on the base when he was in town. Mom did the best she could with what she had. She did not work because we were still very young, and she had her hands full. Amazingly, we never did without; Mom had always found a way. We all had chores growing up as early as five years old, and it changed every week. This is the Filipino culture dad had instilled in us at a very young age. We had the following chores assigned to us weekly: dishes, dusting, vacuuming, setting and clearing the table, trash detail, and folding laundry. If you did not do your part, you would have an ass whipping coming to you when Dad got home, so there was never that issue in our household. LOL. I was fond of doing yard work out of the five of us, maybe because I could spend time outside. I would always be the one to cut grass and pick up dog shit and trash in our yard. Sometimes Mom would ask me to plant flowers and I always had helped dad in the vegetable garden.

Both Mom and Dad engrained this work ethic in us early.

We lived on base housing pretty much all our lives, so you can say that we had this military upbringing crossed with a splash of Filipino culture. So funny how I used to think it was weird to take our shoes off at the door. Whenever we went somewhere, we did this. What I thought was even more weird is that Dad had a pair of slippers for the outside and one for the inside. Now that I think about it, I could remember watching him take his slippers off on the porch and grab his inside slippers, something I never understood and was afraid to ask.

We were all close growing up because we always lived in a three-bedroom house, one room for all three boys and one room for the girls and one mom and dad's room. We would eat some of the best Filipino dishes that Dad had taught Mom how to prepare. Mom also made a very delicious spaghetti as well. Mom also made this ground beef with gravy dish that we all loved. When we used to go to the grocery store or commissary as we would know it on base, we always used to fill up two carts. We would never ask for anything special or treats because we knew not to ask for anything out of the norm.

Those two carts were for about two and a half weeks' worth of groceries. Mom even used to make a menu so we could see what was for dinner. And if you did not like what we were having, you had a choice: eat it or do not. If you did not eat dinner, you could not eat a snack later, and my mom was a great policer for this because if she caught you eating a snack, you got your ass whipped.

I can remember when Dad would get the most out of everything. He wasted nothing. He would even find old toothpaste tubes in the trash and say, "There is still some in there; why you are throwing them away?" He showed us how to get all the toothpaste out; he would hold the tube and take a hard edge of something and squeeze it from the bottom of the tube to the top and tell us not to throw this away and use the next time we brushed our teeth. Dad would save all the insides and whatever my mother would try to discard and make a dish out of later, even parts of chicken that mom cooked for dinner. I used to think this was gross, but as I would learn later, this was how he grew up. We could never leave a drink or food on the table after we thought we were finished; Dad would go insane and make us finish it. Since he taught all of us this at an early age, we grew up not wasting anything. Dad was a big fan of eating leftovers. Whatever was not finished at dinner would be turned into the next morning's breakfast. Dad would always fix things that broke down and never throw them away. I remember telling Dad that I needed new shoes because the soles had split from the shoe; low and behold, he said that he could fix it. Later that night, he found some epoxy and glued the sole back on; this would be a long-standing joke for our family for years. The shoes looked like they were rabid and foaming at the mouth. So, I had to wear these shoes to school. He should have just used duct tape; it would have had the same results. My brothers gave me a lot of shit back then when this happened.

I would always get ridiculed at school by my classmates for not wearing brand-name clothes or shoes, but we were not raised that way, so it did not bother me as much. Mom and Dad would even keep all the condiment packets from fast-food restaurants, sugar, ketchup, and salt; you name it; he kept it. He would also keep extra napkins, so when you set the table, the napkins were always from different fast-food restaurants. The weirdest thing that I thought my parents did in the kitchen was to keep a milk carton by the sink and dump food particles, oils, fish bones, etc. Instead of throwing it in the trash. He said it would make the garbage can smell, and I would say well, I can smell it here when I do the dishes. Dad did not want to waste the whole garbage bag, so this was his method. He would give me this dirty look, and I never questioned it again. We also never took a shower longer than five minutes, or there would be a knock on the door telling us to hurry. We were always in and out of the bathroom. I had fallen asleep after our first meal, and when I woke, I felt like I wanted to brush my teeth, but everything was in my checked luggage, so I took a piece of gum, hoping the gum would clean my teeth. The plane was pitch dark, and I looked at my watch. The time was now around ten p.m.

"Shit, this is not even halfway through yet." I was curious to see outside, so I lifted the window shade and looked outside. All I could see for miles was tundra. I checked the map on the trip guide, and we were over the Northwest territories now and it was something I had never seen before. As soon as I opened the shade, I noticed I had really lit up my portion of the cabin, so I did not keep it open long. Everyone glanced over at me and probably thought about what I was doing. I had finished the movie and was trying to figure out what I wanted to watch next. There were a lot of choices, but me being a homebody, I had watched pretty much all of them. I had opened my planner to recall the last days of my father's life so that I could explain to his brothers and sisters what had transpired from the time he went into the hospital until he passed. It was weird how I never took notes but kept a running diary during that time.

The Disturbing Truth

I had mentioned that my mother died at a young age. She was only fifty-seven years of age and died one evening alone at the dinner table.

My mother had something terrible happen to her while in San Diego. When Dad had deployed, my mother was attacked in our home. I was almost two years old, and my baby sister was just a couple of months. A man had snuck into our house one evening. The attacker had attempted to strangle my mother as I lay in the bed beside her with my sister in her crib. My eldest brother had taken my other brother into a closet in the kitchen and hid while all of this was going on.

As I remember very little about this tragedy, the story goes this attacker told my mother that he would kill both my sister and me if she made a sound. The attacker probably thought he had killed my mother because he eventually left.

When the attacker left the house, my eldest brother ran to the neighbor's house. Soon the police arrived, and things calmed down. This scarred our mother for the rest of her life. After hearing of the incident, the Navy had flown Dad back home. This story made headline news in San Diego as, at the same time, a serial killer was running wild in California. The fact that the attacker was never found gave my mother a sense of insecurity that would haunt her for years to come. Mom had high anxiety and was taking medication for this. Mom would always sit in the back rows that were closet to the exits whenever there was an event. She would not like to attend crowded events. We never really knew of this until we came of age to understand. Mom explained the ordeal to us and even had the newspaper article. That she would share with us. I had a tough problem accepting this. I was heartbroken when my mother told us of this; I was in rage and wanted to find this guy that really changed the course of my mother's life. If I ever found him, he would die a prolonged death, I promise this. We would look and think of Mom from a whole new perspective now. My brothers and I swore to protect Mom. Mom was the glue to our family for all these years and had this burden on her shoulders.

The Early Departure

Mom passed shortly after dad had retired. It was supposed to be their time now.

Mom had sacrificed her entire life to rear all of us. Even though we were poor, Mom made sure we had everything we needed, and we never went without. We grew up a lot differently than most kids. We grew up not having the things we wanted, but we always had the things we needed. A good example was when mom went shopping, we all waited in the car with my dad. We never went into a store and asked if we could have certain things. Mom did her best to involve us in extra-curricular activities, such as baseball, cub scouts, and dance class for the girls. She managed the entire family and did a great job. I think back now to when we were young and imagined how Mom raised us all by herself. Five kids, all a year apart, with Dad being deployed most of our childhood. When there were disagreements between my brothers and me, we would handle the old fashion way with bare knuckles. I would usually get pounded by them, as I was the smallest growing up.

My sisters were hands off because we already knew that Dad would take us apart if he heard we touched them. So, they got away with a lot of shit growing up. Mom had become an excellent cook, and we all looked forward to her putting the weekly menu together. Of course, we all tried to ask her to make our favorites all the time, but mom knew it would come down to what dad wanted for dinner when he was home. On our birthdays, Mom would cook what we wanted and would also bake our favorite cake. We all looked forward to this. Even though it was your birthday, you still had to do your chores; there was no getting out of that. Mom would always make the best of what she had during Christmas time. As we grew older, the significance of a gift became less and less important, and it would be together that was most enjoyable.

When I was in middle school, I remember one of my classmates telling me what he got for Christmas. He then asked what I got, and I told him that I was able to spend the holidays with my family and Dad was home, so it was a very Merry Christmas. This was the mentality that my siblings and I had grown up with. Mom did a fantastic job making us realize what we had and how to be thankful for all of that. On the other hand, Dad will always lecture us on, if we cannot wear it or eat it, we do not need it. Mom sacrificed her life so that we could live ours. I would come to realize this as we grew older. We would all be Momma's boys and crush anyone who disrespected her. As we got older, Mom would be a superb listener and always made things seem like they were ok. Even if you felt like your world was crumbling around you, Mom made things normal. I miss my mom; I miss our conversations.

Anyway, back to my mother's passing. Mom had recently taken a new medication prescribed by her doctor. She was at the doctor's office on a Wednesday morning and died on the following Friday morning. Of course, all of us kids wanted an explanation and maybe even an investigation, but Dad wanted Mom to rest in peace and not disturb her any longer. Dad was crushed and wanted to get through this as quickly as possible. All of us wanted an autopsy to see if it was, in fact, the medication prescribed that did Mom in.

Dad had found Mom around five a.m., slumped over the dinner table. Underneath her was the new medication packet. Mom went down the checklist and marked off all the symptoms that would cause a heart attack. When we looked at the packet, the next box to mark was to call the emergency number right away. Mom never made it.

Dad was having no part in an investigation of any sort. We held the funeral, and it was an unfortunate moment for all of us. We lost the rock that had kept us together for so many years. For as long as I can remember, Mom had been the glue to our family. She had been dearly missed.

The Unique Letter

As Dad was going through moms' things one night, he came across letters addressed to each of us. He called a family dinner so that we all could be there together to read our letters. Mom had written these letters a while back. Obviously, she wanted to tell us how proud she was and offer some words of encouragement for our future. We all met at Dad's apartment and had dinner, then dad passed out the letters to each one of us. He did not read them up to this point. At first, we agreed to start with the eldest and let them read the letters aloud. But as we received the letters, we took sneak peeks to see what was mentioned. As we got into the letters, we found they were very personal and was written for our eyes only. We then decided not to read them aloud. Mom was an excellent writer and had even taken a writing class. Mom would eventually write many short stories and send them to a handful of publishers, but nothing ever became of them. She even kept a file of all the rejection letters; I would guess, to keep her motivated.

Mom's letter to me was special, I am sure, to all of my siblings. She mentioned she knew I would succeed in life no matter how things turned out, because she said I was a hustler. She mentioned I cried a little as a baby, was not a needy child, and always did things independently. Found ways to entertain myself, as she would say. She said I reminded her most of Dad because of my simplicity in life and my work ethic. She could see this in me at a young age. Despite being treated like the black sheep of the family, both Mom and dad knew they could count on me if something needed to be fixed or moved.

As we all got further into our letters, we could see each other's eyes tear up. I tried to finish moms' letter but did not want to get so emotional if front of everyone. I did not want any of my siblings to read my letter. I tried to think back many years and reminisce about what Mom explained in the letter. No matter where I was, they would call me to do something, regardless of my brothers. I would think to myself; my brother is right there; why they do not make him do it? I never understood that for the longest time. As I was thinking back, a memory came across that was hilarious, and I laughed out loud, thinking about it. My second eldest brother would ask to borrow money from Mom, five dollars, I believe. Mom had said no to him. A few minutes later, he came back downstairs dressed up like Abraham Lincoln and asked again for the five dollars.

Mom busted out laughing as we all did but still held her ground. Why I thought of that at that moment, I have no idea. I wanted to think it was because I remember the whole family enjoying the skit that my brother had made up to get the five dollars. Mom would laugh for hours. Later that night, when I got home after receiving the letter from Dad, I would cry like a baby. I would miss my mother dearly.

Living Alone

My siblings all agreed to spend as much time with dad as we could. After the first few months, I think dad was getting tired of us bothering him. He told us we did not have to keep checking on him and that he was alright. Dad adjusted to being alone. He increased his time at the bowling alley from once a week to three times a week. Dad was a pretty good bowler and won a few tournaments with his friends. As time went by, we all realized that he was going to be fine, and we could stop intruding into his life. Dad and I even had a once-a-month lunch planned at his favorite Filipino restaurant. I liked it as well, and it was two minutes down the street from my office.

We met there, and I would always treat Dad. After a while, Dad started adding things to lunch. The restaurant had like a small grocery store in front, a typical Filipino style restaurant and yes, it had a karaoke machine in it. Dad would add his favorite desserts and other snacks there. I laugh about it now. It was like he was back home in the Philippines grocery shopping. I would always ask him if he had enough or needed anything else. It got to where dad would call me to see if we can go to lunch. I would always try to meet him if I were in town. We would talk about how his family is doing in the Philippines and California. I would update him on my siblings as well. This is where I became closer to my father. He would share things about his life that he would never had have done before. At the urging of my siblings, I had asked him many times to go to the doctor's office to get a checkup. His reply was always the same: "I'm fine; nothing is wrong with me." I told him I would go with him to ensure he would be fine, but he shut me down quite fast. I have learned about Filipino men that they never went to the hospital unless broken bones or stitches were needed. Dad was stuck in his ways already and there was no changing that. One day, when my eldest brother and I were there visiting, my dad had a knock at his door. It was a young man selling magazine subscriptions, and he had an appointment with Dad. When my brother asked him what he wanted, he said the matter was with Dad and not him. Dad told my brother that this guy was selling magazines. My brother almost threw this guy out on his ass. He told the young salesperson never to come back or call my father again, or he would hunt his ass down. He then told Dad not to accept any appointments or calls of this nature, as they will try to rip you off. They take advantage of older people, which is why my brother was so pissed. My brother would explain that the subscriptions would turn into thousands of dollars and never to do that again. Like he was talking to a kid almost. I had to laugh.

One weekend, my sisters were asking me if I heard from Dad, and I said no. They told me that Dad was supposed to go to dinner with them Friday night but backed out because he did not feel well. They both said they had not heard from Dad all weekend and tried to call him, but he never answered. So about 11:00 p.m. Sunday, I drove to his apartment to see if he was ok. As I approached the parking lot, I could see Dad's truck there. I then looked up to his terrace and noticed his light was on. I proceeded to the entrance of his complex but did not have the key code, so I had to wait for someone to come out or go in. The way the complex was set up is the first floor was the lobby and the laundry area and storage area were there. As I reached the elevator, I heard someone call out my name. I turned to see Dad in the laundry room folding his clothes. He was surprised to see me. He asked me what I was doing there, and I told him we were trying to reach him all weekend to see if he was alright, but he never answered the phone. He said he received no calls from us. We went up to his apartment to check out his phone. It was on silent mode, and he did not know it. He did not know how to change back to ring mode, so I showed him. I then called my sisters to assure them that dad was fine. Dad made some coffee and fixed us a snack to eat.

We talked for a couple of hours, and then I told him I had to go because I would have an early flight out the next morning.

Dad's Trip Back

Dad had mentioned that he will travel to the Philippines to visit his siblings and will be gone for a month. While he was away, he would ask my sisters to check on his cat and apartment. He seemed excited to be going back home. He said he would fly to California first, meet his brothers there, and then fly to the Philippines. Before his trip, he would ask me to pick up things he could not find to bring back to give to his family as gifts or pasalubong, as they would call it. I bought T-shirts, magnets, and other gifts that had our hometown of Virginia Beach printed on them. I also picked up some chocolates for the family. When I brought this over to dad's place to pack, he just said thanks and put them in his suitcase.

I had spent about $200 for all of this stuff and thought he would reimburse me for it, but he did not. Typical Dad, I thought. Dad packed weird shit like spam and corned beef, lots of it. I asked him why he did that, and his response was that everyone that goes to the Philippines always brought them because it was hard to get anywhere there. He packed cigarettes, all kinds of cookies. He even packed coffee because he said they did not have that brand there. He had two big ass bags he had to check-in. Dad used every available discount he could, military, Senior citizen, and AAA. He did not pay for his luggage at all. He told me after he found out that he would have brought more stuff if he had known he did not have to pay; I laughed and agreed. He didn't agree with me. He had enough shit. I did not know who he would give these things to; I assumed it was just his family.

Unspoken Lessons

The flight attendant woke me up and asked if I wanted a drink and I asked for some water. They would bring our mid-flight snack in a few minutes. We all received a sandwich and a cookie. I asked the flight attendant if I could have an extra serving and she said to wait until they make sure that everyone received it. Sure enough, a few minutes later, she gave me a second serving and more water. Being in the back of the plane had its benefits. The restrooms were located right behind me, and being that there was no one next to me, I had free rein to and from the bathroom without interrupting anyone. I took a peek out of the window again and noticed there was still sunlight out, and it was twelve and midnight according to my watch. We would land in Japan in approximately four hours. I chose to watch another long movie, Saving Private Ryan. One of the best WWII movies ever made, in my opinion. I would fall back asleep halfway through the movie.

Having never been to the Philippines, I did not really know what to expect. I heard it was a third-world country with very little industry. I was told that there are many beautiful beaches there. All the Filipino people I knew would tell me that it was very dangerous there for me because I looked like a foreigner. They would tell me not to walk around alone because I would get kidnapped or something crazy like that. I would be very cautious once I arrived. I would be told to prepare for hot and humid weather every day, but I was already used to that, having lived in Virginia Beach for many years. I had packed all kinds of medications to include mosquito repellent. I also had aspirin, anti-acids, cough drops, and many disinfectant wipes for your face and hands. Again, I did not know what to expect, so I would rather be safe than sorry. I had packed two full suitcases and was worried if I would make the weight when I checked in, but there were no issues at all. I even included some suntan lotion in case I was in the sun for a long period. I was looking forward to that very much. It was still freezing back home. I was so excited to be there for the first time. I kept thinking if I knew enough of the language to get by if my relatives did not speak English. So many things ran through my head. I wished that my father was still alive to make this special trip with me. It would have meant so much to me. The last time he and I spoke about a trip together, he said he did not want to make this long trip again. I would go at it alone if I ever had the opportunity. Dad taught me a lot growing up, and he never knew it. I just watched him closely when he asked me to assist him in fixing things, especially working on the cars. If he had to repeat himself to me, he would get frustrated, so I tried very hard to pay attention. Dad was not a mechanic by trade but knew how to fix things just out of necessity, which I would later learn that all Filipino men had this trait. To this day, I never understood why Dad did not throw things away or waste them. I always thought it was because we were poor and could not afford it. But that was not the reason at all as I would come to find out. Dad had learned survival skills at a very young age because he had to. He once told me we Americans waste so much money not fixing things and throwing away food and other products. We let things expire and simply throw them in the garbage. I always wondered if Dad had this same conversation with my siblings. He would always tell me these brief life stories, but I never knew it was for my benefit. I thought he was just complaining.

The Japan Connection

About an hour and a half before we landed in Japan, they served us breakfast. I quickly consumed everything, had another coffee, then some water. I wanted to make sure I had put everything back into my backpack that I had pulled out and checked the seat pockets to ensure I did not leave anything. I even packed the Delta items, including the blanket that was not used. I really needed to brush my teeth and wash my face; it would be the first thing I did when I landed in Japan, after I smoked a cigarette, of course.

We had made a very smooth landing at the Narita airport, something I thought would be impossible given the size of the jumbo jet. Since I was in the back, I knew it would be a while before I could deplane. Surprisingly, it went by very fast as they had two exits for all the passengers. I followed the rest of the passengers to a customs entrance where we would have to go through security again. I looked at the line and thought this was going to take some time, so I went to look for a bathroom, and low and behold, next to the bathroom was a smoking lounge. I went to the bathroom and made my way into the smoking room. I could not wait to have a cigarette after the long 13.5-hour flight.

The room was crowded and filled with heavy smoke with very little exhaust. I did not care; I had to have a cigarette. I smoked two, then made my way back to the security lines. There was hardly anyone there, so I went through pretty fast. The security was a little different here in Japan versus in the US; we had to show our boarding pass, and passport, and take out our electronics, including cell phones. Everything went in a basket, even my backpack. After emptying everything and giving my documents to security, they asked where I came from and where I was going. I told them I came from Detroit and was heading to Manila. A very quick thank you in Japanese, and I was cleared through.

My first objective was to send my uncle a message to let him know that I had made it to Japan and was on schedule to be there in Manila on time. My problem was that I did not have Wi-Fi to do so. I had to log in to the local airport Wi-Fi to be able to message him. It took some time to log in, so as I was waiting, I went to the store to pick up a toothbrush and paste. I needed to wash my face and fix my hair as well. I used my American Express credit card for the purchases. I then made my way to a bathroom where I could brush my teeth and clean up a bit.

Afterward, I checked to see where my departing gate was located and made my way down to the gate. As I walked through the airport, I noticed a McDonald's and said, "Why not?" I put myself in line. The only thing I had left to do was wait to board. I put my order in at McDonald's and then they said something to me in Japanese. Not understanding what they said, I handed them my American Express card. The attendant quickly waved me off, so I gave her my Visa. She then smiled and bowed to me. My visa was declined, and I immediately panicked, thinking I would have to use this when I was in the Philippines. That would be another issue that I would have to contend with. I pulled out a twenty-dollar bill and gave it to the attendant, and she thanked me in Japanese. I gave her a quick, "You're welcome."

She then gave back change in Yen. I was like, wait I need this back in US dollars, I cannot use this. I tried to explain this to her in English, then the guy before me told me they would only give you change back in their currency. What a crazy thing, I thought. Where the hell would I use this? I took my food and proceeded to my gate. Feeling a little pissed, I thought it was a learning experience, and I ate my burger and fries. I tried to call my bank from there, but it was too late, I would have to wait until morning to do so.

There was a Starbucks located near the gate, so I decided to get rid of the existing Yen. When I arrived at the gate, there were less foreigners and more Filipinos. I stood out in the crowd like a sore thumb. As I sat down, I noticed quite a few people eyeballing me. I was wondering what the reason was. Most of them were older ladies. I had heard about the stories of foreigners coming to the Philippines because of the number of an available beautiful young woman. Maybe they thought I was one of them.

We boarded the same plane that we had just deplaned, and I had the same seat for the very same reason. The flight was supposed to arrive around 9:50 p.m. As we boarded, the first thing I noticed was the flight crew was mostly Filipina. I took my seat in the back and had a quick conversation with one of the flight attendants. She asked me if I had ever been to the Philippines, and I explained to her it was my first time. I told her I had family there, and she asked me if I had married a Filipina: I said no, my father's family is from there. She asked me if I was adopted because I looked and spoke like a full-blooded American, which everyone would tell me throughout my lifetime. She was from a different province but knew where my dad was from. She welcomed me aboard and wished me an incredible adventure there. I was lucky again as the seat next to me remained empty. The flight attendant asked me if I wanted to move up, but I told her I would be okay where I was. Again, all the announcements were in three languages.

As we taxied to the runway, I got comfortable. I put my new pair of slippers on and received a few pairs of earphones. I had stashed all the extra stuff in my bag and would give it out when I got to the Philippines. I had made some notes on my trip to tell my siblings the story when I got back. They gave me some coffee as I watched the movie Goodfellas. The flight attendant brought me some cookies and water as well. She had been very helpful to me when she was not busy. I think her name was Imelda, and she was very hospitable, more than any other flight attendant that I ever spoke to in all my years of traveling, and she was not bad looking at all.

I thought, *Wow, Filipinos are cheerful people. What happened to Dad?*

Growing up, Dad always seemed like he was pissed off at something. I do not know if it was because we were poor or that he had a shitty day every day; I just did not know. You would never want to be lying on the couch during the day when he came home because he would immediately ask you to do some dumb shit just to get you out of the house. He hated we would spend our time in front of the TV for hours. I remember how he once made me cut the grass the day after I just cut it. When I explained to him I had just cut it yesterday, he said it was too high still. I would cut the grass so low that it was brown. I had learned two lessons that time, first not to cut the grass so low and second, not to be lying around the house when he came home. As a child, it would seem like I always got the short end of the stick for getting blamed for things. My siblings would always say, "I think Kris was the last one to use it."

It got to be expected after a while and I did things without being asked to do them. This started at a very young age. After a while, Dad did not ask for my help; when I saw he was doing something, I would just be there to help.

The Toilet Repair

The funniest thing that ever had happened, I thought, was the time he was fixing the loose toilet seat when I was still very young. I would pass the tools to him as he asked. I had to pee really bad, so I told him I had to go. We only had one bathroom back in the day, so he said go ahead. As I was peeing, he asked me where I had put the screwdriver and I told him over there. As I told him my body had shifted, I started to hit the toilet seat instead of the bowl and was ricocheting and hitting Dad in the face. I was so scared that it would be life ending, but dad started laughing and told me to pee in the goddamn toilet. I did not laugh, but that was funny as hell. I eventually had to clean it up, and I apologized for it. Kid moments, I thought. Eventually, we would fix the toilet seat and never talk about the incident again.

When dad was home, he would call for me. I would be upstairs doing something and wondered why he never asked my siblings to do things. I made my way downstairs and dad was sitting in his recliner. He asked me to get his cigarettes. I asked him where they were, and he said on the table. The table was five feet from him, so I wondered why he did not get them himself. I looked at him and then over at the cigarettes and said, really, those cigarettes? I just thought it was the weirdest thing he ever did. And he did it more than once. I did not want to interrupt him while watching Bonanza or something like that; God forbid he would have to get out of his chair.

Imelda

When Imelda was done serving the passengers, she took a seat next to me and asked me questions and told me about certain places I should visit when I got there. Imelda had to be in her mid-thirties with black hair in a bun and a dark complexion. She was a lovely young lady, so I had no problem with her sitting next to me and conversing. She had asked me if I spoke the language, but I said only the bad words. She laughed and asked why. I told her that when my siblings and I were younger and we did something wrong, Dad used his native tongue to curse us instead of cussing at us in English.

I knew the bad words first; she said. She tried to give me a crash course on how to speak with my elders; I mentioned to her I knew to bless my elders when I first met them. She agreed and said that it was very important to do so because that shows respect. She was teaching me how to say yes and no. And if I were speaking to my elders, it was a little different from speaking to my cousins. I realized I had a long way to go to learn Tagalog. The entire sentence structure was unique compared to English, and if you remember, I barely passed English during my senior year of high school. So, this was going to be really hard to learn, I thought. We spoke for a few minutes longer. I found out that she was a single Mom and was never married. I had told her why I was going to the Philippines, and she said that I was a wonderful son to see where my dad grew up. We would laugh about other things, but soon Imelda would have to serve everyone a meal. I told her to come back and talk more if she had the time. After fifteen minutes of talking with Imelda, I really felt comfortable about visiting. She told me that there are worse places in the Philippines and mentioned that there are dangerous places everywhere. It made sense. Imelda sounded like a lobbyist trying to get people to visit the

Philippines. She would tell me how hospitable the people were and how there were so many beautiful beaches and that when it was time for me to leave, I would not want to. She told me the food was so delicious and very cheap. Sounds like my kind of place. She sold me on the Philippines, and I could not wait to land. Imelda was very proud of her country. She was kind and grew on me. I felt this attraction for her. This was crazy for me as we just met. But the more and more I looked at her, I realized how beautiful she was. Imelda had high cheekbones and a signature Filipina mole located just about the right side of her lips. It was a small mole. She had a beautiful smile as well. She actually caught me looking at her a few times, and I felt a little embarrassed. After we finished eating, I checked my watch, and I had about an hour and a half left. I got butterflies in my stomach. An announcement came over the speaker saying we would land about thirty minutes early, thanks to a tailwind. I thought of how I will tell my uncle that I would be there earlier and how he would find me.

I was so eager to hit the ground in the Philippines. According to my watch, it was around eight p.m. that I would never change. The Philippines are exactly twelve hours ahead of us, so I figured there would be no need to change it. Imelda spent another ten minutes with me before we landed, teaching me more words and telling me to see more places. It made me more excited. When we finally touched down, I could see Imelda smiling at me. She was happy that I was in the motherland, almost excited for me. As I deplaned, I went to Imelda and thanked her for giving me attention. I asked how I could reach her in the future if she ever wanted to talk more, and she handed me a piece of paper that was folded. I opened it and saw an email address and her name, along with a line written in Tagalog. I asked her what it meant, and she said I would have to figure it out. I hugged her, something that I never did in my life, at least to a flight attendant. I grabbed my backpack and made my way to the exit; as I was exiting, I stopped to get one last look at Imelda; she had been watching me the whole time. I think she was more excited that I was here. Another flight attendant wished me luck. I did not understand what she meant, so I just went with it. I gave her a wink and a smile, then left the aircraft.

Welcome to the Philippines

As soon as I got in the jetway, I was smacked with the humidity that I had heard about. It was about a ten-minute walk from the gate to customs, and I had noticed the stores were the same store as back in the States. I followed everyone to customs, where there was a long line. The customs agent told me to go to the next line after five minutes in the line. They literally moved me to the very front of a new line. I was like, wow, this is great service. The agent asked me how long I would be here and where I would stay. Once I gave the information to him, he stamped my passport and said, "Welcome to the Philippines."

You normally get a thirty-day visa when you enter the Philippines. I followed the signs to baggage claim. As I took the escalator down, I was hoping to get a hold of my uncle and tell him I landed early, but I did not have any service. I would have to log on to the airport's Wi-Fi. I arrived at the baggage claim and noticed bags already on the conveyor belt. I quickly found my first bag and waited another minute for my second. One thing about Delta is they tag your bags if you have status and usually, those bags come off first. I could not believe from the time I left the plane to the time I got my bags; only twenty minutes had passed. I looked for the exit signs. I tried to call my uncle, but there was no answer. I was thinking this was going to be a nightmare.

As I walked through the exit, I saw about 300 people across the street waiting on passengers. It was deafening and crowded; as I looked around, there were only a handful of us foreigners. I tried to call my uncle again, but still no answer. I went over to the smoking section and lit one up. It amazed me how many people were waiting there; I thought I would never be able to find my uncle in the crowd. One of the few foreigners came over and asked for a light as I was smoking. I asked him if this was his first time here, and he said no, he came here a year ago to see his girlfriend. He had an accent, so I asked him where he was from, he said California. I was so surprised to hear that and looked at him like REALLY?

He laughed and said Australia originally but had transferred to California for work. He thanked me for my light and was on his way. I watched him cross the street and jump into a beautiful young lady's arms, probably half his age. I thought, lucky guy. There is another story to this scenario I will learn later. The people across the street were not allowed to cross over, and there was a lot of security there. I noticed that all the security guards were carrying sawed-off shotguns. I wondered why. As I gazed around, my phone was ringing. I answered it, and it was my uncle. I told him we landed about a half hour early and that I was already at the exit. He said he knew I was early because he saw my plane come in. I asked him, really; you saw my plane. I am thinking, how the hell could he see that? Anyway, he said he was almost there and go to the letter H. I asked him where to go again, and he replied again, go to letter H. At first, I thought we were having a communication issue because I could swear he said the letter H. I had asked one security guard where I can find the letter H? He said it is very easy, just look up and see all the letters in the alphabet spaced apart every ten feet. He was probably thinking, another dumb ass foreigner. I thought "DUH". I found the letter H and stood underneath it. He said that it would be about five minutes. He warned me not to talk to any strange cab drivers.

There were so many drivers asking me, "Sir, do you need a reliable taxi with air-con?"

I told all thirty of them I did not need a ride.

There were so many passengers waiting to get picked up, I did not know how they could find me in this crowd. I kept my bags close to me and remembered Imelda telling me to put my backpack on the front so no one could get into it as I waited. Several people were doing this. I would thank her later for her advice. It was very noisy with all traffic security blowing their whistles and people screaming for their passengers; it was just crazy. I remembered I had a picture of Uncle, so I glanced at his photo again to make sure. I tried not to stare at anyone because I did not want to get a spell cast on me as the myth says. I just kept looking around at all the madness there. So many people in such a small area, cars were moving in and out picking up passengers, everyone yelling, trying to get the attention of the person they were picking up. It was so hot out there I had to take my hoody off. I was sweating now and getting more anxious to see my uncle. Suddenly my phone rang, and it was my uncle. He said wait right there because there was a lot of traffic trying to get into the passenger pickup area and he got out of the car and started walking toward me. He told me not to move out of the H section, and I told him I was still here. But I was not sure if he could get me because only the passengers were allowed where I was standing.

Sure enough, a few minutes later, I heard someone call my name. It was coming from behind me; I turned to see my uncle smiling at me. We embraced, and he told me that his son, my cousin, was driving and that he would be here in a minute. He told me if I wanted to smoke, to do it now because we would be stuck in traffic and not allowed to smoke in the car. After all, my auntie was here also to pick me up. We had some small talk as we waited. I told him that the trip was fine. He asked me if I had eaten and I said yes; I ate on the plane, and he then told me we would eat before we went back to the house. If you have learned nothing about Filipino people by now, you will find out that they are very hospitable and will always feed you, no matter if you just ate, you would have to eat with them again. After a few minutes, my uncle was on the phone with my cousin. He was just pulling up now. I knew very little about my uncle growing up. My dad told me that Uncle Ren married when he was older and had kids later. So, his two children were much younger than I. From what I can remember, my uncle's.

Wife had very close ties to the political parties there. I remember Dad telling me that my uncle's family lived comfortably there. I would soon find out how comfortable.

My cousin pulled up, and uncle escorted me over to their car. My cousin popped out, shook my hand, and gave me a hug. Then my auntie came over and hugged me with tears in her eyes. Someone from Dad's family finally made it to the Philippines, and they were pleased to see me. She placed her hand on my face with tears still running down her face and spoke in her native language. My cousin was translating for me. He said that Auntie was so sorry that she could not make the funeral for Dad and that I resembled him so much that she could see him in me. She missed him so much. She continued to move her hands all over my face. I held my emotions in as much as I could. I gave her another big hug and felt a tear drop run out of my eyes—one of many emotional moments I would encounter there. Uncle said enough of this, he was hungry and wanted to eat, and the traffic would be bad. As we made our way out of the pickup area, hundreds of people walked around and waited for passengers.

Once we left the secured area of the airport, I noticed a lot of these makeshift buses. There must have been twenty of them loading up passengers. I asked my cousin what they were and said they called Jeepneys. The jeepney was a national symbol of the Philippines, created back in WWII from leftover US Military jeep parts in the Province of Pampanga. As this caught on in neighboring Provinces, a brilliant entrepreneur saw an opportunity and started production of the Jeepney as we know now. By the early fifties, the jeepney made its way to Manila and has been the national symbol of the Philippines since. The jeepney can hold twenty-five passengers with its loading and unloading entrance in the rear with a center aisle and seats on both sides.

The driver usually handles all transactions, holding dollar bills between each of his fingers and giving change while driving. There is an honor system as each passenger passes the fares to the front if the change is needed the driver makes the change and gives it to the closest passenger to him and basically, the passengers sort it out. I found it a very interesting concept. Each Jeepney has its own story and is decorated with local flamboyant colors and sayings. It was basically used for local rides going no more than 5 km from one point to another.

I noticed hundreds of scooters and motorcycles with sidecars. They were called tricycles. They were weaving in and out of traffic; I thought how dangerous this was. It was dark outside with very little lighting, yet people would cross the street at any moment. This was the Philippines.

In my first thirty minutes there, I witnessed the "traffic" that I would hear about. It was madness. These were the major arteries going into the airport. It seemed like it was first come, first serve. You could turn in any direction from any lane. I kept saying to my family, this is crazy. Did you just see what that car did? They would laugh and say welcome to the Philippines. I saw buses stop in the center lane and unload passengers; the passengers would walk to both sides of the street, causing more traffic to stop. The area next to the airport was so busy. My cousin would tell me this is nothing; wait until we try to go into Manila; it would be three times as bad. He even mentioned that you can only go into the city on certain days in Manila because of so much traffic. They had odd and even days and was substantiated by your own plates. But he laughed and said no one listens and drives there anyway because you could just give the officer a few hundred pesos and you would be on your way. I could not believe what I was seeing, but it was the way of life there. As we made our way to the restaurant, I continued to be amazed at the number of people, poorly lit streets, and lawlessness in traffic. The more I watched, the harder it was to get my head around what I saw.

The Small Restaurant

We finally came to a small restaurant located next to a gas station. It would be one of my uncle's favorites. We sat down in a booth. My auntie sat next to me and started firing away questions in English. How long would I stay? What was my schedule and when will I go to her house? Uncle explained to her that we will visit them because my purpose was to meet the family that I had never met before and see where dad grew up. My cousin would start calling me kuya from that point. Kuya meant older brother in Tagalog. All of my father's siblings referred to him as Boy. I would hear them talk about kuya boy in Tagalog and wondered what they were saying. Auntie Wen said they will speak English for twenty-four hours only, then I would have to learn Tagalog; I said no problem.

At first, I thought that Uncle Ren was married to Auntie Wen but would find out that they were my fathers' siblings. I could see and hear my father in them. I had a moment of sadness because I saw even the same facial expressions as my father's. I was caught staring at my uncle, and he asked if everything was okay. I explained to him he resembled Dad, and I was just watching him. He probably thought I was a weirdo. Anyway, he excused himself to go outside, and I asked my cousin Rico where he was going. He told me that his Papa was going to smoke. I would join him.

When I was outside, my uncle asked if I smoked as well. I said, "*Opo,*" the proper Tagalog that Imelda taught me. He then asked if I could speak, and I laughed and said no. I recently learned that from someone I met on the plane. He told me to order anything I wanted to eat and that he would pay for it. I thanked him, and after we finished our cigarettes, we both went back to the table. My auntie immediately asked me what I was doing out there, and I said I was keeping my Tito company.

She laughed, gave me a grin, and said, "I know you two were smoking outside. You need to quit."

I told her I was trying and picked up a menu. I ordered some pork adobo, my favorite. My cousin asked if that was all I wanted and I said yes because I ate on the plane. We talked about the long flight I had, and I told them I had met one of the flight attendants. I showed him the paper and asked him what it meant; he read it aloud, "*Sana Makita ka agad bago ka umalis,*" and he said it told "I hope I see you soon before you leave." Auntie butted in and said, "You be careful with these girls here because you are good-looking and American, so they will try to get you." I asked what she meant by that, and she said that many girls here in the Philippines would easily go with American because it will be their ticket to the states. I apologized and told her I was here just for family and nothing else. She told me I was a good boy. I never thought of myself as the overly good-looking guy, and having my auntie tell me this was a surprise. I was not an ugly kid; I always got haircuts from my parents until I graduated from high school. I never thought of myself as a great-looking guy, average at the most. I would think of Imelda and how beautiful she was. I almost wished I had taken a picture of her.

Uncle's Residence

We all ate our meals, and uncle paid the check. I had my very first meal in the Philippines. We got into the car, and I asked how far we were from their house. They said maybe forty-five minutes, depending on traffic, but we had to drop off Auntie first.

I said, "Okay, no problem."

I was excited to see everything on the way. As we made our way onto Macapagal Boulevard, I noticed the craziness again. Traffic was just like nothing I had ever witnessed before. People would say that drivers in New York were the craziest. I think they learned how to drive here in the Philippines. Once we made our way to the Coastal highway and then the Cavitex, things seemed to smooth out to the everyday driving that I am used to here in the states. From the highway, I could see so many lights on the water, and I asked my cousin what it was, and he said it was fisher men on manila bay. I could not wait to see this in the morning—so many things are running through my mind right now. I saw an exit for Bacoor, the family's hometown, and got really excited. I could not wait to see it. We made our way into Imus Cavite where my auntie lived. We dropped her off and proceeded to Kawit, where my uncle lives. The streets in between the two towns were narrow. We ran into a lot of those Jeepneys again and the tricycles; they were everywhere. I thought these were back streets, but they were the major streets. It was barely enough room to get two cars by. I noticed the dogs lying around in the street. They never moved when the cars came by, and I thought that was just as crazy as the traffic I had seen.

While driving, I noticed the houses were very close to each other, and all individually gated. I could tell that they were all made of concrete. Most of the homes were right on the street. It was probably ten-thirty by now, and the streets were still bustling. People walking all over the place, I would imagine there are a lot of accidents because the streets are so narrow and not lit well.

You could reach out of your window and touch someone walking or touch the car passing by as it was so close. Finally, we pulled up to an enormous gate, my cousin honked the horn and in less than a minute, the gates were opened by a kid that must have been around fifteen years of age. The gate was made of a tough wood stained in a dark finish. I noticed the kid closing the gate behind us as we pulled in. I watched him close the gate and then locked it by sliding a thick metal bar through a few eyelets bolted to this huge wooden gate, almost like a castle. In their native language, my uncle gave more instructions to the young kid. The kid then grabbed my luggage and carried it away. I said no, do not worry about that I can do it, but my uncle persisted.

The immense house was made of concrete and crafted by hand. It had a blue-colored aluminum roof and was white. The car port alone could fit four cars. I noticed it was tiled and not just concrete-like back home. There was another door in the carport that led to this inside the house. The door had matched the gate and was thick and heavy. As I walked into this fortress, I could see that all floors were tiled and spotless. The décor was a typical Filipino style with a lot of polished wood and glass. I would certainly ask for a tour in the morning. My uncle asked if there was anything that I needed, and I told him I would love to take a shower. He said there is a shower in my room on the third floor and to go make myself comfortable. I asked him how do I get there, and he pointed to the stairs.

I climbed the three flights of stairs and came to the only room on the third floor. A cool breeze hit me. It felt so good. The kid must have turned on the air-con. The air conditioner was a lot different from ours back in the US. Here they had a compact unit for each room, not centralized. I noticed my luggage was already in the room and thought that this kid was very efficient. I quickly jumped in the shower; the cold water felt so good. I shaved, brushed my teeth, put on a t-shirt and shorts, and made my way back down the stairs. I saw the side door was opened, so I went out to see my uncle and cousin sitting at the table on the terrace. My uncle and I sat in a chair and smoked a cigarette. The house was tranquil as it was late, and everyone was sleeping. I did not see the young kid anymore, either. Uncle asked me if everything was okay, and I told him I was fine.

They would go to sleep now, so I went back to my room. I took out my notebook and wrote what I had seen so far in the Philippines. I wanted to give my siblings all the information that I could since they would not be here. Later, I fell asleep right away. I could not believe I was that tired. My last thought of the night was how hot it was, even at night.

    The roosters woke me up around six a.m. with their loud squawking. I wanted to see as much as I could while there, so I sprang out of bed and brushed my teeth and rinsed with mouthwash. I was told not to rinse with the regular water from the faucet because I would get an upset stomach. I washed my face and fixed my hair, so I did not look homeless to the rest of the family. I was so excited to start my adventure here in the Philippines. Here I was, 8703 miles away from home on the other side of the globe. I could not wait to learn about this country. I ran downstairs to see what the place looked like during the day. I made sure that I had charged my phone so that I could take a lot of pictures. When I arrived downstairs, I could hear women talking in Tagalog. I went to see them, and I guess Uncle never let the maids know I was coming because I had startled them. They looked scared and called for the young boy. When the boy showed up and saw me in the room with the two women, he laughed and explained to them in their language that I was the nephew of Uncle and that I was visiting. It did not convince them at all and acted shy. The boy then asked me, "Coffee Kuya?" and thanked me. The woman would immediately make the coffee. Then the boy asked, "Almusal Kuya?" Since I did not know what he was saying, I shook my head no. I would later find out that almusal was the Tagalog word for breakfast. I would laugh at myself thinking about that. I walked out to the terrace where we sat last night and had a cigarette with my coffee. It was a beautiful morning, and I wanted to take my first look at the Philippines during the day. As I wandered around the yard, I noticed my family was fond of foliage, as it was all over the place. I noticed this large red and white building across the river and wondered what it was. It was an old Spanish-looking building with many Philippine Flags spaced out around it. The first picture I took in the Philippines was when I took out my phone. I went to take a sip of my coffee, and it was delicious. I was so excited to see more, so I went out to the front of the house and snapped a picture. The house was enormous, with a terrace on the second floor; I would certainly explore that later. I went outside the gate to the main street, where it was already busy, even at six-thirty in the morning. As I opened the gate, all the eyes on the street were on me. Weird, I thought, but then again, I looked more American than Filipino, so the people were probably surprised to see a white guy in the street there. I noticed about twelve of those tricycle things lined up on the bridge going over to that old red and white building. I went over to take some pictures; the operators had no problem and even let me sit in one while they took my picture. I thought that was pretty cool. About a half hour later, my uncle was up, and I could hear him giving instructions to the boy. When I went back inside, uncle asked if I wanted coffee, and I said I had some, but yes, I wanted more. He spoke to the women, and they started working on more coffee. I asked Uncle who the women were, and he said they were his maids, and the young boy was the son of one of them. I waived the boy and asked him what his name was, and he said, Marvin. I said glad to meet you. He would then tell me that his mother's name is Rose, and the other girl's name is Marie, the younger sister of Rose. I introduced myself to them properly, and Uncle asked if I had eaten my breakfast yet, and I said no. He looked at the maids and asked them if they cooked breakfast, and they told Uncle, "No." When Uncle asked me why I did not want to eat, I told him they never asked, but he said the maids told him I told Marvin I did not want to eat. I laughed and told my uncle that Marvin did ask me something, but it was in Tagalog. I did not understand it, so I shook my head no. Uncle started laughing and said we will take our Almusal now. Uncle then spoke to the maids and told me to get my dirty clothes.

I said, "It's okay, uncle, I will wash my clothes; I am used to it."

He said no; it is their job and told me to get my clothes and give them. He pointed right at them, and I was a little taken aback. I had never had a maid in my life, so I did not know how to react. I went upstairs and quickly folded my clothes nicely and neatly. I came back down and presented them to Rose; she took my clothes and gave me what I thought was a quick nod. I was so out-of-place doing that, but it was the way of life here, and I kept thinking that things would be different.

Uncle and I were served our coffee out on the terrace. As soon as we sat down, I asked him what that beautiful structure was there across the river, and he said it was the shrine of the very first president of the Philippines. Emilio Aguinaldo was a military leader and politician that played a massive role in the war against Spain and then later against the United States, all during the Spanish American War. President Aguinaldo was born in Kawit in 1869 and died in Quezon City in 1964. As it is named, the Aguinaldo Shrine was the ultimate resting place for the first president. Uncle told me that Rico had been a curator there and that we could probably see it later on during my visit. I answered him affirmatively; I wanted to visit that place; it is a two-minute walk from Uncle's house. Uncle told me later because he said that Rico always sleeps late. My uncle's house must have been in the airport's flight path because there were so many planes flying overhead. I must have counted twenty in the hour we sat outside. So, uncle told me he could see my plane at the airport. I did not understand him at first, but now, you could actually read which airline it was as they flew overhead so close. By now it was scorching, and I was already perspiring. Uncle wanted to take me into Bacoor first to see the resting place of my grandparents. Our family mausoleum was located there. I told Uncle I was here to see how my father grew up and lived here. I wanted to walk the same walk as he did many years ago. After my father's passing, Uncle had me send some personal items, preferably clothing, of both him and my mother. It was customary to include them in the mausoleum. So, not long after dad passed, I sent one of my moms' gowns and a traditional Polo barong of my father's. The Polo barong was used for formal wear here in the Philippines. We would visit there sometime in the afternoon.

We were called into the house; our almusal was ready. We had fried eggs, rice and longanisa with fresh pandesal. Longanisa was a type of sausage made of ground pork, fat, sugar, and spices that could be spicy or sweet. The pandesal is the common bread roll in the Philippines. You want to eat it when it is fresh and warm. That breakfast was delicious. I took another cup of coffee and then went outside to view the surroundings again. I noticed another terrace in the backyard that was not connected to the house. A barking dog stopped me from going over. Once everyone heard all the commotions, they came outside and scolded the dogs. I hoped they would get used to me at some point. When I reached the terrace, a litter of puppies came running over to me. They were so cute. Then the mother came up wagging her tail. I put my hand out so she could sniff me and rubbed her body against my leg like a cat. Uncle told me not to let them do that because the dog was dirty.

Anyway, after the terrace's view, I went upstairs to do a quick set of push-ups and sit-ups. I would push for fifty each. After my workout, I took a shower. Again, the cold water felt so good. It got to where I would look forward to taking the cold showers. After I finished, I made notes of the comical morning I had with the maids. I wish someone had filmed it because they were both scared shitless. After I dressed, I contemplated going back downstairs because the main living area was not air-conditioned, and neither was the room where the television was located. They used electric fans because they were used to it but had the same air-con units in each room for when they had dinner parties. I waited a bit and sat in the air-con for a while. I took out my wallet and counted some cash out that I wanted to exchange; I left the rest in a shoe in my luggage. When I traveled with more than one pair of shoes, I always wrapped the shoes that I packed in a plastic bag, hoping to keep the germs out of my other things, so I thought this would be a good hiding place. I went downstairs to get something cold to drink and to my surprise, my cousin Liza was up talking with Auntie Ways. They were not at the airport to pick me up, so this was the first time meeting them. I greeted them with open arms, and they asked how I was doing and about my long flight. I explained the travel time and the routes and stops I had made. They both seemed excited that I was there as well. Liza had to prepare for work, so she excused herself to get ready. At that moment, Marie came and gave Liza her ironed uniform. Liza took it and ran into her room. Auntie Ways spoke excellent English. She told me Uncle Ren was excited that I was coming and had plans to take me all over the province to show me where dad grew up and other things. She asked if we were going to eat lunch here in the house, and uncle said no, we would be out by then and would just meet Auntie at a restaurant. He asked me to accompany him to the store, and I assured him I will.

Grocery Shopping

We jumped into his old pickup truck and waited for Marvin to open the gate; I told uncle I could open the gate, but he said no, he had already told Marvin we were leaving, and sure enough, the gate was opening. There was so much going there in the streets; everywhere I looked people were walking. Since we were not going far, Uncle would ride with the windows down. I guess Kawit did not get many foreigners there because everyone stared at me. We arrived at a store called Alfa Mart. An armed security guard waved us over to the park. He was carrying some kind of semi-automatic pistol that was holstered. Once we got inside, I realized it was a grocery store. I could not understand why they would have armed security there.

Uncle loaded up on bottled water and asked if I wanted some beer to drink. I said sure if they have light beer. I would soon make San Miguel Light my favorite beer. Uncle bought a case. As we walked around the store, we came to the canned meat section. I saw so much spam and corned beef. I went down the aisle to see how much, and Uncle asked if I wanted some. I laughed and told him no. I was just looking. I thought back to when my dad had packed so much of this in his luggage and laughed out loud. Uncle again asked if I needed anything else, and I told him no. After my uncle picked up a few other things, we went to the checkout, and some young girl seemed excited that we came to her checkout counter. The other girls were kidding her about me being there, I guess. She would keep smiling and finally say, "Hello, Sir."

I said hello back. I told her she did not have to call me sir, and she giggled some more.

My uncle did not know what was going on, so I left it at that. Once our groceries were packed, we said our goodbyes, and I thanked her. I could hear the other checkout girls giving her a hard time. When the clerk packs groceries in the stores here, they use cardboard and tie strings around to keep them secure and also make a handle out of it; I thought this was clever, no plastic bags. The guard stopped some traffic so that we could back out; I saw my uncle grab some loose change and pay him. I asked my uncle why he did that, and he said it was out of courtesy that he paid him. He told me the security guards make very little salary. I understood now. I would witness this act during my entire stay.

As we made our way back to the house, we had passed a bank, and I noticed a guard with a sawed-off shotgun standing there. Uncle explained that every bank had a guard with a shotgun. But he had not heard of any banks getting robbed in his neighborhood. It is used to deter robbers, I guess, and it works.

We reached the house, and a few honks on the horn opened the gate. We unloaded the truck and brought everything inside. Uncle packed a cooler full of water, beer, and soda. While we were still there, I asked my uncle if we could exchange some money. He wondered how much I wanted to change, and I said it was a lot. He asked again, and I said $500 US. He said no problem, he could change it right there. I was like, really, okay. He asked me what the exchange rate was, and I looked it up and showed him. It was around 49.5; he said no problem.

He went into his room and grabbed a bank bag. He started counting out the amount. It impressed me. We exchanged the monies. It ended up being around 24,750 Philippine pesos. And there was plenty to spare. He told me if I wanted to change more, to just ask him because they would charge a percentage to exchange outside. He told me not to take all of it and leave some here. So, I took maybe 5000 Philippine pesos and left the rest in my shoe's upstairs. I told Uncle what had happened in Japan with my credit card and that I would have to call the bank on Monday evening. This time, he made sure I locked the bedroom door.

The Lavish Dine In

We left the house and met Auntie Ways at a Chinese restaurant for lunch. This was a pretty big restaurant. I thought there would be some Chinese people working in there, but they were all Filipino. Again, I received many stares and giggles as the wait staff wondered who the lucky server would be to serve our table. I almost felt famous.

A beautiful and petite young lady walked up to our table, and Auntie Ways immediately ordered our food and asked what I wanted to drink. I told her bottled water. The young lady spoke to Auntie Ways in Tagalog, repeating her order. After Auntie confirmed, the server turned and gave me a quick smile and off she was. I could hear the staff giggling in the back. As they worked the floor, they tried not to look so obvious, taking a peek at me. I thought this was crazy, but cute.

I did not even know what Auntie had ordered. I followed my uncle outside to burn a smoke before we ate. As the food came, Auntie made some excellent choices: beef and broccoli, Yang Chow fried rice and some chicken BBQ on a stick. It was all delicious. We left the restaurant the same way we came in, all eyes on me, with all the staff smiling at me as if it were a contest and I was the judge. Auntie Ways went her separate way from there.

Auntie Wen's Residence

It was about twelve-thirty in the afternoon, and Uncle told me we would pick up Auntie Wen and then go over to the house where they had all grown up. The streets were bustling at this time of the day, so many children were walking around on their lunch break. In the schools here in the Philippines, all children wore uniforms to school. And the style and color determined if you were in elementary or high school. I could not believe how many kids we saw on our drive to Auntie's house. It seemed like thousands. We arrived at Auntie's house, and it looked different from what it did at night. Her husband, Uncle Met, greeted us as we pulled up and invited us in. We would sit on their porch with a slight breeze and shaded. By this time, the temperature was around 33°C or 91°F. If I did not mention before, the Philippines uses the metric system. Uncle Met brought a fan outside. This felt so good. Uncle Ren had brought the cooler to the porch. I took out bottled water. He looked inside and saw the beer and took one of those; I said why not and exchanged my water for a San Miguel Light.

Uncle Met told me stories about my dad in their younger days. It was not long before Auntie Wen came out with a food tray. I told her we had just eaten, and she said eat again. Oh my God, I thought. I am going to get fat by the time I leave here. She had some chicharron, and this dish called sisig. Chicharron is pork rinds, and the sisig is spicy ground pork. It's good with beers from what I understood. As we drank and ate and talked, I would forget how hot it was there.

When Dad passed, all of my siblings would meet at his apartment to go through his things. We would donate his clothes and give the furniture away. Dad had clothes and shoes older than I was still in his closet. All that was left was his and my mother's belongings. I came across an old diary from when my dad was in college. I read through it and found out that he had been courting a young lady. I thought about how cute it was. He wrote that he mailed 777, which, come to find out, was a code name for her, a letter. A couple of days later, he wrote to invite her to dinner. Dad was very attracted to this young lady. I looked at other entries, but they were in Tagalog. I would take the time to translate it later.

Since both of his siblings were there, I thought this would be the proper time to ask about her. I wondered if they had ever heard of this young lady Dad referred to as 777.

Immediately, Uncle Met said he knew who I was talking about. He was very surprised that I knew of this 777; he asked me how I heard of her. I told him I had one of Dad's diaries from college, and he mentioned this 777 many times. He asked me if I knew what the 777 stood for and I told uncle met I had no idea. He would tell the story of how dad would talk about this girl and that her name comprised seven letters for her first, middle, and last name. That is how she got the nickname. Dad courted her for a long time but apparently, nothing ever became of it.

I asked Uncle Met, "Why didn't they get married?"

His answer was a long sad one. He explained that for the longest time they were inseparable. She saw him all the way until the time he left for the Navy. Apparently, the last time he saw her was at Sangley Point. She had accompanied the whole family there to see Dad off. The rumor was he promised to come back home and marry her. Dad would never see or hear from 777 again until after my mother died when he came back home. More than forty years had gone by. I thought about how heartbreaking it must have been for this young lady to go through that.

She eventually married and had a child. Uncle Met told me that she lives here in Imus and if I wanted to meet her, he could take me. I told him maybe not in this condition; we had been drinking. We would plan when would be a good time to meet her. I did ask uncle if there were any long-lost brothers or sisters from this relationship, and he assured me that there were none. He would continue to tell these stories about Dad.

I thought one of the funniest was when my dad was part of a gang of eight kids. They called themselves the Eight Hungry Boys because they would steal a chicken from someone and take it into the jungle to cook it and eat it. Damn bandits, I thought.

Chickens were ubiquitous in almost every household there. You could hear them squawking throughout the day. They could be seen walking all over the place; the dogs did not even mess with them. I laughed so hard at this story. We stayed there for quite a long time, maybe five hours. Uncle Met and I hit it off.

House in Aniban

We all got ready to go over to the family house now for dinner. The beers did not affect me as I probably sweat all the alcohol out. I was excited to see the place where dad grew up in. I took photos of Auntie Wen and Uncle Met, along with Uncle Ren. We jumped back in the truck and drove out of Imus. I noticed a lot of goats were tied up in an empty lot. There must have been ten of them all together. I asked Uncle Ren who they belonged to, and he told me that there were probably a few different owners and that they were there to clean the lot. I said, "Oh, okay."

It still amazed me at how the streets were narrow and how people were everywhere. I asked Uncle what the population was there, and he had said, "Too much." I would later find out, via google, that the population in the Philippines was around 103 million. A third of what it was in the United States with 115,831 square miles compared to US at 3,794,100. No wonder it was so crowded there. School was out, so a thousand children were walking around; the tricycles were very busy. This was everyday life here in the Philippines, and I was so out of touch with what I was seeing. It would help me understand things a bit more. We had driven by some makeshift houses along with one of the smaller rivers. Small houses on top of houses. Again, I asked my uncle what place this was, and he said it was called Squatterville. Squatters would get the name for settling anywhere. Very low- income families had been displaced from all over the Philippines.

There were a lot of small electric lines all over the place, with no method at all. It looks like everyone was tapping into the mainline at some point. It was hazardous. From the brief discussion I had with uncle, there was no running water, and the families would use a community shower and bathroom. Or, as I have witnessed, just go on the side of the road. The strangest thing I saw there was that it seemed like everyone had cell phones and/or an iPad. I'm not judging anyone; I am just curious. As we drove from one neighborhood or barangay to the next, I noticed houses, restaurants, and small businesses all along the streets. This was the common theme there in Cavite. We had driven into Bacoor, where the family had grown up. One thing that hit me suddenly was the sun setting. It was only five-thirty p.m. and it was getting dark already. Then I remembered the Philippines did not observe Daylight Savings Time. The sun would set every day and rise around five-thirty a.m.

We arrived at the house, and I noticed it was also gated. We would have to stop traffic until we could open the gate. Uncle told me that the elementary school that dad went to was right down the street as we waited. It surprised me it was still standing after these years, and he mentioned it was still in use. The gate was finally opened, and we pulled into the courtyard. I could see a concrete house with no color and a red Spanish-looking roof. The lot itself was misleading as it opened up once you went in. Uncle would tell me that it was two lots.

As we entered the house, the main room had an open concept. There were six very small bedrooms, two downstairs and four upstairs, including a loft. There was a semi-spiral staircase laced with many shiny wooden pillars. There were two bathrooms, one upstairs and the other next to the kitchen. The kitchen opened up to a dining area. Out back, you could see the foundation of a second house that used to be there. My first thought was, how could all of them live there? Did it seem tiny? There were his parents, two sisters, and five brothers; for sure things were tight there.

The old clotheslines were still being used outside, something I had not witnessed since I was a kid. There were four coconut trees and a small nipa hut. I went to the Nipa hut to sit and just watch everything going on. I imagined how my dad and his siblings would run around and play back here. There were other fruit trees planted all over the place, kind of like Uncle Ren's yard. Uncle Ren had brought the cooler over to the Nipa hut and asked if I wanted to sit here or go inside, it told him that I wanted to sit here for a bit.

Uncle Met would join me and continue to tell me stories about dad when he was younger. I sat there with both of my uncles while my aunties were inside with my cousin Irene preparing dinner. Irene was married to Auntie Lina's son, so she was like a cousin-in-law, but everyone in the

Philippines did not think like that. If you were a cousin, you were family, and that was it. Auntie Lina had been in the house since Lolo and Lola perished. She and her family would live there and eventually move to the United States, leaving the house for her son, my cousin, and his family. It was still hot outside and between the jet lag and the heat; I felt the time difference. The beers did not help the situation.

Once we finished our dinner, I asked if we could take a tour of the house, and the family said no problem at all. I asked my uncle which room was Dad's; he pointed to the loft. The loft looked a lot like a screened Florida room. It had a small iron spiral staircase leading into the carport outside. It was a small room with shelves. The bed was gone, and the room was used for storage these days. Suddenly, I felt a heavy-hearted as I realized I was walking in the same place my late father once walked. I was actually in the room where he had grown up, and the feeling was overwhelming. We only saw pictures of his house when we were growing up.

I told the family I was going outside back to the Nipa hut to smoke but wanted a few minutes of privacy to let the built-up emotions empty. I cried for a few minutes before Uncle Ren joined me for a smoke. As he walked over, I tried to clean myself up fast, glad it was dark. He asked me if everything was okay. I said yes, and that I was just getting tired. He told me we will go to the mausoleum tomorrow as it was getting late. I could not agree with him more. I was now thinking about that cold shower. After a half hour photo shoot with all the family members, we said our goodbyes and jumped into uncles' truck.

Uncle's Truck

From the family house in Bacoor to my uncle's house in Kawit, it would take about fifteen minutes with no traffic. The streets were not lit well, but I could still see so many people walking around. If you owned property on the main street, you would open some kind of business because that is what it seemed like in Bacoor. I noticed many walk-up type of food spots, small convenience stores, and machine and engine repair garages.

There was one store with a sign that read "24 Hour Vulcanizing." I asked my uncle what type of store it was, and he said it was a tire repair shop. I laughed and made a mental note of that. There were quite a few of these shops.

Since it was cooler outside, Uncle rolled the windows down and said I could because he thought if I wanted to smoke. Uncle's truck was old but ran very well. I could see where they made somebody repairs because of the different color of paints. He was very proud of his truck. He told me the truck was twenty-five years old.

When I asked if he was going to get a new truck, he answered, why? He did not need one as long as this was running and in good shape. Uncle had personalized the truck. It had a roll bar in the back with a thick rope helically wrapped around its entirety. I would think this took some time to complete, as it looked very tedious. There were eyebolts installed on each side of the bed in case anything had to be tied or strapped down. These were regular eye bolts you could buy in any hardware store. You would have to drill through the bed to install these. There were two floodlights installed on top of the roll bar as well. He bought it brand new. He added some splash guards and window guards, the truck was totally pimped out!

Ending First Day

Uncle made a quick call and then said we would stop by the store really quick to pick something up for Auntie Ways. We picked up some more bottled water and some kind of medicine. I had brought all kinds of meds with me because I was told there were none here, and I am looking at two full aisles of meds. Crazy, I thought.

As we walked up to the checkout counter, I noticed my brand of cigarettes there was packaged a little differently than back home. The warning on packs back in the US was printed on the side, whereas in the Philippines, it was a photo of some poor guy missing half of his jaw. I bought a pack just to try them out. I also found the aisle with all the canned meat, and I laughed at what my father told me when he visited here. The Philippines have come a long way since his last visit some ten years ago. Again, I felt like a celebrity walking through the store, as all eyes seemed to be on me. I also felt like a shoplifter. They watched, and every time I met someone's eyes, they smiled and said hello, sir.

I got used to this after a while. We put the neatly wrapped box in the back of the truck and make our way home. Still so crowded outside, I could see some vendors barbequing right there on the sidewalk and, as we drove by, it smelled so good. I want to try this in the next few days. As we pulled up to the house, the gate opened, and there was Marvin. He closed the gate as we pulled into the driveway. He grabbed the box of groceries and carried them inside for the maids to put away. This was still so new to me, and I had to adjust. I found my clean clothes on the counter in the back room. They had been folded nice and neat and smelled really fresh. I told uncle I am going up and shower and probably taking some rest afterwards. He said no problem. Since I was gone, I did not leave the air-con on, so it was still hot in the room. It did not matter because I wanted to take that cold shower. I turned it on and then went into the CR or what they called a comfort room.

After my shower, I opened up my planner and made notes of the day and the relatives that I had met. I mentioned Uncle Met because he was a great guy who knew many stories about dad. I tried to remember all the stories and places he told me about. I just finished my first day in the Philippines, and I was exhausted.

As I lay in my bed, I thought about how I would explain the time I spent with my father in his last few days. I wished he were here and hoped that both he and my mother were looking down on me with a big smile. As a kid, all you wanted to do was make your parents proud, and I feel I did a pretty good job of doing that. Not being one of the smartest children, I went to work right out of high school. I have been with the same company for years and have worked hard. It paid off as I started receiving promotion after promotion. I started off working in the warehouse and I can remember some of the other workers getting pissed at me because I worked too fast. When they told me, it would not get me anywhere, I just simply said we will see. As it turned out, I was very efficient in what they wanted me to do, so any task that I was asked to perform, I would give it 100 percent. Of course, as I was promoted, I would also receive a salary increase. As the time passed, I would work my way to a management position in just about every department. I never understood some people; work is easy; if you just do your job, you will get paid. If you did it well, you would get paid well. I started to make a pretty good living. So, it felt good to hear my parents say keep up the good work, son. I could remember Mom telling me to accomplish one simple thing every day and continue to add to it to become successful. Something as simple as making your bed every morning. At a young age, I would take her advice and do the things she told me to.

I fell asleep around ten-thirty p.m. that night, only to wake up around three a.m. because I was cold. I looked for some type of blanket but found nothing. So, I grabbed the blanket from the plane, wrapped myself with it, and put some pillows on top of me. Soon enough, I was fast asleep once again. I woke up again around seven a.m. to the squawking roosters; man, I could just shoot one of them at that moment. I jumped out of bed and went into the CR to wash my face and brush my teeth. I changed my clothes and made sure that I folded them nice and neat so I could properly present them to the maids when I went downstairs.

The Unique Fishing

I reached the bottom of the staircase and met Rose, one of the maids. She said good morning, sir, and I wished her a good morning. She saw that I had my laundry, and she pointed to the counter, using her eyes and lips. This was so typical of Filipinos to do. Dad always did that as well. Instead of pointing with his hand, he would look in the direction and pucker his lips. I laughed because I knew exactly what she meant. It was the same place I had picked up my clean clothes the night before. Now I would have a system, so I did not have to make a scene all the time. I would just drop off and pick up my clothes with no guilt.

I told Rose that she did not have to call me sir, but just to call me Kuya. She said okay and then asked if I wanted coffee. I told her yes; I would take it out on the terrace. I fell in love with this 3in1 coffee here. It was so easy to make; everything was in the package already, and all you had to do was add the hot water. I went outside to sit on the terrace and looked across the river to see a group of people exercising or doing some Zumba. Music was playing, and they all looked like they were having a good time. It was still early, I thought, but they were used to getting up at sunrise and not wasting a minute of sunlight. One guy I noticed across the river pointed what seemed like a rifle into the water. He would walk up and down the bank until something caught his attention. I looked closely; he would reel the gun once he shot it into the water.

My uncle then came outside and wished me a good morning. He asked me what I was doing, and I told him I was watching this guy across the river shooting his gun in the water; he said, no that guy is fishing. He told me to watch him aim his gun; he would then reel the fish in once he shot it. As I watched, I could see the man stare into the water and follow his target with his sight on the gun. Then suddenly he pulled the trigger, and a splash appeared. He had nailed a fish and quickly reeled it in. As the man reeled away, I could see the fish jumping in the water trying to escape. But the fish would have no chance, as the fisherman was a true marksman, hitting the fish right in the stomach, making it impossible for him to escape. I thought it was not a big fish by any means, but enough for his lunch. This guy would catch a few more fish that way, and I thought it would be cool to video this, so I took out my phone and started filming him. I noticed a cat following him around, trying to grab the fish every time he pulled one in. It was fun to watch. The shooter finally gave into the cat and threw one of his fish to the cat. My uncle told me that the type of fish was tilapia, a great meal when seasoned properly. After filming, I checked the video to see what it looked like and was disappointed at my filming skills. I got so distracted that I was filming the ground. I had a bad habit of doing this, especially when I videoed my children's basketball or soccer games. I would get so into the competition that I would film the ceilings or the sky. My children used to give me a hard time about this. I think it is funny now, but at the time they would get so pissed at me.

The Family Tree

As we sat and drank our coffee, my uncle would ask about my siblings and all of their children. I updated him on how everyone was doing and whose children belonged to whom. We had an enormous family, just like Dad. My mother and father had five kids, thirteen grandchildren, and eleven great-grandchildren. Shit, there were so many I had to write who belonged to who so that I would not forget.

Uncle would tell me a story of how Dad was a good older brother to the rest of his siblings. Uncle was ten years younger than Dad, making him a kid when dad left for the navy. He would say that since Dad was the eldest, he would have the hardest time with Lolo growing up. It was usually like that with the firstborn, as they had to set the tone for the rest of the children. And because he had so many siblings, they all had to contribute to the family's expenses, no matter what. This was the typical culture of the Philippines. Even if they left the country to work, they would have to contribute. Being that dad had five children, he had a hard time sending money back. I always thought this was why he never went back to the Philippines. He might have been ashamed not to send as much. But this was customary for him to do so.

Family Mausoleum

Uncle said we would go to the mausoleum today to pay our respects to my Lolo and Lola and the rest of the family there. He said we would go early before it was too hot outside. I was excited to see this in person as I only witnessed this in posted pictures. My uncle Met built this rest house for the family. As we drank our coffee, I asked my uncle about the house built behind his. He told me that the family that lived there had been the maids for them for a very long time and that he was grateful for them, so he built them a small house in the back of his property next to the gazebo. The family comprised three children and the parents. The father there was a very good handyman and could fix just about anything. He took care of the fishponds and the yard. The mother was no longer a maid and had a job outside somewhere. Two girls had just finished college and the younger brother. Was still in grade school. College was normally two years, and you would go there right after high school, usually in the Philippines you were 16 when you graduated. The younger brother was about six years of age and was just learning to speak English. Uncle had put those girls through college and always helped that family. Uncle Ren was a very generous man if you have not already figured this out. Next to their house were the maid's quarters.

    The back of the house opened up to a courtyard area where all the house's doors would meet. In the courtyard was what they called a dirty kitchen. The dirty kitchen consisted of a sink and a very large grille. Behind that was where the laundry was hung up to dry. The courtyard had been covered with a tarp to offer some shade. The courtyard is where the maids spent most of their time cooking or washing clothes by hand in the sink. I noticed in the backroom before the courtyard the maids had their own comfort room and a resting area with an old 300-pound TV. I have not seen one of those in a while. But every now and again, I could see the maids watching the local news channel on a very blurry screen. There was not an air-con unit in there, only a fan.

Rose and her sister worked very hard, starting at the crack of dawn until dinner was over. They would get a break after lunch, and I would see them in front of the TV watching a movie. When they ironed or folded the clothes, they would watch the tv.

We ate our breakfast, then we prepared to go to the mausoleum. I took another cold shower and threw on a t-shirt and shorts. Uncle said it would be hot. He filled the cooler up again with water, beer, and coke and brought some pandesal to snack on. As we drove through the town, I could smell that barbeque again and asked my uncle if we could stop and pick some up. He obliged, and we stopped at the very next stand. I picked out about ten pieces of the chicken on a stick. It smelled so damn good. The vendor wrapped them up in a plastic bag, and as I reached in my pocket for my money clip, my uncle had paid the old lady. I told him it was okay, and that I had money to pay for this, but he insisted.

I told uncle that he did not have to keep paying and he said that I was his guest and not to argue with him; enough said. As we drove, we ate the barbeque. After all, it was very convenient to eat while driving because it was on a stick. We arrived a little after lunchtime and entered the graveyard site through a small gate that opened up a vast field. I could see many graves from the entrance. In the back, I could see where all the mausoleums were located. We made our way back there, dodging all the joggers in the narrow streets. When we arrived, the first thing I did was take pictures, and then I asked my uncle if he could take my picture in front of the mausoleum. When we opened the doors, I could feel the heat rush out.

I went to grab the cooler as the uncle would open up the windows and turn the fan on. Now I see what he was talking about, being hot in there. The inside was beautiful. Looking out of the front door, we faced a fence on the edge of the site with a lake on the other side. There were two neighborhoods on each side and a makeshift path connecting the two. The trail circled a small lake that was in between the two neighborhoods. The trail was hectic and even some motorbikes used this path. The neighborhoods were for the squatters. I could see so many shacks that had endless additions to them. Clothes were hanging out to dry off just about every window I could see.

On one side of the vault were the wooden plaques with his brother's and sister's names carved out on them. They had died at a very young age. On the other side were the plaques with my mother and father's names. And right in the middle were the names of the family creation, much large plaques. All the plaques had the birth date and the passing date. We lit candles and said our prayers, and uncle greeted everyone and introduced me to them. I kind of felt weird with him doing that, but I did not say anything. It brought to me this one thought I had when I was much younger.

I had the day off and would tell my mother that it was her day, and we could do anything she wished. Well, her wish was first to go eat breakfast, then go straight to the cemetery. I asked her why she would want to go there, and she explained that she and dad had already purchased their burial lots and wanted to go see them. I asked her if she was kidding me, and she said no, that is what she wanted to do. When we got there, she had the lot number but did not know where it was, so we stopped in the office and asked someone to show us. The lady took us to the lot, which was quite a distance from the office. As soon as we arrived, the lady gave me a sales pitch on the lots and had said that the lots next to my parents were still available. I thought, Is this lady out of her mind? I told her I was not interested in talking about that right now, and she turned and left us. My mother was pleased to see both her and my father's name on the nameplate. I told her that this was crazy, and I had enough, but she said she wanted to get to know her neighbors and started laughing. I told her she would have plenty of time to do that. I thought that was one of the craziest things that I ever did with my mom. I would tell my brothers and sisters about our crazy date later on. I love and miss my mom.

My uncle and I sat down and got as comfortable as we could. He turned the fan toward us because there was no breeze at all coming through the room. The floors were all hardwood; the walls were made of thin brick. They were placed as regular bricks but were just half the size, Spanish-like. The roof was made of the old Spanish-style shingles. It was a wonderful resting place. I took out pandesal, and a piece of barbeque and Uncle would follow my lead. He asked if I wanted a beer, and I said why not? It's afternoon anyway.

Dad's Illness

I knew the question would come eventually, and I thought this would be the perfect time to explain to Uncle what had happened to Dad. I just never knew when Uncle would ask. I never prepared myself to answer him. As we sat there, Uncle wanted to know the details because I was the one relaying the information to all the family. I took a deep breath and started from the beginning. I can remember everything like it was yesterday. I explained to uncle that Dad had had a heart attack and had called 911 himself, and would call our sister, his favorite. Our sister would relay the information to my brothers and me. As crazy as it would seem, Dad prepared himself to go to the hospital and even went downstairs to meet the ambulance. Dad had never wanted to go get a checkup, as I mentioned earlier.

Once they had him in the emergency room, we all showed up and waited to hear the outcome. As we waited for the results, there was talk about preparing for the passing of Dad. I was not having that conversation and immediately got defensive. After about an hour, the doctor came to us and told us the bad news. Dad had suffered a heart attack, but that was not the only issue. We came to find out that he also had high blood pressure and was diabetic. All of these things at once, and to top it all off, he had an aneurysm in his stomach. The doctor explained that Dad would need triple bypass surgery but could not be performed until all the other ailments were under control. He would be transferred to the Heart Hospital once he could do so, but the doctors wanted him to rest here before they moved him. We asked if we could see him, and the doctor said that would be fine.

We all went to see dad lying in bed. When we walked in, he was watching TV. His spirit seemed fine, and it was like nothing was wrong with him. I asked him if he needed anything, and he said he wanted some items from his apartment. I took his keys, and I was off to his apartment to pick up some of his toiletries and his slippers. He also asked me to feed his cat while I was there. I was gone for maybe an hour, then back to the hospital with dad's things. I put them in the closet. Dad said he was tired and would rest, so we all said our goodbyes and would be back in the morning. As we were leaving, a nurse stopped by to tell us that only a few people could be in the room at one time and that it was family only. I told her that all of us were his children and to try to throw us out of the room. She gave me a long stare as we walked away from the nurse's station. It was about one-thirty in the morning, and my brothers and sisters wanted to grab a bite to eat. I told them I would pass as I had to be in the office tomorrow but would see them in the morning after I checked in.

I went to the office to speak privately to my boss about my father's situation. They were very lenient and said that as long as I had my phone and laptop, all I needed was the internet; I could work from the hospital. That way, I would not have to leave Dad all by himself during the day. My boss was always very accommodating, one reason I loved working there. I showed up at the hospital around ten a.m. and did not see dad in his room. When I asked the nurse where he was, she told me she could not give out that information because my eldest brother was the point of contact.

I was so pissed. I told her that it was bullshit; I am his son, and I wanted to know where he was. She went to get the doctor that was on call. He explained to me that my brother would be the point of contact and that he could only give information to him. He then said I could see Dad. I was so pissed as I walked into Dad's room, said hello to him, and immediately called my brother. They had all been working, so I was the only one there. Because he was the eldest, my brother told me he had power of attorney and would make all my father's decisions.

This pissed me off. Anyway, I sat next to Dad and asked how he was feeling. He said that he had been fine but wanted a cigarette and coffee, I laughed and told him that those days were over. He would probably get some coffee, but he was certainly not going to get a cigarette. I asked if he needed me to do anything, and he said he was fine. I told him what the doctors told us the night before, that is not normal. I also told him he would not be in this position if he had had a checkup a long time ago. He just blew me off and said that he did not like hospitals. I told him that was not the point. He could have been taking medication for his blood pressure and diabetes, and he would have felt a lot better. He looked at me and said what is done is done; I knew not to carry the conversation on further. I told him that my boss had allowed me to work from the hospital so that I could stay there with him. He told me that was unnecessary, but I told him he would not win that argument. That was the first time I heard my dad say whatever, almost like a kid. He told me they would transfer him over to the heart hospital on Sunday evening. I thought they would wait a few days longer, but apparently, they got things under control quickly. Dad said he wanted to get something to drink, and I told him they will give him a drink when his lunch came, but he could only have water for the time being. He was so funny as a kid not getting his way; I laughed. I told him I would pour a glass of water for him. He turned on the TV, and I took out my laptop. I could not get a signal in the room, so I asked the nurse if there was any Wi-Fi in the building, and she said yes, but because of all the equipment in the room I could not use it, I would have to go in the waiting room to do my work. I would wait until Dad's lunch came, and then grab a bite to eat myself. As he flipped through the channels, he asked if there was anything I wanted to watch, and I said no, whatever he wanted to watch was fine. I am sure he was looking for some old western movie like the Rifle Man or Bonanza. Dad loved those movies. I can see Dad dosing off, so I went to grab something to eat down in the cafeteria. I would bring my laptop and check my emails.

One of my friends came up to me and said hello as I sat there. She asked what I was doing there, and I told her about Dad, and she apologized and asked where he was. She was a nurse there in the hospital and wanted to stop in and say hello to him. I gave her the room number and told her thanks and continued to read my emails. Before I knew it, about two hours had gone by, and I was like crap. I need to check on Dad. I entered the room to find the doctor talking with Dad. My Dad introduced me as one of his sons, and as long as my dad was awake, the doctor could tell me everything, so I pumped him with a bunch of questions. He said that Dad's blood pressure was under control and that they had given him some meds for his diabetes. They wanted to observe him for a few more days before they transferred him. I asked when that would be, and he said maybe Sunday night. As the doctor left, I could see Dad getting worried. I told him not to worry about anything and that he would be fine. I had a convention coming up that weekend for work through Wednesday. This was a trade show that we had planned on exhibiting for a year now. I told Dad about this, and he said that I should go and that my brothers and sisters were going to be here so he would be ok. I told him I would leave in the morning, and he said that was fine. I did not argue with him. That evening, while my brothers and sisters were there, I told them to keep me posted on Dads' conditions. They said they would, no problem.

When I got home that night, I felt so bad about leaving him. I packed my things for the trip, as I had an early flight out to Florida. As I sat in the airport the following day, I could not help but think of Dad. I waited until I landed before I would call anyone. I called my eldest brother to get an update on Dad, but he didn't answer his cell phone. I thought, here we go. Then I called my sister, and she answered and said Dad was acting like nothing was wrong, and he was hoping to go home. I told her to keep me updated with text messages. The next day, the news was that dad seemed to be in great spirits, and he was going to be fine for the transfer on Sunday night. My sister told me that whenever they talked about being transferred to the heart hospital, Dad suddenly got quiet. I told her I knew Dad was trying to be strong for us, but he was getting scared of being transferred to the other hospital. We just agreed not to mention the transfer anymore when they were in his room, and he should be fine.

Dad's Surgery

Sunday finally rolled around, and I was told that Dad was being transferred that afternoon and that they would perform his surgery on Monday morning. I asked if they were for sure because I was told that it would be a few days after they transferred Dad. My brother said they had controlled all of Dad's ailments and that he would be ready for surgery.

I felt so bad because I thought I could not see him before his surgery. I felt like I was cheated. What the hell was I doing in some stupid convention while my father was going to be under the knife? I would never forgive myself for this. I asked my brother to please call me if anything changes and keep me updated.

I slept little that night and was probably as scared as my dad was. Dads' surgery was scheduled for seven a.m., and it was already seven-thirty. I called, and my brother said there was no news and that it was probably a five-hour surgery. This was driving me crazy. I tried to walk around the convention hall to take my mind off of Dad, but I could not help but think about the whole situation. I sat down to eat at a fast-food stand, and my phone rang. I quickly picked it up; my brother told me that they were still in surgery and things did not look good. I started to tear up and asked what he meant. He said the doctors were taking longer than they usually do. I wondered why, and he could not tell me.

I hung up the phone and called my boss. I explained the situation to him and said that I was leaving the convention a day early. My brother called me about two p.m. that afternoon and told me that the surgery had been hard on Dad, and they thought he would not survive it. But he pulled through. I told my brother that I was on my way and would be there sometime Monday night if I could get a flight. I checked out of my hotel, dropped the rental car off, and made my way to the Delta counter.

At first, the lady at the ticket counter was a little standoff ish. She told me that my flight was not until tomorrow night, and I explained to her I had a family emergency. She told me she would work out the fare to see if I could get on a flight that evening. It ended up being around $700. I could not believe it. When she asked for my ID, I could see her entering the information. She said sir; you have status with us, and you did not tell me.

I apologize for the delay, but we will get you on the very next flight. They would have to charge me a change fee of $200, but that was a far cry from $700. I jumped all over it and thanked her for helping me out. This is the reason I love flying Delta. I would give her some accolades when Delta asked for a quick survey. Since I did not sleep well the night before, I fell asleep on the plane. I had a connection in Atlanta, so it was more of a nap. When I finally touched down in Norfolk, I picked up my luggage and raced to my car. I went home first to shower and change.

As I was on my way to the hospital, the thing I could not get out of my head that night was my brother telling me what to expect when I got there. That Dad was not responsive, and the meds will take days to wear off. He had been hooked up to so many machines that he did not know which device did what.

As I drove, I could not stop thinking about how guilty I felt. Would Dad ever forgive me? I reached the parking garage and ran straight into the lobby; I did not realize I would have to check in first, and security stopped me. I showed my ID, and they took my picture and then printed out a sticker that I had to wear. They told me I needed to do this every time I came in. Once I was in their system, I had to show my ID again, and they printed out my sticker. I asked where their ICU department was, and they gave directions. As I entered the ICU, the nurses asked what room I was going to. The ICU unit was very strict with visitors and their hours. She had asked me to wait in the lobby, and she would come out and get me. They had to make sure that only two visitors were in the room. My sister was the one that came out, and I could see her crying as she walked up. We embraced, and I immediately asked what was going on, and she said to just see Dad. As I opened the door, my other brother held Dad's hand. I looked at my father and realized that he was not the same man I had left a few days ago. They had to put Dad in a coma because they found he had an enlarged heart and could not breathe on his own for a while. I did not understand what all that meant. This was the reason Dad's surgery was longer; they did not expect to see this when they opened him up. He would be on some machine to keep his heart pumping for a while until he could gain strength. My heart was broken; I have never felt so much loss in such a short span. Tears ran down my eyes as I went to him. I begged for his forgiveness for leaving him. I grabbed his hand and repeatedly apologized for not being there. My brother soon comforted me and said it was not my fault. But I could not help it. I cried and prayed and then cried again. Dad was motionless and seemed to stare off into space. I could not believe what I was seeing. He had aged that much in a few days. I was just a broken man and could not get it out of my head. I whispered into Dad's ear that I promised I would never leave him again. My elder brother told me that Dad was on a VAD machine, a Ventricular Assist Device. This would help the heart pump blood to other organs, as he was too weak to do so independently.

As I was telling the story, I could not help but become emotional in front of uncle. I paused a bit and noticed that he had become just as emotional as I was. We would both need a break. He stared out into the cemetery and told me a brief story of how he was so proud of my father for being in the Navy and helping the family out when he could. At that moment, I realized I had a gift for Uncle Ren. It was one of Dad's Navy rings. I pulled it out of my pocket and told Uncle I had forgotten to give this to him yesterday. He took it, looked it over, and asked if it was Dads, I said yes; it was. He sat down and wept. I gave my uncle some water, and he thanked me for this precious gift.

Over the next few days, Dad's condition did not change. I stayed with him pretty much all the time except to go home and shower. This would become routine for me. My sister brought some of Dad's music that she had found in his apartment. She thought it would be soothing for him because it was all in Tagalog. A little hometown vibe. I could not imagine what was going on inside Dad's head as he was still out of touch with the world. The nurses were extremely polite in this area of the hospital. Of course, there were many Filipina nurses. I had asked one if she could talk to him in their language as she checked on him. She agreed, and I was so happy that she did this. Even though he could not acknowledge her, I thought the sound of a woman's voice in Tagalog would trigger something. After a while, all Filipina nurses would speak to Dad in his language. Days went by and I continued to work out of the lobby.

The First Movement

Eventually, Dad moved to a larger room, and I could spend the time in there with him. I rarely slept as the nurses were in and out all the time. They would step down his medicine and try to wake him up. About a week after his surgery, I could see Dad move his hands; he was finally waking up. It was about eleven p.m., and I texted my siblings about the great news. They all came first thing in the morning. Dad was still out of it, but at least now his eyes were closed, and he was moving his hands. This was a very positive sign. I sent texts to all of his brothers as well. I had become the liaison between the families. They were happy to hear about Dad's progress.

I remembered Dad's condition the last time I saw him; he seemed nothing was wrong other than what the doctors would tell him. He seemed very normal to me. There was a point where I felt that doctors just needed to practice surgery and practice on my dad. If he were okay then and could live a few more years without the surgery, I am sure that is what he would have decided to do. This never ever came up, and it disturbed me the more I thought about it. I feel that he was cheated and given no options. I felt Dad would want to go on his terms.

Early the following morning, I could see Dad moving more. I went to his bedside and asked him if he needed anything; he just looked at me like I was a stranger. I still did not think he could hear me at this point. I grabbed his hand and held it. Again, he did not seem to recognize me. The doctors said that his medication would have some side effects and eventually wear off. I was just happy to see him awake. I immediately texted my siblings. A nurse came in and was pleased to see that he was awake and said I should turn the tv on so he could watch. I turned it on and tried to find a channel with some old movies that he would like. I came across one that was showing some old westerns and left it on; these were Dad's favorites. I was not sure if he could hear or even notice the TV on, but I did what the nurse suggested. She also asked me to leave the room for a minute so that they could perform an Echo test on Dad's heart. Echo was short for an echocardiogram, which is a test used to monitor the heart's function. They would do this to see if dad could eventually get off the VAD machine. Since Dad was under so much medication, he could not sit up or move. My heart dropped as I watched the nurse as she changed some dressings around Dad's scar. It shocked me to see how long the scar was on his chest. I wondered if he could ever recover from this and live everyday life. He was already old and was a heavy smoker. This was the reason that he had complications. The average recovery for a triple bypass surgery was twelve weeks, but Dad had so much shit wrong with him I assumed it would be longer. He would lay there motionless as the nurse worked him. I know they are trained to do things a certain way, but she was not gentle. I wondered if he could feel anything. It was about seven a.m. now and I would get coffee and update the family in the Philippines with Dad's progress. This became routine for me because of the time difference. I would tell Dad that I have to go home and shower and come right back. I did this week in and week out. I had promised him I would not leave him again, but I had to have a shower.

Dad was still on the breathing machine as he was not strong enough to breathe on his own, and doctors said that his lung had collapsed the night before, so they wanted to make sure that oxygen was getting to where it needed to go. I saw the nurse one time stick a tube down his throat; I asked what the purpose of this procedure was for, and she explained that he would have so much mucus built up that there was not any other way to get it out. If he coughed, it would become very painful. The procedure looked painful. They do this every time they check on him. It usually lasted about only a few minutes. This had to be very uncomfortable, but he still could not move, so he had to deal with it.

Natural Disasters

Uncle asked if anyone else was able to spend the time with Dad, and I told him they had work and that my company had been very flexible with me. I told him that my siblings came during their lunch hours or after work just about every other day, if not every day. I can remember the only time Dad was alone. The National weather service had predicted a hurricane, and all visitors had to leave the hospital. I tried my best to negotiate with the nursing staff, but it was out of their hands. It was hospital policy that all non-essential employees and visitors leave the building. I would have to leave and call the next day to see if they allowed visitors. It would last about twenty-four hours. The storm was not as bad as they had predicted, but there was still a lot of flooding and downed power lines. I made it home just in time as the roads flooded and the winds picked up. It was a long night with the winds howling and the sideways rain pounding the windows; I could barely sleep. I opened up my laptop and did some work. I noticed I had some trips scheduled in the coming weeks, and I would send emails to reschedule all of them. I also logged some more notes into my planner to tell Dad about his adventure when he was better.

The following morning came, and the wind had died down considerably. I looked outside as I drank my coffee and figured I could go nowhere until some of the water had subsided. I called the hospital, and they were open, and visitors were welcome if they could get in. The lady at the information desk where I had called mentioned that many streets were still underwater. I waited until after lunchtime to make that trek through the standing water. That week was weird as far as natural disasters; we experienced a small earthquake earlier, we never had earthquakes on the east coast. So, for a hurricane and earthquake to hit Virginia in the same week was shocking and frightening. The earthquake was small compared to what they have out on the west coast, and for the most part, it went unnoticed. I finished my lunch and prepared for the trip to the hospital.

The roads still had a lot of standing water, and I followed the cars out of the neighborhood and onto the interstate. As I drove, I could see some damage from the winds; large tree branches were sprawled all over the place. Gas station signs were blown down, and I could see a lot of downed power lines. This large tree had been uprooted on the ramp leading to the interstate. A crew with chainsaws worked feverishly to remove the tree from the ramp. It was about a 15-minute delay, but better safe than sorry. The entrance to the parking garage was still underwater when I arrived at the hospital. I watched as another car tried to make it through, only to stall. I thought, what a dumbass; trying to drive through the water. I drove around to the other entrance and found it was accessible. I went up a few levels just in case it rained some more.

I made my way to the ICU department, where Dad had been staying. As I entered his room, I noticed his doctor, who performed the surgery, checked up on Dad. The nurse asked me if I could file all of Dad's paperwork for him. I told them I could not sign it and that my older brother had power of attorney to sign any of Dad's documents. They said that was fine and that they only needed to process his insurance information. That would not be a problem, I said. I wanted to first ask the doctor a few things. I wanted to know when Dad would come off of the ventilator, and he told me that Dad was still very weak and would have to work up the strength to breathe on his own. He gave me a tube and said that dad would have to blow into it and record a certain pressure. Dad was not ready to start this practice. He was still out of a bit. I gathered his insurance cards and brought them to the registration. I explained to the clerk that my eldest brother would sign all the documents and the young lady told me it would not be a problem at all. Dad had the best Insurance in the world. His account would be zero when he left the hospital. Over twenty-three years in the Navy and another twenty in the civil service certainly had its benefits. He did not have to pay a dime.

I do not understand why he never took advantage of this. After I finished there, the clerk wished me the best of luck for Dad and said she would keep him in her prayers. I arrived back in the ICU unit and found one of Dad's coworkers there asking to see him. I explained he could not take visitors right now because he was still in intensive care and that I would call him once Dad could take visitors. He thanked me and told me that all of his ex-coworkers were praying for a speedy recovery. I started to realize that dad touched many people in his lifetime. All this time, we all thought of Dad as a hardass. At least on his children. Dad was different when it came to his grandchildren. He was a hell of a lot kinder and gentler to them.

I always asked Dad to have a check-up, but he always changed the subject. I believe he was too afraid to find out all of his ailments. It would not cost him anything to get checked up, so that had to be the reason. And if you ever brought up his smoking, forget about it. He always said that it is none of our business.

The Will to Survive

Dad was slowly waking up. I noticed the nurse had shaved his face and cut his eyebrows. I thanked her for that. He was moving more and more each day, gaining his strength back. I know most of the moving came from his discomfort of having all these tubes attached everywhere. He had a catheter for his urine and one for his stool. I know this had to be uncomfortable. As he gained more strength, he would try to remove the oxygen tube and the tube going down his throat. He had IVs in both arms for food and meds. I started to see Dad as I had recognized him before. There was more color on his face. He was finally waking up for real. The nurse rubbed his arm and called out his name, trying to wake him up. When he opened his eyes, I felt that there was hope and that he would recover soon. This was not normal for a patient to be out for as many weeks as Dad had been. Dad had been in a medically induced coma during his surgery because of the complexity, the doctors explained. Then he was on heavy meds for about two and a half weeks. I could not imagine what went on in someone's mind during this time. I could see panic every time he got into a coughing mode. All the nurses would rush to his side, and I could actually feel his pain just by looking at his face. Dad was a big-time smoker, so they actually had a nicotine patch on his arm.

When Dad finally woke up, I could see he was looking around the room, probably wondering where he was. He tilted his head from left to right, searching for something he could remember. I walked up to him and said good morning. I grabbed his hand, and he looked at me for the longest time. I remember doing this a week ago, but he was still heavily sedated, but I could see purpose in his eyes this time. He lifted his hand a bit and could see all the IVs attached to him. He was overwhelmed at the sight, and I could feel him getting scared again. I told him that everything was okay, over, and that he just needed to get better. I felt that he could hear and understand me at this point because he watched me as I was speaking. But I did not want to ask him if he could hear me or knew who I was because I did not want to overwhelm him. I told him that the rest of his children would be here soon. I ran out of the room to call my siblings and tell them that dad was finally awake. They were all very excited and had many questions and made their way to the hospital as soon as they could. I then called my uncles to give them the good news. Everyone was so excited. My siblings brought their children in to see their Papa for the first time in weeks. We told them to keep happy thoughts as they would go in and visit Dad because I wanted everything to remain positive. It was sad to watch as the grandchildren came in and saw their Papa; they started crying. Since there were only two visitors allowed in the room, we told them to limit their visit so that everyone else could see Dad. It was a happy and sad moment for me. While we all waited for our turn to visit Dad, the siblings spoke about letting outside visitors in and we decided to wait at least another week to see if Dad was off of all his machines.

I also messaged my ex-wife to see if she did not mind bringing my daughters after school. She said that would not be a problem. This made me very happy. I have seen little of my daughters since Dad was in the hospital, and I needed their hugs right now. So much emotion these past three weeks, and I did not know if I could survive it myself. I called work and gave them the good news as well. I was so thankful to my boss for understanding my situation. They have been accommodating during this whole nightmare, and I was so grateful. My eldest daughter was the first one to show up, and I told her not to be alarmed when she saw her Papa because of all the things he was hooked up to. She was just shocked to see his condition, and tears ran down her face. I explained to her he was in much better shape than a few weeks ago, trying to soften the reality she was seeing. One by one, all of Dad's grandchildren made their way to see him. They all had made "Get well soon" cards and posters for him. I took my second oldest daughter in with me, and she cried right there on my shoulder as she was holding Dad's hand. She wished him well, and as far as I could see, Dad showed no emotion to anyone. I explained to her it was the medication, and it would soon wear off, and then he would realize who he was talking to. Before we left his room, she turned to the window and pointed out two rainbows. She told me she would think of her Papa whenever she saw two rainbows in the future. We went back into the lobby to let the other grandchildren in. It was fascinating to hear some of their stories about Dad while waiting. Most of them were funny stories. They all agree that Dad had the loudest sneeze. He practically screamed when he sneezed, and it scared everyone. They all told stories about when Dad frightened them. Then they talked about Dad's pants. He always wore what we called highwaters, pants that were above his ankles. They all tell their stories that were very entertaining to the rest of the family. There would be laughter and tears by the end of the night, but we all needed this at this difficult time. The only grandchild that had not been there to see Dad was my son. He had been on duty, but I kept him informed. The following week was kind of comical for Dad and me. As he gained strength, he tried to take everything off. He could not walk so he was still hooked up to the catheters and I can see him trying to wiggle his body because I knew it was uncomfortable. Dad still has trouble speaking, so he pointed and shook his head yes or no. He could move his arms pretty well and started trying to talk. I brought in a whiteboard to see if he could read and write. He could, but not clearly. The first thing he wrote was the word home. I explained he could not go just yet and that he needed to get better first. He gave me a dirty look and wrote home on the board again. I wrote to him saying that he needed to show some improvement before they let him go and that he was still here for his own good. After he read it, I felt that if he had enough strength to smack me, that is what he would have done. He was pissed. I told him we needed to practice on the breathing machine every day so that they could remove the oxygen mask and tube from his throat. The nurses kept the tube in because Dad had a lot of mucus built up, and the tube was removing it. If he got into his coughing mode again, it would be more painful for him.

 The nurses told me it was time to move Dad into a stepdown unit, another department that did not require the critical care he was getting in the ICU. That meant that he was getting better. This was good news. But Dad was still going to be too weak to walk and eat, so they would keep all of his IVs and the catheters in. I constantly fought with him about keeping the IVs in. I remember the one night he kept me up until 3:00 a.m. trying to pull the IVs out. I told him I would let the nurses secure his hands to the bed rails if he kept this up. He gave me the dirtiest look. The next morning, I told him I had to go home to shower and come right back. When I arrived back at Dad's room, I noticed they had secured him to the bed rails. I asked the nurses, since I was there, could they remove the restraints? They said to give it a few more minutes so that he understood they would restrain him again if it happened again. I removed the oxygen mask and started having Dad inhale and exhale into the practice tube. I missed the fact that they had removed the tube down his throat, so this was good news. The new nurse there told me I could now give him some water and ice chips if he wanted them. I asked Dad if he wanted water, and he shook his head yes. It pissed him he was being restrained, and I told him I would untie it. He must have been thirsty because he drank half the cup of water using the straw. After I untied him, he pointed to the whiteboard; I gave it to him, and he wrote "Home" on it. I told him that as soon as he got better, he shook his head no. Then he looked away from me. Inside, I felt so bad for him because he was far from his comfort zone. He wrote on the whiteboard to take down all the get-well cards and drawings the children and grandchildren had made for him.

Dad was miserable at this point. So, I let him be for a while and went to get some coffee.

The Extended Relations

As I walked back to his room, a young nurse stopped me and asked if she could speak with me. I said no problem; how can I help you? She then asked if Dad was from Bacoor, in the Philippines, because the name sounded familiar. I told her he was born and raised there, and she seemed delighted. When she first saw the name, she said that it was familiar to her, and that she called her auntie in California to tell her. She gave me her Auntie's phone number and asked if I could call her and I said I would, no problem. I then asked her if she could go to Dad and speak to him in their native language and tell him her findings. That her auntie and my dad were second cousins. She said that she would, and I wanted to see his reaction, so we both went into the room together. She greeted him traditionally, with the blessing and then spoke, "Kumasta Po, kumasta ang pakiramdam mo? Naninwala akong ikaw ang aking tiyahin ay unang pinsan mula sa Bacoor."

From what I could understand, she asked Dad how he felt and said that her auntie and my dad were cousins from home. Then she continued, "Ang aming pangalan ng si ay Eusebio."

I saw Dad look at her and nod his head slowly; yes. She smiled at him and then kissed him on his cheek. She was so excited to call her auntie and let her know it was him. Before she left, she turned to me and said, please do not forget to call my auntie; she wants to hear from you. I asked her what the last thing she had told Dad was, she said her family name was Eusebio. I told her that was his middle name and his mother's maiden name. She said yes, now she could tell her Auntie. I promised her I would call that evening. I asked her what her name was, and she said it was Angelina and I said you or your Auntie? She said her name was Angelina and her Aunties name was Maricris. I said okay. I thanked her, and she was off to call her Auntie herself. She seemed so excited. After about thirty minutes later, Angelina returned and started to pay attention to Dad more than ever now. I was happy that she took care of him and spoke to him in their language. I could see Dad react to her more than any of the other nurses. I see more and more of her now that she realizes that there was a family tie. Maricris was a relative from my Lola's side of the family. I really knew little about them. When I spoke to my siblings, I mentioned it to them, and they were all excited to meet her. They even asked her if she could be the only one to take care of Dad, but she said she could not because of how they have to rotate in and out. But I noticed she would always come by and speak to Dad when she started her shift, even when she was not assigned to his ward. I thought what a small world we live in for this to happen. Just from the last name, this young nurse made the connection to my father. I called her Auntie that night and spoke to the daughter of Maricris. She mentioned she talked with Angelina about Dad and wished him well. Maricris would be asleep by the time I called, so I promised to call her back the next day.

The Grandson Visit

The following morning, I received a text from my son asking where Dad was. I told him the room number and asked when he could come to see Dad and he said he would be down this afternoon. I was so excited to see him as he had been gone for a couple of months and had not seen his grandpa since he had been in the hospital. So, I told the rest of the family that he was finally going to see his grandpa and they all wanted to be around. I went back into the room and told Dad that his first grandson was coming to see him for the first time. He did not seem too excited and pointed to the whiteboard again. He wrote, "I want to go home now." I told him he could go home soon, and that he had to gain more strength.

Uncle Ren was a little confused by this because he thought Dad was out of harm's way and in full recovery mode, the reason they transferred him into the step-down unit. I explained to Uncle that he must remember that I called him and gave them the good news about Dad's progress. I said yes; he was making progress but in tiny steps. Usually, after this type of surgery, patients were already dismissed from the hospital, but he had been there a month in recovery in Dad's case. I explained to Uncle that they had to put Dad in an induced coma for the surgery. It took Dad a long time to recover from this, the reason for his long stay in the hospital. Uncle understood, and I explained Dad was progressing slowly.

That afternoon, I met with my son in the hospital's lobby and prefaced him on Dad's condition. I did not want him to be surprised when he saw his grandpa. He had come straight from his post and was still in his Army attire. I thought back to when his grandpa pinned his bars on him when he became an officer. I was a total surprise for Dad. He did not know that he would be the one to pin the bars and give him his first salute. We waited for my son's name to be announced; when that time came, they also announced if Mr. Hermoso would please approach the center stage. Dad looked around totally surprised, and I said, "Dad, that is you; they are calling you up there."

Dad made his way up to the front of the reception hall, where he met with his grandson. The Major then handed the bars to Dad and announced Second Lieutenant Hermoso; then Dad pinned the bars on each shoulder. He was so proud of his grandson and would not miss it. It was a very proud moment for me to see Dad pin second lieutenant bars on his first grandson. Dad made his way back to me and whispered, "You should have told me I was going to do this. I would have worn my dress uniform."

I told him that his grandson wanted this to be a total surprise.

We walked into the room, and I saw Dad's expression. He had finally seen the last of his grandchildren. He reached up and touched his grandson's face and held it there.

Tears immediately ran down the side of my son's face and mine. My son grabbed his grandpa's hand and apologized for being so late to see him. Dad kept shaking his head as if he were saying it was okay. I could see Dad tear up, something he had not done at all. Dad brushed his hand across his uniform and then looked back at my son. I took a tissue and wiped his eyes. He pointed to the whiteboard, and I handed it to him. He wrote once again, "Take me home."

I looked at my son and explained to him that dad could not leave until he got better, and we all had to stay positive so that we could help improve his condition. My son excused himself and I walked outside to check on him. I knew this was not comforting for him to see his grandpa this way. I looked around and asked my siblings if they saw him, and they said they think they saw him go to the elevators. I made my way out to the main lobby downstairs and saw my son sitting on a bench outside. He had his head buried in his hands. Crying as I walked up, he apologized for not being there earlier. I told him not to worry; everyone understood he could not come right away and not to worry about it. He was so broken to see his grandpas' condition. I told him that his condition was a lot better now than when Dad first came out of surgery. We spoke for a few more minutes, then we went back up to see Dad. I just wanted to make sure he had settled down before we went back in to see Dad. I know seeing his grandpa for the first time in his condition was overwhelming for him.

When we got back to the room, Dad's demeanor had changed. He did not care about all the get-well cards and drawings hanging up; he literally pushed the whiteboard towards me. I asked him if he wanted to tell me something, and he just looked at me with defeat in his eyes, knowing he would not leave for a while. He stopped, trying to rip the tubes from his arms, and lay there motionless. I felt him; I knew what he wanted to say for the first time in my life. I looked at him, shook my head, and said, "No, please don't give up now; you came too far."

Dad passed away with another minor heart attack triggered by a coughing episode that evening. I had to make calls to all of his brothers and sisters. I found this very hard to do, and there was a ton of emotion on both sides. As my siblings and I gathered the following day in his room to take his items, young Angelina came into the room crying and apologizing for what had happened to Dad. I told her I believed Dad wanted to say goodbye to everyone and had held on as long as he could until he could see his grandson. I asked her if she could inform her family for me. She asked for my address, and I kindly gave it to her. She told me she would be transferring back to California to be with her family, and we exchanged goodbyes.

Things We Left

After I told Uncle, we sat there quietly staring out of the mausoleum into the fields. My dad's passing changed who I was. I do not know how to explain it. It is like all my family is gone; I did not have any grandparents or parents that were still alive. I felt cheated that my parents were gone so early. I was alone for the first time with no one. The following weeks, I kept to myself, still wondering how I went through my whole life not knowing my father because he was always out to sea or working multiple jobs to support us. So, I focused on the times we had together, good and bad. As my siblings and I went through Dad's apartment, we started to separate the things we would keep, donate, and trash. Going through all of this was going to take some time, as he still had a lot of Mom's stuff in the apartment. We started moving stuff to the trash bin and I must have made a dozen trips to Goodwill to donate their belongings. I felt so sad just giving all of their possessions away like that. I could see Dad up in heaven getting pissed off because we were going through all of his things. We all laughed about it at one point. Those two weeks were met with happiness and sorrow. I had been an emotional wreck but kept everything inside and never let anyone know. I would cry myself to sleep every night. Even though I had children, none living with me, I felt so alone.

We discovered Mom and Dad also had a storage unit they were renting. Since my company was very flexible, I volunteered to inventory the unit. When I arrived there, I explained to the manager that I did not have access to my parent's unit and that they had died. The manager was very sorry to hear this news and gave me everything I needed to gain entrance. She told me not to worry about the rent any longer and take as much time as I needed to clear everything out. She mentioned she adored my father because every time he made Chicken Adobo, he would bring some over to her. It was her favorite Filipino dish. She also said that he was the only customer that ever did that for her. His apartment was only ten minutes from the storage facility. She would miss him as well. I never knew that Dad did this for anyone. Hell, I love Adobo as well, and he never brought me any. I would soon learn about some of the little things that he did that made an impression on many people. I never knew him to be like this.

I reached the unit and realized it was a ten by ten-foot unit. When I opened it up, I found the damn thing was full all the way to the top. I thought, another entire week cleaning this out. I took a snapshot of it and sent it to my siblings. I went through everything the following day. They could not believe all the shit that was in there, considering all the stuff in Dad's apartment. I told them I would go back in the morning to break everything down and give them a complete inventory.

The Worst Movie Night

That night, I looked through one container that I had brought from Mom and Dad's apartment. The container had old photo albums; as I glanced through them, I came across a photo of us at the drive-in movies. I remembered back to when we would go to the drive-in movies. That was a treat for all of us because we would stop by McDonald's first. Back in those days, you could feed a family of seven for under ten bucks. We would all load up in the station wagon with our snacks and drinks. Usually, the days before our special treat, we would be on our best behavior so that our drive-in date was not canceled. This one particular time, we went to watch the Green Berets. Of course, this was a movie that Dad wanted to watch, but all of us boys also loved to watch this army movie.

It had started to thunderstorm in the middle of the movie, so we all had to get into the car and roll the windows up with just enough space for the speaker to fit. It got very hot, and Dad's favorite daughter began to cry. All of us boys were trying to keep her quiet, and of course, Dad would intervene and ask her what was wrong. When she said she wanted to go home, we all freaked out and argued with her. Finally, Dad threatened all of us boys with a severe ass whipping if we did not shut up. We all immediately shut the hell up whenever Dad got to that point. It did not matter where we were, Dad would beat our asses. The ride home was even worse. We would whisper to our sister that she ruined the movie for the rest of us just because she was afraid of the thunder. We continued to harass her, saying things like she was a baby and always got her way. Our oldest brother even told her that when Dad was not home, he would smack her. She immediately told Dad, and with no warning, he backhanded me right in the face while he was driving. I tried to complain

Kenny Hermoso

to him it was our older brother and not me, but he just said for all of us to shut the hell up. This was the story of my life growing up, lol. I just dealt with it. I figured one way I would understand him more was to see where he grew up and how he lived. I got excited thinking about it. I planned the trip to his hometown shortly.

Family Visit at Sangley Point

Uncle Ren asked me if I was hungry, and I told him no. It had to be around four in the afternoon now. I popped open another San Miguel Light and lit a cigarette. Uncle told me a story of when Dad left for the Navy. The family was very proud of Dad when he signed up for the US Navy and sad because they knew he would be gone away from them for a very long period. Dad came back after his initial training, and the whole family could visit him on base at Sangley Point Naval Station. Uncle was just a boy but remembered seeing Dad in his navy uniform. They were called dungarees, the working uniform worn by the junior enlisted sailors. The dungarees comprised the traditional Navy white dixie cap, a white t-shirt with a blue chambray shirt and the bell-bottom jeans with black leather boots called boon- dockers. His name had been stenciled in black right above the right chest pocket. I could see some pictures that Dad had of this, but never knew who was in these photos. I promised my uncle I would bring them on my next visit.

The friend of Dad's, 777, was there to see him off. This would be the last time she saw him for many years. Dad had been courting her for some time before he was shipped off. Dad never discussed this girl with anyone, and as the story goes, he broke her heart long ago. He didn't see her again until my mother died, and he visited the Philippines. I asked Uncle if we could go to Sangley Point, and he said we could go there at another time, and it was close to Cavite City. We would visit many sites where Dad grew up. I was very excited. We soon left to go back home.

When we arrived back home, I went to shower and cool off; the cold water felt so good. I looked for the piece of paper that Imelda had given me and tried to message her. I figured she was probably traveling but sent her an email, anyway. I wanted to tell her about my first couple of days in the Philippines and how easily I adapted to everything. I also wanted to thank her again for her excellent hospitality during my flight from Japan. I left my number for her if she had some free time and wanted to have dinner or something like that.

After emailing her, I took out my notebook and made more notes of the day's events and places. I went to drop off my laundry and found my clean clothes ready. I could smell something good being cooked in the kitchen and I would surely be ready to eat again. I swear I ate more in the Philippines than I did back home in the states. I walked into the kitchen to see my cousin frying chicken. She said this was her specialty, and it sure smelled like it. I had forgotten what day it was already and had to look at a calendar. I spent two whole days already and thought, wow; the time is flying by. As I was waiting for dinner, I went out to the terrace while the sun was setting and thought what a beautiful place this is. The streets were still busy from the hustle and bustle of workers coming home and students getting out of school. I could not imagine.

Dad growing up here because I only knew the way of life in the US. Of course, growing up here seventy years ago is a far cry from what it is today. Anywhere for that matter, with all the technology these days.

Extended Visit

I can remember as a kid, we did not have color television until the late 1960s and only maybe four channels. Now you can get thousands of channels on a smart TV that I don't even know how to operate. If there was one thing that Dad taught me growing up was to keep things simple. I still remember the aluminum foil he used on the TV's "Rabbit ears." He says that this made the picture clearer. If a plane were to fly overhead, the entire picture would be destroyed for a minute. The TV stations typically shut down after the late shows, so there was nothing to watch by midnight.

A few minutes later, Liza called us in for dinner and bragged about her special fried chicken. It smelled so good I could not wait to taste it. Along with the chicken, Liza served rice and some type of sour soup called Sinigang. The soup was delicious, as well as the rest of the meal. Fresh fruit was served after our dinner. I was so full. I gave Liza a great compliment on the dinner, which made her very happy. I asked her to prepare it again before I left; I liked it so much. After dinner, we watched some TV.

A movie that had just started, called *A Mother's Story*, was about a mother who left her family to work overseas. I watched the movie and realized how true it was for Filipinos to work abroad to make money for their family. It was sad, but she got rewarded big in the end. I will not ruin it for anyone that has not seen it, but it is a must see.

It was now late in the evening, so I said my goodnights and headed to my room. A few minutes later, there was a knock on the door. It was my cousin Rico asking if I needed anything. He stood in the doorway to have a conversation, so I asked him if he could come into the room. He asked me why, and I explained that the cold air would leave the room, and the mosquitoes would come in. He said he would not be that long, so I would say okay.

A few minutes passed, and the damn door was still open. I acted as if I was exhausted and ready to sleep, so to make him close the door and let me rest. He got the message and left. As I lay on the bed, I heard a mosquito buzzing. I tried to run them away because I could not see the damn thing. I started thinking, "God damn it. I told him to pull the door shut."

I pulled out my laptop and read some emails from work. I answered as many as I could.

Came across one email from my boss asking me about a client here in the Philippines. The client reached out to my boss, and my boss told him we have our sales manager there in the Philippines right now. The client was happy to hear this, but I was not ready to put my vacation on hold. He asked me if I would reach out or possibly meet him. I emailed my boss and explained that I was on vacation and probably would not meet him. To my surprise, my boss had just read the email and replied, "Maybe I should contact them."

My answer was that I would email him and if he had some time, could he possibly meet with me? My boss's reply was that he would let me expense the airfare and hotel if I could meet with him. I immediately searched my contacts for the client and shot off an email. I will not hear back from the client until tomorrow, probably. So, I continued reading some other emails and suddenly got a reply from the client saying he could not meet me next week, but for sure the following week. I emailed my boss back and told him what our client said, and he asked me if I would not mind staying there in the Philippines for another week. Yes, I told my boss. I will stay. He said I could expense all my hotel, food and travel costs just like I was in the states. I then decided to visit a few other clients that I knew from a few years back that we did business with. I was so excited to see more of the Philippines. Plus, I could stay another weekend here in paradise. I will put this together sometime this week.

I made some more notes of the day's experience and shot off some text messages to my family back in the states. I could still hear that damn mosquito. I soon fell asleep. I woke up to my favorite chickens squawking at each other. I looked at my phone, and it read six-thirty. I got up to use the "CR," or comfort room as they call it. I did my business, then washed my face and brushed my teeth. Then I looked into the mirror and noticed that my eye was swollen and had a big, red mosquito bite right underneath it. I was so pissed. All I could think of was my cousin standing in the doorway last night with the door open and talking to me. I finished washing my face and brushing my teeth. I went downstairs to get some ice to see if I could reduce some swellings. I went back upstairs to get my laptop to make some more notes, then came back downstairs. The maid asked me if I wanted some coffee, and as I turned to answer her, she was startled to see my swollen eye. I immediately told her it was fine and was just a mosquito bite. She nodded but stared at me as if I had a horn growing out of my forehead. I asked her to bring my coffee to the terrace, and she nodded yes. I set myself up on the terrace and quickly noticed a cool breeze. This morning felt so good. I opened up my email, and to my surprise, there was an email from Imelda.

This put a smile on my face, even with this fat swollen eye. She said she would not be available until two weeks from now. That was perfect because I would be in the city by myself at some hotel by then. I emailed her back and told her that it would extend my stay because of work, and I looked forward to meeting her. I emailed her later the hotel's name so we could meet somewhere close to there. I also asked her for her local phone number. I was excited about her return email.

Alfonso Trip

Around seven-thirty in the morning, my uncle had just woken up. He came outside on the terrace to make sure I had coffee already, and I said yes. He looked at me and asked what had happened to my eye. I told him I believe I got stung by a mosquito last night. He said he would get Rico to spray the room when he woke up. I said okay. The whole time I thought, it was his fault, anyway, damn it! He told me we would leave around noon and not be back until very late because we had about an hour and a half drive. I asked him where we would go, and Uncle said to meet more family in Alfonso. I was excited to see this place because I remember Dad telling us about the family property there and how he was hidden there during the Japanese invasion. This was going to be an exciting day.

Recently, I saw some pictures Dad took during his visit to Alfonso when he was here last. As I went through the plastic containers in the storage unit, I could not help but think about what my siblings and I would do with some of the possessions of our parents. There were so many things that we would split up once we went through everything. I started pulling the containers down and setting them out next to the storage unit so I could take a picture of their contents. I found picture albums, Christmas decorations, and some of my sisters' things. There were also clothes, shoes, and coats. Dad also had a lot of tools stored there, including some of his old gardening tools. If you remember, I mentioned Dad did not throw shit away. There was not much to keep from the unit other than the pictures and my sisters' things. The clothes would be donated along with all the Christmas decorations. After I took pictures of everything, I packed it all back up and put it back into the storage unit until my siblings and I decided what to do with it all. I sat there and opened one of the plastic bins with the pictures and looked through them.

There were a few pictures I remembered about Alfonso. Dad had mentioned that the entire family went there during his last visit. He said it was the family farmland. Dad was always proud to tell the few stories of his family and the properties back home after his visits there. There was a picture that I recognized from before, from the Philippines. It was a photo of Dad walking down the street when he was in his late teens. I tried to think of where this picture had been taken because Dad was dressed up. But the picture was black and white, but I had to admire how Dad was dressed because he looked sharp. I thought, wow, Dad knew how to sport threads back in the day. I tried to look at the picture and imagine what Dad was thinking. Did he know he would join the US Navy and have five children? Was he going to spend the rest of his life in the Philippines with his girlfriend 777? How come I did not know him? Who was Dad? What was he like when he was a kid? What were his likes and dislikes? Was he an excellent student? I did not know any of this. How could I go through my whole life not knowing? I broke down and cried out there in the middle of the afternoon in the storage facility. I felt cheated that I did not get to know him better. Did I make enough effort to find out who this man was? Why in the hell did I feel this way about him?

Rico finally woke up and came downstairs. I could hear him ask the maid for some coffee. He took his coffee out on the terrace with Uncle and me. Uncle said to him to spray the room because there are mosquitos in there.

He looked at me and said, "Wow, Kuya, what happened to your eye?"

I wanted to say, "Remember when you kept the door open last night, and I was trying to get you to close it, and you did not? You just stayed in the doorway and let the mosquitos fly right the fuck in!!!"

But I said, "I guess a mosquito got in the room somehow last night."

He then told me that I should keep the bedroom door closed at all times.

I looked at him like, are you saying that shit to me right now? I let it pass and agreed with him. "Rico, we must make a better effort to keep the door closed."

Uncle said we would leave around noon, so we needed to get ready. I jumped into the cold shower, followed by a shave. When I opened the bathroom door, I smelled the mosquito spray and saw Rico spraying it all over the place.

I asked Rico, "Why are you spraying when I'm in here? You should have waited until I was done in the room."

He just shrugged his shoulders. That mosquito repellent was strong. I grabbed my things and told Rico to make sure he shut the door completely. I went into the bathroom downstairs to continue getting ready. It was warming up there. I rolled my eyes at the thought of why I was in this heat, getting prepared. As I thought about it, the whole situation was comical.

We loaded the cooler with water and brought some snacks for the drive. We drove Uncle Ren's old truck. Something he was very proud of. He took excellent care of it. As I mentioned before, it was a 1995 Isuzu Strada, and he pimped it out. The drive would take approximately two hours with traffic. We stopped off at a gas station to gas up first. To this day, all gas stations in the Philippines are still full service. We pulled up, and a young kid spoke to uncle, "Magkano Po?"

Uncle answered 1000Php regular.

"Sige Po" was the answer from the kid. As we drove down the highway, Uncle told me stories about when they were kids on this same route, that he only used to see a few jeepneys and only about ten cars all day. I thought, wow, how things changed because as far as I could see, there were thousands of cars, buses, and jeepneys. So much traffic and we were not on the main road yet. We made our way through the municipalities of Kawit, Imus, General Trias, Dasmarinas, Silang all the way to Tagaytay before reaching Alfonso. We stopped in Tagaytay at Starbucks for a quick cup of coffee and to see the famous Taal Volcano. Starbucks had a beautiful view overlooking the Taal lake. I would take a couple of pictures there. The Taal volcano was probably the world's smallest volcano, but one of the Philippines 'most active. It is in the middle of Taal Lake in the province of Batangas. Unlike other volcanos, Taal was not a mountain top type volcano. It is also part of the Pacific Ring of Fire; a belt where volcanic eruptions and earthquakes are most common. From the mountain ridge of Cavite, this was one of the most picturesque views in the Philippines. The location was even used in the movie Apocalypse Now, an old Vietnam War story. We finished our photoshoot, grabbed our coffees, and continued on our way. Alfonso was less than a half-hour away.

From the Aguinaldo highway, we entered Alfonso off the primary route, Tagaytay- Nasugbu highway. There was a huge welcoming sign for Alfonso as we approached the entrance. I thought, wow, this is the motherland and where my dad's side of the family was created. My first impression of Alfonso was that it was full of rolling hills and farmlands. Like other municipalities, storefronts and small, personalized shops were located right on the street. We continued our way down Luksuhin-Mangas Road. Uncle Ren suggested we roll down the windows now because it was a lot cooler in the mountains here than in Kawit and turned the air-con off. Plus, he wanted to smoke. As we drove deeper into Alfonso, I noticed the houses were further apart than in the city. I saw lots of banana trees and more and more bamboo. The terrain looked like jungles to me. We turned left onto a dirt driveway where a small concrete house was located. We parked the truck and got out. An old lady was sitting on the porch and as we walked up, a young man and another lady appeared in the doorway. They were relatives, first cousins to my dad. The boy was my nephew. They spoke very little English, so Uncle did most of the translation.

When Uncle told the older woman that I was Boy's son, she waved me over to sit by her on the porch. She ran her hands all over my face and spoke in Tagalog. Uncle said how she could see him in me and that she was very sorry that he was gone already. I got all choked up for a while and sat there quietly. Lola continued to hold my hand as we sat and did not seem like she was letting go anytime soon. She spoke about Dad when he was younger and how all the ladies say how good-looking he was. She said they all wanted to be his wife.

I smiled at her after Uncle translated this for me. Uncle then said to Lola, "That apple didn't fall from the tree," in his native tongue.

Lola smiled and put her palm on my cheek and said, "Nasa dugo" or in English, it is in the blood.

I had to smile back at her and say, "Opo."

After a few minutes of sitting, there was this God-awful smell. I looked up at Rico and asked if he had passed gas. He shook his head. Laughing, he mentioned that there were pigs in the back. That explained the smell for sure. We took a stroll around back to the covered pens to find eight giant pigs; They separated one because she was pregnant, and another one separated because she had some piglets. It was very noisy, with them all squealing, especially when we got close to the piglets. The heat and the smell made it unbearable to prolong our visit back there. We took a stroll further back into the property and found chickens running all over.

There were plenty of coconut trees and other fruit trees I had never heard of. They were native to the provinces in the Philippines. Some of them were Atis, Lanzones, Rambutan, Chico, Balimbing, and Caimito are the most common in just about every area. Then they have jackfruit and, of course, mango and banana trees. There were so many I would get confused talking about them. We ate some fruits right from the trees. The Rambutan, or ugly fruit as they would call it, was lovely. I ate a few of them. The Atis was a big, lumpy fruit that was sweet as well. They would never run out of fresh fruit, for sure. There were even a few coconut trees there. We made our way back to the front of the house to see the old auntie still sitting there. We said our goodbyes and told them we would be back before I left. We drove a few kilometers down the road and came to the family's property.

From the roadside, it looked tiny but stretched out in the back. The house was tiny, with addition after addition in the back.

We met there with Dad's nephew, Jhonnie. A man in his sixties who was still in perfect shape. Uncle introduced me as the "Boy's anak."

He looked at me with surprise. None of my siblings have ever been to the Philippines, let alone this deep in meeting family members. Jhonnie immediately greeted me and asked if I needed anything to drink. I answered no, I am fine right now. He motioned me to sit there on the porch and asked his wife to make some coffee.

Uncle Ren then said, "This is your second cousin."

I said, "Wow, how many cousins do I have here?"

Uncle answered, "Too many. We cannot meet them all while you are here."

We sat and talked about how the family was doing back home, and I said fine. Jhonnie's children made their way out onto the porch to meet me; five in all while one was not there. They were all nieces and nephews, and then they had children.

The temperature was lower in the mountains there but was still very warm. They asked if I wanted to see the natural spring down the hill. I could not wait to see this. Dad had pictures of this on his last visit. I took a peek out back, and it looked like a jungle to me. I had asked Jhonnie if I would be okay going back there in shorts, and he said I would be fine. Jhonnie spoke a little English. It was only one or two words, just like when I spoke Tagalog. I thought this was funny, and he was my counterpart. Jhonnie was wearing shorts also and no shirt. He had a machete slung across his body.

I still could not believe how fit he was at his age, even being a smoker. I could not believe his physic at sixty-five. I commented on his condition, and Uncle Ren said it was because he would get fresh water every other day from the spring. I was not even thinking about how and where the spring was. I just said, "Okay."

We made our way through a winding path, thick bamboo clumps everywhere; It amazed me to see how tall and thick each bamboo was. There were mahogany trees around as well. They were planted there some forty-five years ago with the idea of harvesting them for profit, eventually. There were so many different trees there, unlike anything I have ever seen. I was introduced to all the many other fruit trees as well. This was where they hid my father during the Japanese invasion. I had asked Uncle to show me the spot where it was. Uncle said it was further into the jungle. As we made our way down the path, we came upon a small shack with a dirt floor. This was where they would hang out and cook when they were younger. They would stay there overnight sometimes. I asked my uncle where they slept, and he said on the dirt floor. Even though it was in the afternoon, the exceptionally high canopy of the jungle kept it looking like late afternoon. There was no breeze there, so it became hot again as we walked. We came to a spot where there was a vast area of bamboo clumps. This was the area where our Lolo had hidden Dad for weeks. I took a photo of this place and imagined dad as a kid surviving out here day in and day out. The bamboo was so high that to look at the top, you were bending backward to see the tops. At the top of the canopy was a small breeze; I knew this because the bamboo made a frightening sound when they shifted or knocked into each other. Cracking wood is what it sounded like, and the wind would vibrate down to the bottom of the bamboo, making a humming sound. Dad was a kid when he was brought here, so he must have been scared to hear this in total darkness. The bamboo was so thick and tall that I couldn't believe that anyone could have any makeshift home.

We proceeded further into the land and could notice there were some pretty steep cliffs in front of us. We made our way to the edge and continued alongside the cliffs. I could not believe that Jhonnie was still without a shirt and walking in flip-flops. We came to a valley where artificial steps were carved into the side. They spiraled along the hillside. We took the steps down into the valley and went to a small, flattened area. The foliage was so thick that we still could not see to the bottom, and the path we were taking continued to spiral along the hillside. We took a quick break and then continued. We came across some more carved out steps that seemed steeper than the previous set, making it more challenging to get down to the bottom. Things became very slippery as we got closer to the end. I felt a cool mist as we reached the very bottom of the valley. We can see a stream flowing in between the hills and was on the family property. Jhonnie brought us to the side of the hill, where we could see many makeshift fountains coming out of the side of the hill. This is where the fresh spring water came from. Jhonnie had cut bamboo in half, making a pipe that would lead to some buckets. Jhonnie then carried the buckets back to the house. This is the reason he was still so fit at his age.

The overflow spilled into a small stream that moved through the very steep valley. Jhonnie spent a lot of time there, constantly fixing the cut-out stairs and makeshift plumbing. You could see how steep the hills were and wondered how we made it down there. The area opened up to a bed of small stones with more enormous boulders displaced from the hillside scattered all over. We stayed there for a few minutes longer so that I could take some photos. Uncle Ren said we should go soon because the sun would set and soon be dark. I quickly found out that the climb down was much easier than the climb back. I did not realize how far apart the stairs were as we made our way back up the side of the mountain. We all stopped for a minute to catch our breath and drink water. After about twenty minutes, we reached the top of the hillside. It was getting dark in the jungle, and we had to pick up the pace, because we did not bring any flashlights. We made it back to the house just in time. I could smell food and had built up an appetite with all the climbing and walking.

As we walked in, my nieces had set up the table with banana leaves and all kinds of meat, rice, and vegetables lined down in the middle of them. This was the traditional "Boodle Fight" of the Philippines. It originated from the Philippine Military Academy, having its commanding officers and the ordinary soldiers eating together as a symbol of brotherhood and camaraderie. There were not any utensils; we stood side by side and picked the food with our bare hands. This was Philippines culture at its best. You picked some rice, ball it up, add meat and veggie, and then down the hatch. You poured many sauces in front of you and dipped a handful of creation into it. Some spicy and salty. Either way, I ate like a pig and could not imagine my siblings doing this. Afterward, we all met in front of the house and sat and smoked and had some drinks. They gave me a shot of Alfonso liquor; it was a powerful brandy that I had to chase with some San Miguel light beer. After three shots in, I was feeling pretty good. Uncle Ren and my cousin Rico did not drink at all. Since I was the guest of honor, I was given the attention of the liquor. I finally said, no more, that I am fine. Whew, that shit was strong.

I gathered all the children together and played a game with them. I held a 100-peso bill down and said they could have if they could catch it with their two fingers. The game's object was that they had to catch the bill with their thumb and pointer finger only. There must have been eleven children there. They all were excited and lined up for their turn. I gave them a demonstration, so they knew it was possible. They failed to catch the bill and would go to the back of the line one by one. Soon the whole family watched and laughed at the kids and tried to coach them. There were about forty family members there that I did not even know existed before I arrived. One of the more minor children was next, and I let him win, and all the other children charged me. I took out about 2000 pesos, all 100-peso bills, threw it up in the air and let them have at it. The family cheered and had a great time watching all the kids fighting to get the bills. In the end, one little girl cried because she could get none of the bills in all the madness. I called her over to come to sit on my lap. I comforted her for a bit until she stopped crying. Then I gave her a 500-peso bill. And the crowd exclaimed, "Wow!"

It took thirty minutes to say goodbye to everyone. I thanked Cousin Jhonnie and his wife for having us over and preparing the delicious meal for us. They wished for me to come back before I left, and I agreed. It had been a long, tiring day.

On the way home, Rico dosed off, and I soon followed. I had quite a bit to drink today.

I woke up halfway through the ride home with Uncle yelling at another driver for blocking his lane. He cursed the driver in Tagalog. I asked if everything was okay, and Uncle was determined that the driver was purposely blocking him. The car in question was a Jeepney, and the driver pulled around a parked vehicle and would not back up. Uncle was not backing up either, so we were at a standstill. There was not enough room to pass for either of us; someone had to move. By now, the streets were dark, and I suggested to uncle to let him pass first, but uncle said that the other cars behind him would also have to back up. There were far too many cars to get this done.

Rico got out of the car and went to talk with the Jeepney driver. He explained we could not back up and that he should because he had some space to do so. Rico told the driver that we would hold the traffic behind us once we pass so his Jeepney could pass and not wait. The driver eventually backed up and gave Uncle a dirty look as we passed. fifteen minutes had passed since the standoff. Uncle told Rico to get into the truck and not wait for the other cars. I laughed the whole time because Uncle was so pissed that he did not live up to Rico's bargain.

Fishpond Fun

We finally arrived home around tenant night. I helped bring some things inside and then went to my room to shower. I could still smell the mosquito spray from this morning. It was still strong. I made notes on the day's events and then checked some emails. I noticed an email from my boss asking how the vacation was going and if I had reached out to the clients. I messaged him back to let him know I did trade emails with our client, and they wanted me to travel to the project sites in Bohol and meet with the end-users. I also told him I had reached out to other clients and set up more meetings. He would be happy to hear that he was getting his bang for his buck.

I checked my emails and was happy to see an email from Imelda. She had been in Japan but wanted to meet shortly. I sent her an email explaining I would check into the hotel on Manila Bay in about a week. I had searched for a nice hotel in the Manila area, knowing that I could expense it. I found this beautiful hotel on the shores of Manila Bay and very close to MOA, the Mall of Asia. Not overly priced and great location, I made my reservation for a few nights' stay. I noticed the pool area was beautiful, and there were lots of pictures of the sunset there. A very picturesque setting. I wrote to Imelda that we could even eat at the restaurant there because it looks pretty nice. I was excited to visit there soon. Hopefully, she will make it there as well. After all, she mentioned she would be off that week.

Day three was now in the books. I slept with my head inside a sheet to not smell the mosquito spray as much. I was soon fast asleep. I woke up around seven and showered. I arranged my dirty clothes to bring them downstairs and pick up the clean clothes. I dropped my clothes off the spot and picked up my clean clothes. Rose gave me a nod and asked if

I was ready for my coffee, and I replied yes. I took my clothes back to my room and then went outside onto the terrace to have my coffee. I sat down and waited for Rose to bring my coffee. Across the river, the Zumba class was in full swing. The music was loud, and there were lots of people working out. There were so many children making their way to school as well. Some of the young girls were walking with umbrellas to block the sun. The day was already hectic. Rose brought my coffee onto the terrace and asked if I wanted some breakfast; I said sure. I imagined Dad sitting on the terrace with his coffee and cigarettes, enjoying the view. He did this in his apartment back home. But had to prepare things himself there.

Today we would visit Sangley Point, the Naval base where Dad originally joined the US Navy, and some schools he attended. I was excited to see these places. Uncle was up and came outside to have his coffee as well. He mentioned that there were some changes in our plans today. There would be a family gathering on the fishpond today so that we would postpone our trip to Sangley Point until tomorrow. I told Uncle it was not a problem at all. Outside of their gate, there was a small opening to the street from the river, a makeshift boat ramp, where all the river dwellers docked when they came to get water and groceries. It was always busy down there. The style of boats on the river was called Basnigan without the outriggers. They were some twenty feet long and about three feet wide at its widest spot. They resembled a canoe but had a motor built into it. The driver sat in the very back, where he could steer the vessel. The small boat ramp was always busy from the early morning until dusk. Few boats were on the water after dark there. We left for the fishpond around noon. I did not know what to expect to see, so I was curious to go there now.

Uncle Ren and I sat out on the terrace. I asked Uncle how far it was to the pond, and he said it was only right there, maybe a 15- minute boat ride. I told him I've seen so many boats come and go, and he mentioned that these are the people that live on the water. I then told him I could see that some people made their home right there under the bridge. He said they were squatters, and the government cannot stop all these people from building makeshift homes because so many of them were there. But they have been getting better at helping these people find places to live. Most of the squatters have been displaced by a natural disaster and some are just relocating because there is no work in their province. Mostly, these are all normal Filipinos that had hardship fall on them and are decent hardworking citizens. The culture is God, family, then work, a tradition that most of us forget about in this modern world. I learned more and more about my father each day I spent there. I kept trying to imagine his demeanor while he was here. What was different for him being here in the Philippines versus being in the states? I know it was very different for me, but I grew up in the states. This continued to bother me, not knowing. How I wished my father and I could have traveled here together.

I kick myself now and think I should have been more persistent.

We prepared the coolers for the trip to the fishpond, loading soda, water and beer. We also loaded food that we would cook out there. It sounded like a lot of fun. Uncle asked if there was anything special that I wanted, and I said no, everything was fine. I did not want to become this burden to the family. I kept everything very simple. It did not want to be labeled a "Prima donna" from the states.

I went upstairs to shower and charge my camera and phone. This was going to be a fun day, and I wanted to take a lot of pictures. I checked some emails after I finished preparing. There were a few emails that caught my attention. Some clients I reached out to in the Philippines got back to me and agreed to meet with me while I was there. So, I now had four appointments spread out over two weeks. I would have to prepare a show-cause report for my boss to approve the two weeks instead of one week. I worked on this later and noted completing this in my calendar.

The first boat arrived, and we loaded the food and coolers on it. We then took five of us on the first trip. Two boats ferried us back and forth. As we made our way down the river, we came to the bridge I spoke of earlier, where their families made homes underneath it. I made a video of this and took pictures to remind myself and my siblings how life is not so hard for us. The makeshift home looks like it had two families there. A couple of kids were playing on the shore, and as we passed, they waved. I waved back and thought how hard their life was living there, but they were still happy. Teenagers were looking at something on their cell phones. They had their boats docked alongside the riverbank. Life seemed normal for them.

We made our way down the river and came to a split. We bared right and continued on. I started to see artificial barriers used to separate the boundary lines for each property. They were made of rocks and dirt that you could walk on. As we went further, I could see houses built on the river. These were wooden-built houses, not like the ones on land. It is hard to believe that these houses could withstand a typhoon.

We came to the first property of the family. It looked like an enormous deck with lots of room for parties. We pulled up beside the dock and started unloading the coolers. As soon as we finished, another boat pulled up. Our boat went back to make another pickup. I cracked open a San Miguel Light and wandered through the enormous deck. Made of bamboo, I could hear the floor creak every time I took a step. I would have to be careful as it probably was not made for a 180-pound American.

I noticed that there was a bathroom and a kitchen area. The entire platform had to be around thirty-feet by thirty-feet. They built it around trees, so it was cool to have shade out there. I looked across the river and saw some dogs running around on the artificial seawalls. These dogs were known in the Philippines as street dogs or as Askal. These dogs were just about everywhere I had traveled in the Philippines. They all looked the same, just different colors. They were just free as a kite without a worry on their minds.

In each of the ponds, I noticed these nets that were used to catch all the fresh seafood one can eat. We would eventually go to another pond and check the nets there, as the nets were checked here this morning. Uncle said we would have to take another boat ride to get to it. So, we had a few minutes of wait time. I took some pictures of the ponds; so many of them. They eventually empty to Manila Bay. There were lots of coconut and banana trees lining the shores as if they were purposely planted. Before the waters reached Manila Bay, thick mangroves outlined all the fishponds, a filter of sorts. During storms, the waters are polluted with plastic bottles, bags, and other trash. You could see some of this in the mangroves, and river dwellers were cleaning this. I had asked Uncle if these people were city workers, and he said no, they were just normal citizens that wanted to keep the mangroves clean. I thought, what outstanding citizens they are.

We took the next boat over to the other fishpond that seemed more open and more significant than the one we were just on. We pulled up to the dock, where a few Askals ran wildly around the artificial barriers. After disembarking the boat, we went to a small hut that provided shade. I told Uncle I wanted to go around and see the place; I did not mind the heat or sun so much. The Askals followed me wherever I went. They were not mean dogs, but I kept my distance, anyway. Who knows what they were carrying? I found a private spot where I could take a piss without being bothered. As I peed, one dog was drinking it right before me. I tried to turn away, but another dog was thirsty as well. I had to laugh and ask myself what was wrong with these dogs. I pissed right into their mouths. That was gross. For sure, I would not touch or try to pet them. I went back and told Uncle Ren of the incident, and he laughed and said to me he forgot to tell me they would do that.

My uncle had a man that took care of the fishpond every day. Rex pulled a net in, and I watched. As he pulled it in, I could see lots of fish splashing, trying to escape. When he finally pulled it out of the water, he had crabs, prawns, and plenty of fish. I was amused; how fresh does it get? Rex took two small fish and threw them at the dogs. The dogs ate the fish alive, which I had never witnessed before. The crabs had enormous claws, and I thought about all the meat there. I could not wait to taste it. We ended up with about twenty crabs, fifty tilapia, and twenty prawns. The prawn resembles the likes of large shrimp. How I wish I could fry them up, lol. We took one small crab and threw it at the dogs; I wanted to see if they would eat it live like the fish. One dog grabbed it and immediately started chewing on it. They must have had a crab before because they bit it right in the back and instantly killed the crab. I could hear him crunching on the shell. These dogs ate anything and would learn that this was all they ate daily. Sometimes they would go days before eating again, which explains why they ate everything.

We noticed a big splash in the middle of the pond, and I was curious what it was. My cousin would tell me that a couple of big catfish in there have never been caught. They were too smart to go near the net.

We packed up the day's catch and made our way back down the river to the deck. I noticed more people there now. I would certainly have to meet them, as there were some that I did not know. They were friends and relatives from all over the waterway. I could smell the hot coals from the barbeque starting up. It smelled so good, and I was getting hungry now. We sat around the table as all the questions had started. Questions from if I were married to how many children, how long I would stay, and if I wanted to meet someone's niece. We talked for hours, and I could see Dad sitting there telling stories of his family and adventures in the United States. All conversations led to Dad. As the day got longer, I cooled myself with San Miguel light. It was like water to me. All the women were busy preparing today's catch.

I could smell my favorite marinated chicken being barbequed, so I got up and went over to one auntie and asked if I could sample a piece. She gave me one, and I devoured it. I went back to the table to hear more storytelling. I learned Dad was a very hard worker back in his younger days. The typical family culture of the Philippines was that everyone worked for the family, not individually, like many Americans. I had to think about that and realized that they were right in a way saying that. We Americans lived a liberated life. We had everything at our fingertips and worked to buy things we wanted, not necessarily needed. Some watermen talked about working every day to live for that day. One older man asked me how many pairs of shoes I had. I had to think about it; I had work shoes, dress shoes and many tennis shoes or athletic shoes. I told him that maybe I had twenty pairs in all. The old man said, wow that is many pairs; why do I own so many? He then explained that most of the common people had maybe two pairs at the most. They did not buy them if they did not need them. I made a joke about Imelda Marcos having over 500 pairs of shoes.

They all laughed and said she was THE exception and that most Filipinos did not live the way she did. I remember Dad or Mom would always sew or patch our clothes. We never threw them out. And if you had new clothes, you had better take care of them and make them last. It is funny how I still live under those terms with my things. My brothers and I all shared the same jacket during our high school graduation photos, so I understood the culture back then. I was used to having these hand-me-downs all the time. So, growing up, we would take care of our clothes, knowing they would be passed down. To this day, I still have clothes in my closet that are older than my children. I remember my daughter coming to me one day before school and saying, "Dad, it's Nerd Day in school, so I need to borrow some of your clothes."

I told her that my clothes were nice clothes, not nerdy at all. She laughed and said okay.

We all sat down to eat, and the very first thing I noticed was that everyone was eating the crab bodies and not the giant claws. I asked why, and they explained that this was the healthiest part of the crab. I thought, the hell with health right now; I am cracking open those claws. There was plenty of meat in those claws. I dipped them in a sauce that my auntie made up. I think it is comprised of vinegar and soy sauce. After a while, everyone started piling up their claws in front of my plate. I told them to keep the claws coming.

Along with the crab claws, I ate rice, barbequed chicken, and tried a piece of fish and some vegetables. I bet I gained weight while I was there just in the week that I had spent there already. Uncle and I would move from the main table to smoke. He mentioned how happy he was to have me as his guest. The entire family welcomed me, he said. He spoke of how it brought back memories of my dad. He could see Dad in me, some of my actions and thoughts. I explained I was close to my dad's side growing up but far from him as in a relationship. Being around him and watching him do things just grew on me over the years. I told my uncle that I was so happy to be here and how I wished Dad were here as well.

During my dad's funeral, I catered to all of his siblings that attended. Uncle Ren and Auntie Wen could not get their visas in time, so they didn't attend. We did not hold the traditional Filipino burial ceremony, the Nine-day Novena. This is very traditional in the Philippines, where family and friends will gather each evening after the passing and pray. Once you start it, you are committed to praying each evening.

I would later receive an email from my uncles and aunties that attended, thanking me for entertaining them. This email made me feel like I was close to Dad. My uncle mentioned that all of his siblings said out of all dad and Mom's children, I am most closet to the Filipino culture and that I resembled my dad the most. This made me want to visit the Philippines more and more.

Night had fallen on the fishpond, and the mosquitos were out in full. We turned on some large fans, yes; they had electricity there, crazy. They also lit a lot of citrus candles to keep them away. I continued to enjoy the ambiance of the tropical island life at night. All the women would check on me every five minutes, asking if I wanted more food or drink.

We would make our way back to the house; it was amazing how the boat driver could navigate at night through some of the narrow passages; he had been on the water for a long time. We passed under the bridge where the squatters lived, and I could see some lights on, and music was playing. Life goes on for them. As we approached the house, I could see the Aguinaldo Shrine was a wonderful site lit up with different colors. I snapped a few pictures.

When we hit the small dock, I told Uncle I wanted to run over there really quickly and snap some more shrine photos. Rico followed and said that they were having a festival there as well.

That explained all the music I was hearing. As we approached, I could see many small booths set up for vendors selling anything from food and clothing to handmade souvenirs. I picked up a couple of homemade bracelets and magnets to bring home. Again, it seemed like I was the only foreigner there, as all eyes were on me. I felt like a movie star walking around. Some girls in the booth spoke excellent English. They asked me where I was from and how I liked the Philippines. Am I married? The same questions over and over, but it was okay with me. As I would leave one booth for the next, I could hear the girls giggling. Some of the food booths had my new favorite food, chicken barbeque. But I was still so full, I could not eat anymore, but it smelled so damn good. There were many vendors, and we tried to see as many as we could in the short period we would be there.

Naval Base

We finally got home, and I desperately wanted to take that cold shower now after being outside most of the day. After the shower, I made notes on the day's events. I always wanted to make sure that I did not forget to write anything down. It would make for a good story one day, I thought. I opened my laptop to check on emails, hoping to find one from Imelda. I know she is busy flying everywhere, so I did not expect to find one. There was an email that I was happy to see. She mentioned that she would be pleased to see me in a week and be on leave the entire week.

I wrote her back saying that I would first stay near the airport because I have to fly to another place called Bohol. I would be there for an overnight trip, then transfer to the hotel by Manila Bay, maybe Wednesday afternoon. I was looking forward to seeing her again. I wrote a summary of where I have been so far and what we have been doing.

I can't believe that I have already been here for one week. It felt like over a month. I looked over my notes from the trip and realized how much information I had taken down. The family here has been so accommodating. I learned so much about my father in only a week of being here. Something about taking the same steps he took when he was alive here in his hometown gives me some peace and understanding. I tried to imagine him being there, and how he reacted everywhere that I had gone. One thing for sure is that I know he would not be outside in the heat as much. I closed my notebook and soon fell asleep.

The following day, I woke up to loud music being played across the river. I went out onto the terrace outside my room to see all the commotion. It was like the entire community was doing Zumba. It was only six-thirty a.m., but the town was already so busy. I could see cars lined up, ready to turn into Aguinaldo Park. There must be some type of festival going on there. I took a quick shower and made my way downstairs. The maids were already up and must have heard me coming because they were making my coffee already. I think it was Saturday morning now; I wondered what would be in store for the day's adventures. I took my coffee on the terrace as I usually did in the morning to watch the town wake up. Over the years, I have learned that people watch me. Being in another country, I tried to watch more and more, but I realized people are the same all over the world. They have their daily plan, and they wake up and go do it.

Uncle met me out on the terrace. We said our good mornings and then got into our daily discussion. Of course, I asked him what was going on this morning at the park. He told me a festival was going on there, and vendors would set up their booths all morning. Most of them are food vendors, but he said there would be a lot of vendors selling arts and crafts of sorts. The first thing that popped into my mind was the chicken barbeques. I could not wait to get some. Uncle mentioned Uncle Met was in a band, and they would perform at a local bar and grill this evening. I said it sounded like fun and would love to watch. We would revisit the mausoleum this morning to put down some termite control. He wanted to do this early because the smell was strong, and it would have to sit for twenty-four hours before anyone could go inside. So, I went upstairs to shower and get ready. I checked some emails and found that one of my appointments was pushed back a week. I had to immediately communicate this to my boss for his advice on whether to stay. I would not hear from him for a few days as it was Friday night back in the states.

The roads were bustling so early in the morning. So many Jeepneys and tricycles are already crowding traffic. A typical weekend morning here in the province. As we made our way into Bacoor, Uncle showed me where Dad went to school as a kid. I could not believe it was still there and Uncle said that it was still in use. After maybe 70 years and still in service. You can ride around town there, and there are few empty buildings like back in the states. If they build it, there is a purpose, not just putting it on the market for commercial sale. No space is wasted here, and for perfect reasons. The landmass is not as large as other countries because of the number of islands.

While we were on our way to the mausoleum, we stopped around the corner from Dad's old elementary school so I could take photos of the old school; I wanted to show my siblings back home. Then I tried to imagine my dad walking to school as a kid in his uniform. From where the family house was in Aniban, Bacoor, it might be a ten-minute walk. The streets were not as busy back then and the houses were fewer and farther between. And the street corners were probably set up by Japanese checkpoints during that era.

Since we did not have any pictures of Dad when he was young, I asked Uncle if any of the family here did. He said he was not sure, but he would ask around. I wanted to see what he looked like when he was a kid. In all of those photos that I found in Dad's possession, there was none of him when he was a kid.

I could not wait to see the city in a couple of weeks. My only view was driving from the airport, but it was at night and not really in the central city of Manila. I heard about all the casinos, restaurants, and malls. That is one thing I noticed even since I have only been in Cavite is that there are a lot of malls.

We arrived at the mausoleum, and Uncle sprayed the termite repellant all over. On the way back, I asked Uncle if we could stop and pick up some barbeque; he told me that there would be plenty of the barbeque back at Aguinaldo Park. I said, okay, sounded good. I asked Uncle what kind of kid Dad was, and he told me that Dad was a good kid and did not get into a lot of trouble. Being the eldest of his siblings, they all looked up at him. There might have been a twenty-year spread from the eldest to the youngest. Lolo was hardest on Dad and wanted Dad to set a good example for his younger siblings. When Dad left for the US Navy, uncle was still a kid, so he had a few stories to tell. Dad had graduated college from the University of the East and held an accounting degree. He would log some of his assignments in his diary and when they were due. He also wrote letters to some women he was interested in and dated it. I just thought about how cool that was, being some fifty-eight years later, and how technology has changed. He grew up in a household with only a radio and no television. He worked small jobs wherever he could to help support his family. Uncle mentioned it was a sorrowful day when Dad left for the Navy. He can still remember the whole family being there and having a picnic on the base before leaving. Like I mentioned earlier, his girlfriend was there as well. I still have those photos of them at the picnic. I asked my uncle where Sangley Point was, and he said maybe only thirty minutes from his house. I asked if we could go there, and he told me we would eat lunch first and then go there. I was excited about going there.

We got home, and my cousin and I went to the park to get some barbeque. I saw some of the same vendors there from the other night. All are selling the same things. Some vendors remembered me and asked if I wanted to buy more. So, I picked up a few more handmade bracelets with wooded beads. I also picked up some t- shirts for my children.

After lunch, we made our way out of Kawit and into Cavite City. Cavite City is where the Philippine Navy is based. Cavite City was like the parts of Cavite that I had seen already. Storefronts were right on the street side and lined up the street. There were so many restaurants also boasting of having the best food. Uncle was correct as it was not far from home. As we approached the gate, I could see its resemblance to the US Navy bases back home. I got out of the truck and quickly snapped some photos of the prominent signage and of the gate itself. I got back in the truck and asked Uncle if we were allowed in. He did not know, so armed guards came out of the guard shack and stopped us as we pulled up. The guards were dressed in their fatigues; they must have been hot. They asked us for identification and Uncle explained to him we are not in the navy but only wanted to visit because my father was recruited from here many years ago. The guard apologized to my uncle and said we could not proceed onto the base. I had asked the guard if I could at least take some pictures from the main gate, and he told me to do it quickly. After all, it was Saturday, and there was not much traffic coming into the base. I took as many pictures as I could. As we passed by the guards, my uncle thanked them for letting me take the photos and we were soon on our way back to Kawit. We talked about the Navy there and I asked Uncle where are all the ships? He told me they have a few here, but most of them are out patrolling the waters all over the Philippines.

I was told that the main headquarters were in Manila, close to the US Embassy. I did not realize that they had so many vessels, around one hundred or so with some aircraft. The Philippine Navy does not have any aircraft carriers. Back in the US, I lived most of my life around naval bases because of the many years Dad had put into the Navy. I could see three aircraft carriers in port and supporting vessels in my hometown. These aircraft carriers were so big they could be seen from miles away. I live pretty close to the most extensive naval base in the world. So, I always felt pretty safe. In the Norfolk and Virginia Beach area lies the largest concentration of military. All branches are here, along with the Joint operations base. We could always see and hear the fighter jets making practice runs. So amazing how fast and loud they can be.

I Became Him

When Dad was on his way home from deployment, we always got excited; we started cleaning the house and fixing shit a week before he got home to make sure that he did not have to do anything upon his return. Mom would be so excited she would almost forget to take us with her on the day of his arrival. We packed into our Rambler station wagon and made our way to the base. When a fleet was coming home, there would always be a shitload of traffic, so Mom would always leave hours before the boat was due in. A Naval support team on the base would keep the wives and families updated on the fleet's arrivals, including the dockings. Because it would take a whole day to dock the fleet, we were only interested in Dad's ship, so we would leave the house three hours before he was due to dock.

When the ships pulled into port, the sailors were lined up on the upper deck in their dress white (traditionally worn by enlisted sailors in the Navy). Even as a kid, it made me very proud that my dad was out there defending our country. They would stand there until the ship was docked and secured and until they were dismissed. Once this happened, it would take another thirty to forty-five minutes for each sailor to make their way down to their quarters, grab their gear, and then make their way back out to the ship's gangway. There were so many sailors on board that it was almost impossible to tell who Dad was when they were on the deck. Of course, hundreds of families would be lined up in a cordoned-off area waiting on their sailors. A few times, there would be some crazy lady that broke through the makeshift barricade and ran to her sailor. Everyone would always applaud when they saw this, and security did not stop them. So, we would wait, and all eyes were on the gangway to see when dad would make his way out. When Mom would finally see Dad, she would start crying; then my baby sisters would start crying. All of us boys would grab his heavy ass bags and stay out of Mom's way.

The first twenty-four hours were always great. Dad would have some stories and always brought gifts from other countries where they would dock. Dad always would go back to the ship the next day to get the rest of his things. I always looked forward to the sea rations he would bring home. Some of that stuff was pretty tasty. Dad would find out if we were bad during the next few days while he was gone. Mom used to say, "Wait till your father gets home; I'm going to tell him how bad you were." I was never sure whether Mom kept a list, but my brothers and I wondered when the Kraken would be released. Dad seemed like he took inventory of all of his shit, and if he found something missing, the world as we know it would just stop until it was found, or a suitable solution was accepted. It did not take long before Dad was back to his usual self. When he got pissed, we would typically stay out of his way.

It was now mid-afternoon in Cavite, and the sun was hot and high. Mostly everyone walking around had umbrellas to block the sun. It was busy there in Kawit. I wanted to go across the street to the little store just to experience it and see what was available. The store was probably a ten foot by ten-foot room with a shallow ceiling connected to the main house. There was no entrance, so you had to look through the gated counter to see what you wanted. In the store's corner was a small color TV broadcasting the local news. There was a fan on the wall in the opposite corner. In the middle of the room was a table with lots of food for sale there. From the outside looking in, you could see some fresh baked goods in the window below the gated counter.

Pastries, bread, and even prepared food like fish or chicken were stored here. To the right of the window was a Coca-Cola cooler full of coke products, small water bottles, and cold San Miguel. There were also some meats like sausage and siapao. There was a shelf running the length of the store in the back packed with small, canned goods like sardines, spam, corned beef and vegetables, and sauces. Again, I thought how Dad said they needed the spam there. Along the ceiling were strings tied from one end of the store to the other, with chips and candies clipped to it. Some meds were there as well.

In such a small space, I could not believe how organized everything was. There was not an inch of space that was wasted. They sold my favorite new coffee, 3in1, in single packs. A young girl welcomed me and asked what I needed as I approached the counter. I did not want to say I just wanted to see the place, so I quickly asked for a pack of cigarettes and a candy bar. She put it on the counter, and I asked her how much.

She said like 80 pesos. I was like, wow, did you add the cigarettes also? She said yes, and I gave her one hundred. She opened an old cigar box and made the change. Right away, I knew I loved this place. That is like spending three dollars on a pack of smokes. Wow! And I got a candy bar. I asked her if I could take a picture, and she said it would be okay. I took the picture and imagined what the little girl was thinking. Those foreigners are weird.

I was back inside Uncle Ren's compound gate in just a few steps. Now

I know where the maids got the fresh pandesal every morning. I went out onto the terrace to see what was going on, and Uncle asked where I was. I told him I went across the street to the little store on the corner. He asked if I went by myself, and I said yes. He told me to be careful out there; I might get lost. My uncle treated me like I was one of his kids. Auntie told him I am a grown man and to let me experience things on my own if I wanted. I had to laugh, but he was just concerned about my well-being. Uncle told me we would leave to watch Uncle Met and his band around eight-thirty p.m. He said that I would be just casual so I could wear shorts if I wanted. Sounded good to me.

Local Festivities

I went upstairs to my room to record more notes and check some emails. Even though it was now Saturday late afternoon, I hoped to see one from Imelda; I did not. I knew she was always busy, so I was not disappointed. I started searching for hotels near the airport as I would go there on Monday morning. I found a Marriot, and since I was a member of their program, I booked a room for one night. I checked out their website photos and saw that they have every amenity as the hotels in the states. I was excited as this would be the first time I would be on my own there for a while. The Marriot was located right across from the airport, so a quick hop in a taxi and I would be there in a few minutes. On a Sunday, I would check in early and spend time at their pool.

I was soon falling asleep with my laptop at my side. I fell asleep for about an hour. I woke up and had these horrible bags under my eyes. I went downstairs to put ice on them. It looked like I had not slept for weeks. I did not want to look so old when we went out later.

The maids were busy cooking something in the kitchen that smelled so good. I was hungry. Uncle came and said it was time to eat. I sat down in my usual seat; it was becoming routine; me being there. We had some pork chops with rice and soup and fresh fruits. I stuffed myself, knowing I would drink later. I went out to the terrace to relax before we went out. The park across the river was very busy with festivities, and music playing; the community was alive here on this beautiful Saturday night.

I took a shower and prepared for our festivities this evening. Uncle Met and his band would perform in a resto-bar this evening. I was looking forward to getting out into the community and enjoying some nightlife in the Philippines for the first time since my arrival.

The streets were dark but bustling. Lots of jeepneys and tricycles littered the roads. I could see many bars along the way that were lit up like Christmas trees. You could hear the music as we passed by. We made our way onto Tirona's Highway, one of the primary arteries in Bacoor. This was a bustling street and seemed to be lit up more than the back streets. We did not have to travel far to get there, maybe ten minutes. The place was packed and as we walked in, all eyes were on me. We took a table next to the stage. Uncle Met greeted us as well, pulled up, and introduced me to all the band members. The lead female singer was a middle-aged woman that took care of herself. She was gorgeous. Her long dark hair made her much more attractive; I was a sucker for long, dark hair. They would start their first set in about fifteen minutes. So, the lead singer Anna sat down next to me and started ripping off questions. She was interested in talking with a foreigner because I guess there were not too many visiting there. She asked me where I was from, how long I would be there if I am married. I believe she was single from the content of the questions. I heard her tell Uncle Met that I was very gwapo, good-looking. I smiled back at her as she made her way to the stage.

The place was relatively small, seating maybe sixty people, with another air-conditioned room in the front that seated about thirty more people. There were some stairs on the side of the bar, and I asked my cousin what they led to. I had seen servers make their way up and down there, and he did not know. I asked the server what was upstairs, and she said come with her she would show us. We still had a few minutes before the band started, so we headed upstairs with the pretty server. As soon as we walked in, we were greeted by about fifteen women, prettier than the next. They immediately grabbed me by my arm and escorted us into a booth. I asked what this was, and the beautiful young girl, who could not be any more than twenty, said we have fun up here and drink. There was music playing, and the lighting was very dim. The girl flirted with me and asked me if I could be her boyfriend tonight. That was the point I understood what this was; I kindly declined her offer and said we were here to see the band. I grabbed my cousin and got out of there faster than we had arrived. We laughed as we made our way back downstairs. We took our seats at the table, and Uncle Ren asked what was so funny, so we told him what was upstairs. He told us to stay away from there because those girls were bad. We continued to laugh for a few more minutes.

The band finally took the stage and opened up with some songs from the 1970s. I would later find out that it was the type of music we would hear throughout the evening. They sounded perfect and practiced a lot. Anna had a fantastic voice and looked very attractive up there on the stage. I was embarrassed as she dedicated the very next song to me over the microphone, "I want to dedicate this song to Kris, who traveled from Virginia, USA to see us here tonight. This is for you." They shined the spotlight on me, and I felt embarrassed as everyone clapped. The song was the hit "Endless Love," now I was really embarrassed. The server came by and asked if I would like something to drink, and I said yes, could you bring me a San Miguel Light? She explained that if I bought it in a bucket, it would be cheaper. I said sure, why not? Uncle Ren did not drink as well as my cousin. The server brought us a bucket of beer and some juice for my cousin. He asked if he good sees a menu. My cousin could eat. He was still hungry, I guess. I think I finished my first beer before her song was over. While on stage, Uncle met gave me a quick thumbs up, and I nodded back at him.

After their first set was completed, Uncle Met joined us at the table and grabbed a San Miguel Light. He would eventually become my drinking buddy there. I told him they sounded perfect and that the lead singer's voice was amazing.

In between sets, they would play karaoke for the guests. Some people had no business singing, but that is the beauty of it, I guess, because they did not give a shit if others thought it was bad, they were having a good time, and that is what mattered. There was one song that was a duet that was in Tagalog, but I loved the melody. It would become one of my favorite songs. It was a love song called Bakit Ngayon Ka Lang, which translates to why are you alone now? In English. I heard a woman's voice and wondered where it was coming from. She had a beautiful voice. It was a server singing, and I was just in awe. We had consumed the first bucket of beers and were feeling pretty good. I asked the server to bring another bucket. My cousin said one server wanted to meet me, and I said sure. He told the other server to bring her over. She was timid, and I felt awkward meeting women like that. It was the same server that just finished singing. She introduced herself as Jen. Jen was beautiful with long dark hair and a dark complexion but was very young. I remarked what a lovely voice she had. I asked her how old she was.

She said twenty-one.

I was like, damn; I have children older than her. I told her how old I was, and she said that I did not look that old and was still very handsome.

I thanked her, and we flirted back and forth all night. She would drop a note for me at the table. It read, Age is only a number, and that she found me very attractive. She wrote her number and hoped we could get together before I left. As soon as I read it, I caught her watching me and smiling. I was a little embarrassed. I gave her a quick nod and continued watching the band. I could see her talking with the other servers and they would all giggle. She was a little cutie, that is for sure.

By the end of the night, I was feeling pretty good. I went over to the Band's table and tipped them; it seemed like it was customary to do so. I then bought them all a round of drinks and they invited me to sit with them. It was not long before we ordered another bucket of beers. I went over to the server stand to grab our tab because, for sure, Uncle Ren would try to pay for it. The tab was only 3500 php, and I tipped another 1000. They were very appreciative. Then I went over to say goodnight to Jen. She was pleased that I came over to say goodbye and reminded me to call her sometime so we could get together. She gave me a hug and a kiss on the cheek.

I went back to our table, and I could see Uncle Ren asking the server for the tab; she pointed at me and smiled and spoke back to uncle. He asked why I paid for the tab, and I told him because I did most of the drinking and the food was not that expensive. I did not want uncle paying for everything that I did. Uncle Met joined us at our table before we left and thanked us for coming out. He smiled at me and said that I had a new admirer. Jen found out that I was the nephew of Uncle Met and had asked him a lot of questions throughout the evening. I thought that was cute. The evening was enjoyable. It was 1:00 a.m. and Uncle Ren was tired; it was way past his bedtime. We got home, and all of us went directly to sleep.

SM Mall

I woke up the following day with a headache; knowing this would happen, I took some Advil before sleeping. It did not work. I took a couple more and headed downstairs for some coffee. This was the latest that I have slept during my stay here in the Philippines. Maybe this is why I had the headache as well. I only require about five hours of sleep to function properly. By now, it was nine in the morning and already hot. I stepped outside onto the terrace to have my coffee and a smoke. Uncle met me on the terrace and told me today we would just relax and go to church in the evening. That was a great idea; I could use some R&R right now. My cousin asked me if I wanted to go to the mall nearby, and I said sure. He was going for a haircut, and I said I would like to ride along with him. I just thought of another experience for myself. He told me we would go there around lunchtime. The name of the mall was called SM Bacoor. Since I was there, I have seen the SM symbol everywhere and wondered what that stood for. I googled it and was surprised to find out that it was a single man named Henry Sy, an entrepreneur that formed his first shoe store in Manila back in 1958 called ShoeMart. He would import shoes from the US and Europe and sell them in his small store. His business flourished and soon would become a department store, a strip mall, and then a mall. SM became one of the largest investment corporations in the entire Philippines. His signature malls are located all over the Philippines. Sy, originally from China, learned the language at a very early age and would become one of the richest men in the world, actually number 52 by Forbes. What a great story, I thought, from rags to riches.

We made our way out of Kawit and hit a bunch of traffic for a Sunday; I could not believe it. The reason was that we were at an intersection that did not have a light. My cousin was telling me there were supposed to be some traffic coordinators here, but there were not any that I could see. I told him maybe they were at lunch and laughed. Cars and trucks inched their way through.

When it came to driving here in the Philippines, there was no courtesy, and I felt terrible for the people in the Jeepneys because there was no air conditioner, and it was hot. The whole situation was a cluster fuck. After about fifteen minutes, we finally made it through the traffic and onto the main road. While driving, we came upon the makeshift neighborhood they called Squatterville.

I have only seen this from a distance, and it was surprising. It was like a maze, with one room after another. I could see the main paths from the road that looked like they went on and on. I felt so lucky to have what I have after seeing this. We take so much for granted. There were so many children running around. There were a lot of mom-and-pop types of stores there, and food stands. I could not imagine living here like this. I saw many young ladies in uniforms waiting for the bus or jeepney. Some of these ladies were so beautiful it was hard to believe they came from here. But life is hard everywhere, I guess, and we each live and learn our ways. We create our paths and here; the struggle is more evident than anywhere I have seen. The Filipinos have a tough mentality and rarely show emotion. I have seen this in my father. I would use thick skinned as the term. They never give up.

We arrived at the mall and had to go through security, where the guards were all carrying what looked like ARs. They would walk alongside the car with mirrors that reached underneath the vehicles and then ask you to open the trunk. So much precaution, I had to ask my cousin about this. He explained that years ago, an Islamic group set bombs off during Rizal Day that killed so many people in the airport, a mall, a train station, a hotel, and a gas station. These bombs went off almost simultaneously. The Philippine government made drastic measures to ensure this did not happen ever again. He explained that when you go into Manila, it is even more security in every office building, hotel and casino.

We made our way inside the mall, only to go through security again. They checked your bags and patted you down. This was some serious security that I was not used to back home. But I felt safe. Back in the states, everyone complained about the additional safety measures put in place after 911, but here the people appreciated the extra precautions. We entered through the SM store. I could not believe the number of people working there. There must have been five people in every department, and they were very courteous. Some people we saw on the side of the road on our way here must have been coming to work here. Everyone was in uniform, not like back home. Rico wanted to get a haircut, so we went in the barbershop's direction. Again, I felt like a celebrity, as everyone seemed to watch me. I noticed a Dairy Queen and told my cousin that we had to get an Oreo Blizzard right now. He laughed and said OKAY. This was one of my favorite desserts back home. I was in heaven. While Rico went to get his haircut, I walked around the mall to see what kind of stores were there. They had many brand-named stores like back home and many specialty stores there. I walked into an athletic store and noticed all kinds of Pacquiao paraphernalia in here.

Being that my brothers were big fans, I picked up some things. For those of you that do not know who Manny Pacquiao is, he was the poor kid from the streets of Mindanao that would become one of the best pound-for-pound fighters in the world. Manny "Pacman" Pacquiao made boxing history by winning twelve major world championships in eight weight divisions. A feat that no one in the world would come close to. He was an icon for all Filipinos. Dad was a huge boxing fan as well, and when there was a Pacquiao fight, we would always get the family together, and Dad was always there. My cousin was a big fan and told me that there was a fight this coming Saturday. We would have to find a place to watch it. We left the mall and made our way back home. We would have to prepare to go to church soon.

Sunday Mass

We attended mass in one of the oldest churches in the Philippines, St. Mary Magdalene church, or what the locals called "Kawit Church." The church was old. The beginning was said to be around 1638. They restored it in the 1700s and again in 1990. There is a long history here dating back to the Spanish-American war. The church looked much bigger once you were inside. The mass was in Tagalog, but being a confirmed Catholic myself, I was able to follow the entire mass. It surprised my auntie to see me following the mass, and I would later tell her that the Catholic masses were the same globally. The only thing different was the sermon. Like I said before, Mom and Dad made sure all of us were practicing Catholics, even though they both rarely attended church. When we were just kids, all five would walk to church. My brothers and I were even Alter boys at one point. Luckily, we would never be exposed to the sinful altercations with some Priests. Thank God for that. Both Mom and Dad would get pissed at us if we said we did not feel like going to church, but we never questioned why they would not attend. We would all eventually become confirmed Catholics; I was the last one, and later on in life.

After mass, we all went out to dinner at a local restaurant that served traditional Filipino food. The restaurant was a small family-owned shop that was open-air style. It would only seat about twenty people, but we were only six, and nobody else was there. The owners were friends of the family. They introduced me as Boys son. The lady behind the counter then came to me and said she knew my father and was sorry to hear of his passing. Then she remarked about my resemblance to Dad. I thanked her for saying that. I was finding more and more about Dad everywhere I went. The lady even said that Dad was handsome, and all the girls wanted to date him. I had to laugh because this was not the first time I would hear this. Dad was a good-looking guy, no doubt.

Aguinaldo Shrine

When we finally got home, Uncle and I sat out on the terrace and talked more about his memories of Dad. I asked Uncle if Dad ever visited the Aguinaldo Shrine as a kid, and he told me that Dad used to work there as a staff accountant before he joined the Navy. I remember some black and white pictures of Dad in a white shirt working at a desk and never asked him where he was when the picture was taken. I was like, wow, Dad worked for the very first president of the Philippines. Of course, he was not the president at that time, but I just thought it was cool. Uncle told me we should go there tomorrow for a tour. I was excited about going there now. I told my uncle that I would try to rest early tonight. I went upstairs to shower and made some notes of the day's events. I sent Imelda an email telling her I was very excited to meet with her in a couple of weeks. As each day passed here in my dad's homeland, I grew to know him more and more. I felt closer to him than ever before. It saddened me I had never had some personal conversations with him about his childhood. Still, like I mentioned Filipino men are stubborn and prideful, they show no emotion and keep their beliefs close to their chests.

I quickly fell asleep. During my sleep, I felt that someone was watching me, like a presence was there. I woke up around two a.m. and wanted to get something to drink. I opened the bedroom door, and it was pitch dark; I did not want to turn any lights on, so I was just cautious going down the stairs. The whole time the feeling was still there; someone was watching me. As I opened the refrigerator to grab bottled water, I tried not to think about it. I quickly made my way back upstairs. I could only assume it was Dad, but I remember my uncle and cousins telling me a few stories of seeing Lola after her passing. Now I was freaking out. The bedroom had a balcony as well, and I would open the door to go outside and have a cigarette. I felt a little better getting some fresh air. I looked over the balcony and saw all the puppies still playing with their mommy, even this late. This took my mind off things for a bit. I would go back to my room and grab some cookies in my bag from the original flight here. I broke them up and dropped them down to the puppies. The first drop shocked all the dogs as they froze to see what it was. I was three floors up, and they could not see me. I then dropped another piece, and one puppy went over to see it. As soon as he smelled it, he started to eat it, then all the dogs came to him. I kept dropping them piece by piece and was amused at how the dogs reacted. Never once did they look up to see where it was coming from. They probably thought it was raining snacks. The Alpha dog then came and pushed his weight around. This pissed me off, so when he would be in a spot by himself, I would pour the water on him. He would take off running. I had to hold my laugh so they would not hear me.

I continued to do this until the cookies ran out. I went back into my room and did not have that feeling again. I was able to go back to sleep. I didn't mention this feeling to anyone.

The following day, I woke up and went downstairs to have my coffee. I made sure I brought my clothes down because having to climb the stairs was wearing me out. It had become my daily routine. As soon as I woke up, I washed my face, brushed my teeth, and did my core workout, which consisted of sit-ups, push-ups and some leg lifts and planks. Then I grabbed my dirty clothes, folded them nice and neat and brought them downstairs. I was excited to see the Aguinaldo Shrine now that I knew Dad was a part of this many years ago. I would have to wait until my cousin woke up, and I knew he was a late sleeper. I asked Rose for some coffee and told her I would be on the terrace. It was a lovely day out, and the park was as busy as ever. Many children were making their way to school. I could see the mothers walking with them, holding an umbrella over their kids. It was so cute. I felt the culture here and became more and more acclimated with things. I could live here. I learned more and more about Tagalog as well. I never felt closer to Dad than now.

Uncle joined me out on the terrace, and we both said our good mornings to each other. I told him I was excited to see the Shrine today. He would not join us, as he had to take Auntie somewhere. Rose called us in for breakfast, so we finished our cigarettes and went inside. I liked the fried rice for breakfast, along with the spam. The only other time I remembered this was when Lola had visited years ago. She was always the first one up and would make breakfast for my siblings and me before school. After breakfast, I went to watch some TV. There was a movie just starting called Metro Manila; it was actually on the Netflix channel. It was in Tagalog but had captions on so I could understand it. I immediately was drawn to the actress in the movie, as she was gorgeous and resembled Imelda. I ended up watching the entire movie. It was a great story. I would look for this back in the states. The young actress was just amazing.

I jumped in the shower and prepared for a trip across the street. I made sure my camera was charged to take many pictures. As soon as I was done, I checked on my cousin. Since he was not downstairs, I went to his room. I could hear him on his phone, so I knocked on the door. When he answered, I told him I wanted to go next door to the Shrine, and he would shower and then we would go. I anxiously waited for my cousin downstairs. He had been a curator there before, so he knew his way around the place pretty well. A half-hour later, we were walking across the street. We would enter on the side of the building because children were taking a tour. My cousin greeted everyone and introduced me to them. They were the current curators and staff members. One of the members was the grandson of Emilio Aguinaldo himself. I told him it was my pleasure to meet him. He told my cousin to go ahead anytime.

As we walked through the shrine, I tried to place the picture that I saw of Dad. Many of the walls were dark polished wood, similar to what I saw in the picture. But there were so many different settings that I could not place it. We went to the top floor and climbed the latter that said, "Do Not Enter." This leads to the steeple at the very top. My cousin told me to open up the shutters all the way so we could look out to the city. It was a fantastic view; you could see Manila from here. I thought how lucky I was to be doing this.

I took many pictures from this and even zoomed in to Manila. You see all the mountains surrounding the city. I looked out of every opening and could see that there were mountains in every direction. What a sight. We stayed up there for a while and talked about the shrine. There were many hiding places and escape routes within the walls of this five-story fortress. I also took a bird's-eye picture of Uncle's house since he lived right there across the street. I never realized how big his house was until I saw this view. We must have stayed in the tower for an hour just talking and taking pictures. It impressed me that my cousin knew about the history of the shrine. We went downstairs and outside to the garden area and saw an old car that was placed in a large glass room. It was a 1924 Packard limousine that Aguinaldo used back in the day. It looked like it was in perfect condition. The entire tour lasted about an hour, but my tour was a lot longer because it was only me, and we had free rein of the entire shrine. Uncle met us in the garden, and we talked more about the tour. I told him I wanted to get some souvenirs before we left. I ended up buying a book on the history of Emilio Aguinaldo.

We walked back to the house and some of Aunties friends were visiting. I was introduced to them all, including one of my auntie's cousins. She told me to call her Auntie Jo. Auntie Jo reminded us of the Pacquiao fight this weekend and invited us over to watch it. Auntie Jo was quite the entrepreneur, come to find out, owning a water park there in Kawit and a couple of restaurants that would become well-known establishments in Tagaytay. Auntie Jo wanted us to visit the water park tomorrow, so we agreed it sounded like fun. I excused myself and went upstairs to drop off the souvenirs I had purchased at the shrine and check on emails, mainly from Imelda.

I did not find any emails from Imelda. Before dinner, I laid down. I looked at my luggage and thought if I bought any more souvenirs, it might not fit anywhere. I had all kinds of things, and I had not been to the city yet. Maybe I should buy another piece of luggage, I thought. After about an hour, dinner was being served. I went downstairs and took my place at the table, as I usually do. Uncle asked me what I thought about being here for over a week now, and we talked about some of my experiences. I told him that my company is extending my stay here so that I can visit some of my clients here and that I would go into the city sometime on Saturday or Sunday of next week. I was not sure just yet. I also told Uncle I would come back here before I left to return home. He told me to be careful and that I could leave the things I did not need in my room. I thanked him for that. After dinner, we sat out on the terrace. It was a lovely evening with a cool breeze. Uncle asked about my children and how they were doing. We talked for hours about them and all of my sibling's children. He had met my family briefly when he came for Dad's surprise birthday party. I would turn in early this evening, after all, we climbed a lot of stairs today, and it was a great work-out, and I was drained. When I opened my laptop, I noticed a few emails from work. It was about nine in the morning back home. I looked them over and did not see anything worth keeping me up. So, I laid down and tried to fall asleep.

Waterpark

I woke up the following day around six-thirty to what had become my alarm clock: the squawking roosters. I was eager to see the water park Auntie Jo spoke of yesterday. But I know it would be a while before we got to go because my cousin would not be up for a few hours. I finished my daily routine and made my way downstairs with my laptop. I wanted to answer some emails I received from work. I dropped my clothes off and asked Rose for a cup of coffee on the terrace. I ran through my emails quickly. It probably took me thirty minutes to finish them all, then I went back to the ones I thought needed attention. I spent another thirty minutes just answering basic questions. I saw one email from our client here in the Philippines, he just wanted to confirm our meetings. I quickly shot a reply to him confirming our appointments. My cousin woke up early and said he wanted to get to the water park before it got crowded. I told him that is fine with me and all I had to do was take a shower and change.

We met Auntie Jo at the water park entrance, which was only a few minutes from the house. She gave us the full tour and asked us if we wanted a cabana while we were there. The cabanas were really nice, almost like hotel rooms with beds and bathrooms. We passed on the cabanas and told Auntie Jo that we just wanted to go in the pool. She told us to come to see her at the office if we change our mind. She then took us to the snack bar and told the staff that if we wanted anything, it would be in the house, whatever we wanted. I thought these were some pretty good perks.

The water park was very crowded now. It had to be around noon, and we grabbed a couple of hamburgers and washed them down with some bottled water. We were in and out of the pool for a few hours and finally decided to go back to the house. We stopped by and thanked Auntie Jo for her hospitality and told us not to forget about the fight this weekend. My cousin had told me that Aunties Jo's house was as big as their own and that they had a separate place just for their movie room. I could not wait to see this.

Games

On our way home, we passed some young guys playing basketball. I asked my cousin if he played and he said not so good. I told him we should go there just to shoot around. After all, the court was right next to the shrine so we could just walk there in minutes. We changed our clothes, put on my shoes, and walked over to the court. We asked the guys if we could shoot around, and they said sure, no problem. I played a lot of basketball in my day and was still playing for a team in the Filipino league back home. Before we knew it, there were a lot of kids watching us shoot around. The guys decided to play a pickup game, and I said no problem. Some kids were in flip-flops while the others were barefooted. That is how they played here, I guess. Had to hurt. I started to really heat up from long range, and the kids seemed to be impressed. I was well beyond the three-point line and every time I got the ball outside the arc, the crowd would cheer, wanting me to take the shot. We had a good time playing with the kids and they thanked us for playing with them. They went to see if they could match the range from which I was shooting. I impressed my cousin with my skills, especially at my age. I told him I played my entire life. Outside of golf and fishing, this was my favorite pastime.

We got home and sat out on the terrace to cool down. My cousin had asked what I wanted to do later this evening. I told him I have no plans and if he wanted to do something, we could. He asked if I played billiards, and I answered, of course. We would go play after dinner somewhere. I went upstairs to make some notes on the game before I forgot. I wanted to point out that these kids were playing in bare feet and flip-flops. Dangerous, I thought, but that is how they played. Rico and I went down the street to a local pool hall. We started to play, and I soon realized that Rico was a pool shark. He was very good at billiards and reminded me of another famous Filipino named Efren Reyes. For many years, Reyes remained the World 9 Ball Champion and Rico had the same style. He was making some unbelievable shots and quickly retired me every game. Some people in the room would watch and eventually challenge Rico. He dispersed them quickly as well. I sat and watched as I drank a few beers. Rico ended up going undefeated the rest of the evening. I lost all desire to play against him.

Ternate

The next day we took a trip to Ternate, Cavite. Uncle told me there were mountains and beaches, so I was excited to see this. It took us about an hour to get there. We brought the young son that lived in the back. I asked the little boy if he wanted anything when we stopped to buy snacks. We bought a few bags of cookies and some bottled water. We drove up some very steep mountains. There was a Marine Base located at the top of the hill. You could see out into Manila Bay from here. Rico told me that the islands were very famous during World War 2. He told me of Corregidor Island, a US Marine base, and Fort Drum, a tiny artificial island shaped almost like a battleship, to deter the Japanese Navy from entering Manila Bay. Rico told me we could take a tour of Corregidor Island tomorrow if we wanted.

I loved history, so I quickly said yes. As we were looking at the sights, a few monkeys came out to see us. Never being around wild monkeys, I would certainly keep my distance. I told the young boy to throw a cookie at them and he did. He laughed at how the monkeys would run to the cookie quickly. He did that many times. Well, all the excitement caused more and more monkeys to come out of the trees. As the young kid threw the cookies, the monkeys got closer to him. He became frightened and cried. While laughing, I chased the monkeys away and told him that everything was okay. We will not let the monkeys get him. It was so funny.

We looked down at a beach. Yet another cousin of Auntie Ways owned that. They called this beach the "Boracay of Cavite." It was a beautiful beach with white sands and looked empty. I asked Rico what was going on with it, and he told me that his auntie had closed this to do some upgrades and cleaning. The resort would not be open by the time I would leave; too bad, I thought. We drove around the mountainside

I Became Him

only to come to a recently built tunnel. The Kaybiang tunnel was built to cut down the travel time to Batangas from four and a half hours to two hours. It was the longest tunnel in the Philippines. There was what seemed to be a landside about twenty meters from the entrance. I was not sure if the authorities were notified about this, but a couple of enormous boulders and some trees had fallen onto the side of the road, taking the two lanes down to one. We pulled up to the entrance of the tunnel to just look inside. Uncle was probably afraid to go into the tunnel, but he would never tell us.

The views of the mountains and beaches from up here were spectacular. We went back the same way we came and could see the mountains in Bataan. The peak was some 4500 feet up. This was the province where, in April 1942, the Japanese army marched both Filipino and American soldiers that had surrendered at the Bataan Peninsula on a sixty-five-mile trek that would last six days to a prison camp in Tarlac. This became known as the Bataan Death March. I read a story of this march and found it to be bothersome, as thousands of prisoners had perished brutally. The US military later tried the Japanese Lieutenant Commander and a few of his officers of war crimes and executed them by a firing squad in 1946.

Corregidor Island

The following day, Rico and I made our way into Manila to take the ferry to Corregidor Island. I was excited to see this.

We passed by this huge globe, and I asked him what that was. Rico told me the Globe of MOA lights up when the sun goes down. MOA was the famous Mall of Asia. They mentioned the mall to me, and I would get to see this later on when I transferred to a hotel nearby. This was my first time in the city, and it was jam-packed with buses, jeepneys, and tricycles all competing for space. There were twice as many pedestrians as back in Cavite as well. There was so much construction going on in every direction. It was a good thing we left early in the morning, or we would be stuck in this mess. The ferry was located close to MOA. The day trip was inexpensive and served lunch as well. We got onto what they call a fast ferry.

This one was small compared to others docked at the piers of Manila Bay. Our ferry could hold maybe forty passengers and had the name Corregidor Island painted on its side. The ferry ride was a little more than an hour, and the tour would last all day, with the ferry departing Corregidor Island at two-thirty p.m. and back in Manila by four p.m. Manila Bay had just gone through a transformation. The government had declared the area off limits until they cleaned the beaches and waterways. Although the water seemed clean, it still smelled like a horse's ass. The ride had been smooth, and we arrived at the very dock where General MacArthur escaped via Navy PT boat on March 11, 1942. His famous saying, "I Shall Return," was written on a placard there, but history had him saying this once he reached Australia. I could not fathom the number of military relics that had littered Manila Bay near Corregidor Island. There had to be subs, planes, shells and casings, and probably many bodies. As we made our way from the docks, we could see where some bombs had blown away portions of the pier. The story goes, the Americans and Filipinos both were on Corregidor training.

They considered this the stronghold of Manila Bay; if the Japanese could penetrate Manila Bay, they would overrun Manila. The Japanese bombed the island by air. We made our way onto a tram that took us around the Island. We came to one of the most significant battery positions on the island. We could get out and view this area. You could still see the devastation on the roofs where bombs had pierced through the concrete fortress. Some of the artillery located at this station were 28-inch anti-aircraft guns still in place. We then came across the "Nine Mile Barracks. "The barracks were not nine miles, but a long four- story building used as living quarters for the marines. Its skeleton still stands and has been untouched since WWII. Some myths say that these halls are haunted. It is hard to imagine what happened here years ago. The once home to some 2500 marines was now an empty bomb-shelled dwelling. History has it that the Japanese captured the island shortly after MacArthur left in 1942. Continuous bombings throughout the days and nights were too much. The remaining Filipinos and American soldiers became prisoners and were transferred to Bataan. MacArthur was true to his word as he came roaring back to the Philippines and took Corregidor back in 1945.

After the tour, I stood on the docks and looked back upon the island, then across to Bataan, and finally to Manila. I realized the sacrifice that many people, both Filipino and American, made for the freedom of the Philippines. I have read many books on WWII and thought I was pretty educated on the subject; however, putting my feet on the ground here gave me a much- needed awakening. I never realized the importance of the battles here in my father's homeland. How did he perceive all of this? So many deaths, so much cruelty, and so much unknowing as a kid. Maybe this was why Dad was a hard man that did not show emotion. I realized his appreciation for the little things, the simplicity of life, the craving just to survive.

We landed back in Manila precisely at four p.m. I was tired after all the walking, and I was emotionally drained. Rico asked if I wanted to go anywhere else. I told him to take me back home.

He agreed, and we started our journey through the traffic. The drive from the port to Kawit took us two hours. It would have been thirty minutes if there were no traffic, but this was normal here. When we arrived back home, I took a shower and wanted to rest. I made notes about the day's events. The trip was a humbling experience. It marked a change in how I perceived things. I had this same feeling one other time after visiting the Holocaust Museum in Washington, DC.

After dinner, I checked some emails. I found an email from Imelda. She was stuck in Japan overnight. She mentioned she felt like she had known me longer than the week and a half that we communicated. After all, we spent a lot of time together on my four- and half-hour flight. I mentioned our trip to Corregidor Island and how I could use a hug right now. I had asked her if she could send a picture for my keepsake. Then I sent my phone number to her if she ever wanted to call. I wanted to hear her voice. I guess I missed her.

I watched a little TV and then slept quite early. It had been a long day. I brushed my teeth and laid on the bed. Suddenly I could feel my phone buzzing. I picked it up and saw a number that I did not recognize. I let it ring through to voice mail. I was soon fast asleep.

Birthday Party

I woke up the following day, not knowing what day it was. I laughed at myself that I had to open my calendar to see. I noticed a voice message on my phone; then I remembered I had a call last night. I listened to the message and wanted to kick myself in the ass for not answering it. It was Imelda, and she was calling me. I did not think she would read my email so fast and call.

Her message was that she would be back home this afternoon sometime, only to fly out again in the morning. She said that she was excited to meet with me. This made my day. By the way, today was Friday. I prepared myself and then went downstairs to get some coffee. I brought my laptop to the terrace to do some work. My client's message reminded me about the meeting at the airport on Monday morning. I messaged him back, confirming our plans. Then I spent the next hour answering emails from clients back in the states. Uncle met me outside on the terrace and said they had a birthday party to go to around dinner time. He asked if I wanted to go, and I said sure I would love to go. It was a cousin of Auntie Ways. I asked him if I needed to wear anything special and he said no, just jeans and a polo shirt would be fine. Not knowing where the party would be, I just figured it would be at somebody's house. As it turned out, the party was in Manila at one of the high-end hotels. The party was in the ballroom, and I immediately regretted what I was wearing. As we walked in, I noticed the men wearing the traditional Polo Barong shirts, the formal wear of the Philippines. The women wore dresses. My appearance embarrassed me.

Uncle was wearing jeans and a polo shirt as well as Rico, but I would for sure stand out because, as I looked around the room, I was the only foreigner. Damn it!! This side of the family obviously had some money because the ballroom was huge, and you could see the city through the windows in any direction. There was a gigantic chandelier hanging over the center table, where the guest of honor was sitting. Rico, Liza and I grabbed a seat at a table with some children and their Nanny. I told Liza that I felt so out of place here because I was the only foreigner and because I was not dressed properly. She told me not to worry about it because they were all family here. A waitstaff served the dinner to us. First, they served everyone a salad first. Then there was a second wave of servers taking drink orders. I asked for bottled water. The waitstaff would serve prime rib with red potatoes and asparagus a few minutes later. I looked around the room and counted maybe sixty people minimum and thought, this will cost someone a lot of money. After the waitstaff cleared the dinner plates, they served the cake. Uncle Ren wanted to introduce me to the guest of honor.

As we walked over to the table, Uncle told me that the guest of honor, thought Liza and I were a couple. I had to laugh at this, but I can see why he felt that. We approached his table, and the man stood up and greeted me. Uncle then asked me if I knew who this guy was, and I told him no, I did not. He introduced him as one of the senators here in the Philippines. He was the first cousin of Auntie Ways. Now I was really embarrassed at my attire. He was an older gentleman that was one of the favorite senators of the Philippine people. He told me he was from the province of Bicol and asked if I had ever been there.

I explained to him that this was my first trip, and I wanted to see where my father grew up so that I may understand him more. He asked where my father was now and did he make the trip with me? I told him he was in heaven now, watching me. He gave his condolences and asked what his name was. When I told him, another gentleman overheard our conversation and approached. He said, "Excuse me, but I heard your uncle talking, and I was a friend of your father's. We both joined the Navy together in Sangley Point. He continued to say that "He was a very honorable man. I am sorry that he is gone.

Please give my condolences to your family." I thanked Mr. Ernie for his kind words.

Soon after, they started the photo session. If there is one thing about Filipino people, they love to take many pictures. This probably took 45 minutes in all. They even asked me to join in on the family pics. The whole time I thought about what a bum I looked like. Then we took another half hour to say our goodbyes to everyone. We were deep in Manila and things were much different here. Skyscrapers after skyscrapers, new construction everywhere. Manila was developing into a metropolis, and I was excited to spend some time here in the coming days and learn more about the motherland of my father. We arrived home around ten p.m.; I grabbed my laptop and checked on some emails. There was nothing pending, so I quickly closed it and dialed Imelda's number. I could not connect right away, and my service from the states was pretty weak out here. I had to connect to the internet. I received a text from my service provider saying that my calls and text messages would be expensive. Did I want to sign up for their international plan? I declined and shut my phone off, disappointed I could not make the call. I emailed her to see how she was doing. Before I knew it, I was fast asleep. Knocked out.

Pacquiao Fight

I woke up around seven in the morning feeling refreshed. To my surprise, my cousin was already up. I asked Rico why he was up so early, and he said that the Pacquiao fight was today. I said yes, tonight, correct? He said no, it's this morning. I had forgotten the time difference. The fights start around eight am here. This I was not used to, lol. The main event, back home, probably will not be on till around eleven p.m. Here it is Saturday morning. I took a peek outside of the terrace and it was like a ghost town. The entire Philippines shut down for the Pac-man fights. Of course, he was the hometown hero. Rico told me we would leave for Auntie Jo's house around nine a.m. So, I went upstairs to shower and change. I was excited to see the fight. I could imagine my siblings getting together for the fight back home, as they always did. We drove through Kawit and the streets were just empty. It was amazing to see some immense houses in this town. We arrived in the subdivision where Auntie Jo lived. The guards at the gate asked Rico where he was going, and then the guard rang into Auntie Jo. We were cleared to proceed to her house. Even though the neighborhood was secured at the entrance, the individual lots were still gated.

We arrived at Auntie Jo's place, and Rico beeped his horn. Soon the gate was opened by a young man wearing what looked like a uniform. I asked Rico why he was wearing such attire here at Auntie's place, and Rico's answer was that the young man was probably a staff member. Auntie Jo met us at the car, excited that we had arrived. "Come, let's eat before the fight."

I told Auntie we had already had our breakfast, and she looked at me and said, "It's okay. I can afford to eat more."

I laughed. We made our way into her big, beautiful house. I saw maids and staff members all wearing the same color. I guess this was to distinguish them from guests. I told Auntie that she had a beautiful house and she immediately asked me if I wanted a tour.

As we made our way throughout the house, I realized that there were as many staff members there as were guests. We ended up in the main room with a huge TV screen. I asked Auntie if this is where we were watching the fight, and she laughed and said no, we would watch the fight in the movie room. The movie room was detached from the main house. I went outside to walk around the yard and smoke a cigarette. I walked around back to where the staff members took their breaks. It was funny because as soon as I turned the corner and they noticed me, they all stood up at attention like I was a general or something of the sort. I told them it was okay and just to relax.

They were a younger group and spoke excellent English. One of the male staff members asked me how I knew Madam Auntie Jo as I knew her I told them that I had just met her for the first time, and she was my auntie. They all said that I do not look Filipino. I told them yes; I have heard this many times during my visit here and laughed. I explained that I am half Filipino and was visiting here for the US. The girls jokingly asked if I wanted a Filipina girlfriend. We all laughed, and I told them it was nice meeting them all, and I made my way back to the front of the house. Rico told me to go inside the Movie room because the fight would be on soon. The movie room was just amazing. There were two rows of recliner seats. Twelve in all. The big screen was almost as big as the wall that supported it. I thought, this is how you watch a fight.

The surround-sound made you feel like you were right there. There was a full bar in the back. We still had to take our shoes off at the entrance. As the fight started, we grabbed a seat. We all cheered for the hometown hero Pac-man. Manny was fighting a trash-talking fighter from Mexico, who told the world he would pound Manny into retirement. This was a bigger fight outside of the ring, as both training camps had altercations with each other a few different times. From the opening bell, Manny took the fight straight to the Mexican, determined to make him pay for his trash talking. Throughout the fight, it looked like Manny could easily have dispatched his opponent, but seemingly wanted to make him pay for his prediction of retiring the aging Filipino. Wishful thinking on his part for sure. Manny destroyed this younger and bigger boxer and totally rearranged his face. The entire Philippines was joyous for the victory, and the streets' celebrations began. After the fight, everyone gathered around the massive buffet, and we gave thanks and praise to not only God but also to Manny. We ate so much that we were ready for a nap by the time we got home. We thanked Auntie Jo and said our goodbyes.

Karaoke Night

When we arrived back home, I was tired and told Rico that I would lie down for a few minutes. I put in a good hour and a half before waking up again. I was ready for a drink this evening. This was my last night before I had to leave for the city in the morning, and I would not be back until next Friday.

I messaged Uncle Met to see if he was performing tonight. Uncle Met messaged back fast and said he was playing at the same place tonight. I asked Uncle Ren if he wanted to go, but he said he was taking Auntie Ways to a batch reunion party with her friends. I asked him what that was, and he explained that when a group graduates from college together in the Philippines, they are called batch mates. I assumed it was the same thing as a fraternity. So, I waited for Rico to wake up and see if he wanted to go. I was going either way. By now it was almost time for dinner, and I was still full from the buffet this morning. I would just grab something to eat at the bar later.

Rico finally woke up, and I asked him if he wanted to go tonight, but he declined because he was not feeling well. I messaged Uncle Met and told him I will be the only one attending. He messaged me back and said that he would just pick me up and we would go to dinner first. Uncle met would be on his way in a half hour, so I had to get ready immediately. I ran upstairs to grab a quick shower and shave. I was prepared in record time. Uncle Met was right on time, and we were soon off on another adventure. On the way, we spoke of my time spent here so far and he mentioned how everyone was so happy that I came to see the home of my father. All the relatives could not stop talking about Boy's son. I was just as happy that I had the opportunity to come and meet everyone. I talked about realizing who Dad was and how he became the man he was.

The trip was very emotional for me. His siblings looked, laughed, talked, and had the same expressions as he did, so he was always on my mind the entire trip. Everything I looked at, I tried to imagine him being there. We did not take long vacations together as a family, so I couldn't imagine how dad spent his days here on his last trip. Dad always kept to himself, busy working and then bowling in his off time. So, I asked Uncle Met about my dad's last visit here. Uncle Met went on to tell me that Dad was pleased that he was in his homeland, and just like me, he wanted to visit all the relatives and see all the places he remembered growing up here. Uncle Met told me he really saw the resemblance in me and that I reminded him of my father so much.

We pulled up to a restaurant down the street from where Uncle Met was playing later on this evening. We walked in and grabbed a seat. Immediately, the server addressed Uncle Met, and he introduced me to her. Uncle told me that the staff knew him because his band has played here in the past. We ordered our food, and I asked Uncle to have a beer with me. The server soon came with our drinks. They were singing karaoke, and in noticed some songs were back from the time I was growing up. A young lady asked if I could sing a duet with her and I told her no, that I was not a very good singer. She persisted and said it was just for fun, anyway. I was very cautious, as Uncle Met would critique me. But then he told me just to try it. I told the young girl to pick a song, but I had to agree to it first. I wanted to make sure the melody was familiar to me. She chose an old song and one that I knew.

The song's name was "How Do You Keep the Music Playing." I said sure, let us kill this song together; it was for fun. She asked my name and then opened the mike; I was so embarrassed because they announced it to the entire restaurant. So, I asked the server for a quick shot of tequila before we started. I sang the song pretty well but could not hit some notes.

The young lady was marvelous; made me sound great. Afterwards, I would receive more requests to sing more, which is why I have no idea. It was probably because they wanted me to stay and buy beer rather than hear me sing. But it was a great time. Uncle Met said that he had to leave to go set up, and I told him I would just meet him there. It was only a few blocks away. My singing partner would just wave down a tricycle when I was ready to go. Since Uncle Met knew them, he knew I was safe.

The singer's name was Linda. She stayed with me at my table, and we had an excellent time for about another hour. We had a couple more drinks before I left. I was feeling pretty good. I thanked her for her time, and we exchanged numbers. She was a beautiful girl as well. This was actually my first ride on a tricycle. I thought it would be cool to videotape it with my phone. The ride was only twenty pesos, and I was there in only a few minutes. The tricycle was uncomfortable and challenging. But it was how people got around there, and I wanted to experience everything.

I walked into the restaurant and immediately saw Jen. Jen was the young lady I had met here on my first visit. Uncle Met must have told her I was coming. When we met at the door, I gave her my greetings and a kiss on the cheek. This made her very happy. Jen sat me at a small table near the restaurant's rear, next to a huge fan. I could see straight to the stage and had a little privacy. She quickly asked if she could take our picture together and I agreed. So, she sat on my lap and posed for a selfie of us. She must have taken ten pictures. For sure, she wanted to look her best. She asked if I wished to have another bucket of beers, but I told her I had to get up early the following day so that I would take one for now. Uncle Met was already on stage with the rest of his band, fine-tuning their instruments. He gave me a quick wave. Uncle's band played a lot of music from the sixties and seventies. Since I grew up in that era, I was familiar with the songs. I enjoyed listening to them perform.

When another server approached my table to ask if there was anything I needed, I could see Jen rush over and snap at the server in her native tongue. I thought this was so cute. When the other server left, I asked Jen what she said to her. Jen told the server that I was her guest and that she would take care of me. She was marking her territory. Then she asked how come I never messaged her. I explained that I would have to download the apps to communicate with her and that if I was out and about; I did not have any service. My service originates in the US and not here in the Philippines, and it has costly roaming charges.

Terrace Sleep Over

A smile came across her face, and she said okay and that I should download the apps soon. I had a few more beers and did not realize how time flew by. It was already midnight, and I knew I still had to get ready for a trip into the city in the morning. Uncle Met said that he would drop me off with no problem. I finally reached home around one a.m. and quietly checked to see if the gate was unlocked. I turned and gave uncle a quick thumbs-up, and he was on his way. Thank goodness it was because otherwise, I would have to scale this seven-foot fence, and I was in no condition. I walked up to the front door to see if it was unlocked; it was not.

Shit, I thought, *what do I do?* I did not want to wake everyone up, so I sent Rico a message to open the door, no answer. I pulled up several chairs and made a makeshift bed on the terrace. If Uncle Ren was anything like my father was, there was no way I was waking him up.

I can still remember Dad telling us we would have to sleep outside if we were not home by midnight. We would never knock on the door after midnight. Instead, we would throw rocks at our sister's bedroom window, hoping to wake her up. When she woke up, we thought we were in the clear, only to peek inside and see Dad coming down the stairs. Our sister had sold us out and Dad was pissed that we had come home so late. Of course, we were all older now, but dad made us feel like we were still kids. My brothers and I had been out with some friends and had a few beers. When we saw Dad coming down the stairs, he was in his whitey tighties, and his hair was all messed up, cursing all the way down. We laughed until the door opened. Dad cursed us badly, and all I wanted to do was go to sleep at this point. But he continued to lecture us. I would not look at my brothers in fear of we would start to laugh at the situation. I did not think

I would make it out of this situation alive, but Dad must have been tired and told us to lock the door and go to bed. We continued to joke about the situation. This would be one of the stories we told our children at family gatherings.

I fell asleep on the terrace and woke around six-thirty a.m. as I heard the maids inside already. I went around back because I knew the door was open now. Rose looked at me, smiled, and said, "Good Morning, Kuya, coffee na?"

I passed and went straight upstairs to grab a few hours of sleep.

I woke up about an hour and a half later, knowing I would have to pack my things for my adventure into the city. While having my coffee, I made notes about last night's outing and what a great time we had. I jumped in the shower and then got dressed. I was excited about going into the city. I made my way downstairs and ran into Uncle, he asked if I needed a ride, and I said I would just catch a Grab. Uncle asked me when I came home last night, and I told him maybe 1 a.m. He then asked me how I got into the house. I told him I did not want to wake anyone, so I slept out on the terrace. He laughed and asked why I did not wake him? So, I told him the story of Dad and did not want to wake anyone up. He looked at me and asked what a Grab is? So, I explained to him it was like a taxi, only the fare was better, and drivers were all checked out to make sure they can legally drive passengers. He wanted to make sure that when the driver showed up to let him know so he could speak with him. I told him I would.

The driver was coming in about fifteen minutes, and I showed him how the driver was making his way to our place. He asked me how much I had to pay him, and I told him I thought the trip cost 850 php, and Uncle said wow, that was expensive. I told him that my company reimburses me for my expenses this week while I see clients. I said my goodbyes to Auntie and my cousins. I told them I should be back on Friday. Uncle then told me he would give me a key next time so I would not have to sleep on the terrace. Laughing the whole time, he said that was crazy.

The Visit to The City

The driver showed up right on time and it impressed Uncle that he could watch the driver's progress on my cell phone. I explained it works like Uber in the states. I grabbed my small bag and backpack and made my way to the Grab car. I thought again, Did I forget anything? I figured I could probably pick it up at or near the hotel if I did. I can see Uncle talking with the driver seriously. I gave Uncle a hug and got into the car.

When I got into the car, the driver said to me that my uncle was very concerned about my safety and asked him many questions. I said to the driver, yes; Uncle still treats me like a kid because this is my first time in the Philippines. As we made our way out of Kawit, the driver told me about things close to where I was going. He told me there was a casino connected to the hotel where I was staying and thought that would be nice to visit. I told the driver that I would only be there for one night but would try to make the best of it. The drive on Cavitex, the main freeway from Manila to Cavite, was different from when I arrived here because it was dark and now it was the morning, very sunny and hot outside now. As we drove towards Manila, you could actually see the metropolis from the highway.

Manila bay was bustling as I could see many of the fishermen still on the water. I could see all the nipa huts on the water that I could not see during my arrival, I just remember seeing a lot of lights. The nipa huts were tiny one-room huts, and there were so many of them. Next to Manila Bay was the Bacoor shoreline; I could see many of the squatters' makeshift homes. It was not a pleasant sight, and I felt for those living there. The conditions were terrible. I have seen nothing like this at all. The houses were constructed with plywood, with some rooftops made of scrap metal. There were old tires piled up on the roofs to hold them in place. The windows were not windows but just cut-outs on the sides of the huts with make-shift curtains. Some of them extended into the water and were built on stilts. I saw so many people just walking around there with their children. It made me think of how blessed we are in the states and do not even realize how good we have it. I paid little attention to the drive we made earlier in the week because my cousin and I were very busy talking. I asked the driver why the government does not help these people. He told me there are too many and that the government cannot keep track of them. People come here from the provinces all over the Philippines looking for work; most have had life-changing events from earthquakes, typhoons and floods. I am slowly learning that Filipinos are a proud people and will do what it takes to feed their families. The driver explained his people do not wait for the government to help them during natural disasters; they fend for themselves, especially in remote areas where they have no choice. He said that is why the community is strong and comes together when these things happen. They help each other rebuild and feed everyone during these disasters. I told the driver I understood him, and that is a great thing. Many people in the states wait and blame the government sometimes for the lack of assistance. It brought me back to when Dad was very thrifty and upset, when he thought we did not take care of things. But one thing is for sure, Dad never waited. If something needed to be repaired, he did it immediately. I understood my father more and more as I spent time here in the Philippines.

We reached the end of Cavitex freeway, which turned into Coastal Road. This is where the traffic started. I could not believe what I was seeing. It was a Sunday morning and there were still people everywhere. So many tricycles, jeepneys, buses, cars, trucks and pedestrians. The pedestrians would just walk anywhere in the street. When we came to a stoplight, all the motorbikes would weave their way to the very front of the line and wait for the green light. Some cars would even make their way to the front. There were three lanes, but they made five lanes out of it. I thought this was madness. There were men with safety vests that read "Traffic Control." I laughed because they were all in the shade and the traffic was fucked up. My family would think this was funny and I would take a picture. I noticed there was also a lot of construction going on. The driver told me they are building a skyway to lead to the airport and other major highways. There were so many skyscrapers here in Manila mixed in with smaller apartments that were basically right on the road. So many businesses lined the streets and small vendors. I could see the barbeque stands and thought how good they would smell. There were condominiums after condominiums as well. The driver mentioned that many of the residents are foreign nationals that spend months at a time here. I could see so many restaurants like back home. There were plenty of Starbucks here, so I would not have a problem if I wanted coffee or American food.

The Hotel

We arrived at the hotel, which was heavily guarded. There were armed guards at the entrance gate with heavy-duty metal barricades. They had bomb-sniffing dogs there as well. The security checked the trunk and inside the car and walked around with mirrors to check underneath both car sides. I was shocked and asked the driver why all the security. He told me it is a precaution because some of the factious groups there try to make trouble in Manila and some of the other groups. We pulled up to the entrance and were immediately greeted by the staff. They guided me to an x-ray machine-like in the airports. My bags would go through a scanner as well. After going through, they gave me the wand. I thought; this is some serious security. Once I passed security, two beautiful ladies in long gowns greeted me at the door. They asked me if I was checking in and I replied yes. They guided me to the reception area. The hotel was huge and classy. The young lady at the front desk greeted me as sir, as did everyone else. She explained that the check in was not until ten p.m., and it was only ten in the morning. I told her that was fine and asked if I could drop my bags somewhere.

She asked for my passport so she could make a copy and get me pre-checked in. She made a copy and punched my name into their system. "Sir, you are a platinum member here, so we can check you in right away."

I told her that would be great. Status has its privileges.

She upgraded me to a suite rather than a room and put me on the hotel's top floor where all the elite members stayed. I felt like royalty. Once she confirmed my room, my bags disappeared.

I asked her what happened to my bags. She said they would be delivered to my room, so I went with it. She welcomed me to the hotel and instructed me on the elevators, pool, and bar times. She also gave me a bag of goodies and thanked me for being an elite member. I thanked her and made my way to the elevators. They greeted me every step of the way by the hotel staff. They were very hospitable.

I arrived at the top floor and swiped my key card to get into my room. There I found a note from management on the bed welcoming me and offering fresh fruits and drinks placed on a table by the balcony. My room had a balcony that faced a golf course, just a beautiful sight with the golf greens and trees and Makati in the backdrop.

Picturesque, I thought. I immediately went and took photos. There was a knock at my door; I assumed it was my luggage. The young man with my bags was in the door. I told him he could just put it anywhere and gave him fifty pesos. I sat out on the balcony for a few minutes and ate the fresh mango. There were caddies holding umbrellas for the players on the course. I changed into my swim trunks and made my way down to the pool on the second floor of the hotel. When I arrived, only a few people were there, so the pool was wide open. A young lady named Sherry greeted me.

She was the pool attendant and had asked for my room details. Once I gave them to her, she told me I could sit anywhere I wanted. Of course, I wanted to be in the sun. After I got situated, Sherry returned to me and asked if there was something I wanted from the bar; food or drinks were available. I asked her if I could get a San Miguel Light. She soon bought this over to me. I put suntan lotion on and laid there for about thirty minutes, listening to some R & B that I had on my phone.

It was not a minute after I laid the empty glass of beer down before Sherry arrived again. I thought this was great service. I told her I would like to have another. She went back to the bar, and I lit up a cigarette. When she returned, she told me I had to smoke at the bar, not in the pool area. I told her no problem and made my way to the pool bar. I grabbed a seat, and the bartender brought me over an ashtray. She asked me how I was doing, and I told her I was doing just fine.

The pool attendant came over and entered our discussion. She asked me for my name, and they would call me Sir Kris from then on. We continued our conversation and found out that they had worked at this hotel for about five years each. I finished my cigarette and went back to the lounge chair. I continued to listen to my music and started wondering what Dad would do if he were here. I remembered all the places I visited and tried to place him there. The family had little pictures of Dad when he was young, and I had asked them why. Their reasoning was they did not have a camera in the family back in those days. Since Dad was the eldest out of all the children, he had to set the bar for the rest of his siblings. If we thought growing up was hard under Dad, I can imagine it being ten times as hard growing up here in the Philippines under my Lolo's rule. My uncle told me that Lolo was stringent and mean. Lolo would take a stick and beat you with it if you messed up. Dad had always asked for my help with things. No matter what I was doing I was always required to stop what I was doing and help him. When I finally turned sixteen, it was the age at which I could get my driver's license.

I still remember it so clearly, as Mom and Dad did not think I was ready to drive. I argued I had passed my class course with no problem making me eligible to get my license. They both felt that I was not mature enough to drive. This was the first time I questioned them. I was in a rage, saying things like, I had always done everything you asked of me. I always felt that you were harder on me than the rest of my siblings; why is this? I tried to understand all the years why I was different. I admit I did not have the best grades, and I did a lot of stupid shit when I was growing up. From an early age, I felt different. The black sheep of the family, the middle child.

Mom and Dad asked everyone to leave the room so they could talk to me one on one. I thought, *Here it comes. I was adopted or something like that. That is why they wanted me alone.* When I thought about it, my hair was lighter than everyone else, and my complexion was darker. My siblings resembled each other, and I did not.

As soon as the room was clear, Mom started off. Since I was born, I had never been a needy child; I cried little or needed my parents' attention, as my siblings did when they were growing up. She loved me as much as she did all my brothers and sisters, but each differently. If that makes sense, she continued I was always doing things independently and never asked for anything. Mom saw something in me she did not see in my siblings; she explained I could withstand anything because I needed little to survive, a simple kid who could always entertain myself. That is when Dad chimed in. He told me I reminded him of himself when he was a kid, as a naïve kid. He told me he saw it in me at a very young age. Dad did not want my life corrupted with easy things; the reason he said he was so hard on me. I could remember one time when Dad told me you must work for what you want in life. He thought I could do anything I wanted and was disappointed with me most in my schoolwork because I did not make my siblings' effort. He followed with he could always depend on me to do things when he needed me to and that I learned at a very early age to do the things that need to be done and not have to be asked to do them. Then they both told me how much they loved me, something that I never heard from them, not because I needed to listen to it all the time, but because they felt I did not need the reassurance growing up. That was the first time that Dad had ever said those words to me.

The pool attendant had asked me a question, but I was still in deep thought; I felt terrible because I ignored her until she brought another beer to me and told me this was on the house. She had my full attention at that point. They asked what places I had seen so far. I answered with, only to see my family in Cavite. They told me I should go to the Mall of Asia. It was close and was an excellent place to have many options to eat. This was a great idea, I thought. I grabbed my things and paid for my tab. I gave them both a nice tip for the short time I was there.

Mall of Asia

I took a quick shower and went down to the main lobby to grab a taxi. Everyone there was so hospitable. It impressed me. I told the desk that I wanted to get a cab to MOA, and she directed me to be a stand in the hotel's front. As soon as they procured the taxi for me, I got in and the driver asked me where I was going so; I told him MOA. He then gave me a flat price, and I asked him why? He said because of traffic and maybe he will not have another fare to come back to the area. Since he negotiated with me, I asked him why he could not use the meter. He just shook his head and said it was broken. The hotel's doorman knocked on the window and asked if everything was ok. I told him that the driver was trying to negotiate a fare for me to go to MOA. He immediately got pissed and yelled at the driver. The doorman told me to get out of the taxi. He then told the taxi driver to leave and not come back. The doorman made a note of the taxi company and number.

As I stood and watched, I realized the driver was trying to make an extra fare. The doorman came over to me and said that when the drivers see a foreigner, they will always try to get more money because they know we would have it. The doorman made a call on his phone, and soon a private car arrived. He told me that this was the hotel's private car, and that the driver would take me there for free. I asked for his name and then I thanked him and gave him a nice tip for helping me. I hopped in the car; we drove out of the cul-de-sac. The hotel was not off the main street, so we drove a few blocks. I saw all the electrical wires hanging on the utility poles. I could not believe my eyes; they were massive amounts of wire; a human could probably walk across them. There were so many. This went on for the entire trip until we reached Pasay. The hotel was located in Pasig City, near to the Mall of Asia, but traffic made it seem like it was far. When we arrived in Pasay, I could see so much construction. I saw so many high-rise condos, office buildings, and municipal buildings. I was in the heart of the Philippines now. Manila, the capital of the Philippines, was growing into a metropolis.

There were so many restaurants lined the streets, chains that you would see all over the world. Manila was thriving with business; people were everywhere. I could not believe it was a Sunday afternoon. As we got closer to MOA, I could see traffic getting worse. We drove by this enormous church, and I asked the driver about it. He told me that this was the Baclaran church. It had a long history and was one of the most famous churches in the world. I would later learn that Baclaran was a small town in the city of Paranaque, in what is now known as Metro Manila. In 1932, the city of Baclaran opened a small wooden chapel dedicated to Our Mother of Perpetual Help. It was not long before the chapel grew into a church with thousands of parishioners and missionaries. Some of the earliest ties to the Redemptorists go back to the 1700s. I told the driver that I would eventually go to the church after visiting the mall. I asked the driver why there was so much construction going on, and he told me that there are a lot of casinos and condominiums being built. Since tourism is one of the most significant incomes of the Philippines, they wanted to make a Las Vegas of Southeast Asia.

The driver spoke excellent English and had been very helpful. He was a very proud Filipino and knew his history in the Philippines. He also told me that the mall's area used to be part of Manila Bay. I asked him what he meant by that? He said that there was a reclamation project back in the late 70s to add land to this area. It was part of the bay. I could not believe it; he said the area had been filled with rocks, sand, and dirt, and he laughed and said maybe some bad people. I had a wonderful conversation with him on our ride. When we finally arrived at the Mall of Asia, I gave him a few hundred pesos, and he said no sir, there was not a fare; I told him it was for the brief history lesson he had given me. He thanked me and told me to enjoy my stay here in the Philippines.

As I entered the huge mall, I was checked by security, another scanning and x-ray machine, and a quick pat-down. I felt safe. I saw the same stores there as we have in the states. Crazy, I thought. I know they did not have these when Dad was a kid, so I wondered where he went to buy his things? I remembered Dad was born a few years after the Great Depression and lived with the effects of it. Since the Philippines was considered being a colony of the US, it felt the impact of the depression. But most Filipinos were used to surviving on their own with no government assistance. Even to this day, they take care of their problems independently. A trait I saw in Dad. If something broke, Dad would fix it right away.

As I walked around the mall, I noticed many older foreigners walking with young and beautiful Filipina women. I thought, What's going on here?

As I walked by many of them, I noticed the women would crack a quick smile at me. I first thought that maybe these were working girls, but later found out that these girls were looking for a better way of life. They would come from provinces all over the Philippines to meet a guy here in Manila and hoped to be taken out of the country to start a new life in a new country. I remembered what the two girls from the pool told me, "Many Filipina women are attracted to foreigners simply to be taken care of." They told me that many older men would come to the Philippines and seek a beautiful young girl to take care of them. So, it made sense that there were so many foreigners here. Filipina women, by trait, always cleaned and cooked and took care of the man. And they were in abundance here. I could see a big difference in the age gap between the men and women.

Some foreigners were so out of shape it was disgusting. But I had to remind myself, it is what it is, or the infamous saying of the Philippines, "Bahala na" or in English, "Come what may." The phrase was coined during WWII during the invasion of the Philippines. As the story goes, a group of American soldiers crashed in New Guinea and had been rescued by a Philippine task force staged in New Guinea awaiting the raid on the Philippines. This would be led by none other than the infamous General MacArthur. I read a book about this story. Fascinating read.

Like other malls in the states, the mall had all the usual high-end stores. I probably walked about a quarter of the way through before I got hungry. I found a Shakey's pizza in one corridor and ate there.

I sat next to a foreigner and his girlfriend. He was speaking rudely to her, and it bothered me. I tried not to pay them any mind as I ordered my food. The server came and took my order. I have not been to a Shakey's since I was a kid back in Maryland. I ordered a pepperoni crunch pizza. I tried not to notice the couple sitting next to me as I sat there, but he was loud and obnoxious. He was a foreigner; I could not place his accent, European, I thought, sitting with a young Filipina girl probably half of his age. When their food came, he complained to the server about it taking so long. The server politely said, "Sir, we are swamped and trying to get everyone's food out on time."

The perfect answer, I thought. I looked to see what they ordered; it was a pepperoni pizza and some wings. The man tasted one wing and immediately complained. He called the server over.

I could see the girl was embarrassed by her foreign boyfriend's actions. He told the server that he had ordered some hot wings, and the wings that she brought over were not hot enough. The server, frightened by now, walked over to her manager and explained the situation.

The manager, another young lady, came over to the foreigner and asked what was wrong, and I heard the foreigner tell her that this was not what he had ordered. The manager tried to explain that these were the hottest wings they offered.

Then the foreigner got mad and said, "You people can't get anything right; I'm not paying for this."

The manager told him she would deduct the wings from the order as he continued to eat them.

He said to her she better.

By now, I had had enough of his attitude. I chimed in, "Excuse me, sir, but if these are the hottest wings on their menu, pay for them; after all, you are eating them, right?"

He told me to mind my own business.

I told him I was, but his ignorance was too much for me not to include myself as I was sitting right next to them. Then I told him, "You are right. This is none of my business, but you are being very rude to the entire staff. You mentioned to the server, you people. Well, you included me in your conversation by saying that I am half Filipino. So, I do not appreciate you using that tone at me or anyone else in this place."

His girlfriend smiled at me while he was not looking.

Then he said, "Why is this your problem?"

I stood up, looked him straight in the eyes, and told him we can discuss this further, but not here in the restaurant. I asked him to step outside if he wanted to discuss this further with me. I could see fear overcome him, and he eventually shut down.

The manager did not make him pay for the wings, and he paid his bill. He turned to me and said, "You Americans think you own everything."

I stood up again and said to him, "Sir, if it is a problem, like I said, we can discuss this further outside."

He was speechless and left the restaurant. I told him and his girlfriend to enjoy the rest of their day.

Almost everyone in the restaurant had been watching and clapped as soon as the guy left the restaurant. The manager came to my table and asked if there was anything that she could get for me. I told her no, I was fine.

She asked if I was really half Filipino, and I told her yes. I asked her what happens when the customer orders the food and does not pay for it? She said that she and the server would have to take it out of their salary.

I told her, "No, add it to my bill, and I will pay for it." Then I apologized to her and the server for the foreigner being so rude to her and told them both that not all of us are like that. I left them a nice tip as well.

As I started to leave, the manager and the server returned and thanked me again. I told them no problem and to enjoy the rest of their day. It amazes me how some people think they are better than others. I see this back home when someone thinks that the wait staff is beneath them. It makes me sick to see this. The difference with me is that I will call you out. At an early age, I did this when I felt something was not right. Sometimes it got my ass whipped, but at least I stood up for what was right. Dad was the same way. When he tried to explain to someone in the store that something was wrong, they automatically thought, "Oh, another boat person." I have seen Dad get so pissed at people that they become scared. Dad always spoke up, always. I guess this is where I got it from. Dad never backs down either. I remember one time I was playing in the front yard when Dad came home. He was parallel parking and the car behind him pulled up so close he could not back up. The drivers in the other car kept beeping their horns, and Dad got out and yelled at them. I ran into the house and got my brothers in case Dad needed any help. By the time we got there, the car was finally backing up, and Dad continued to yell at the young drivers. They eventually drove around and cursed Dad as they passed him. I noticed they were teenagers from our high school. I told my eldest brother that I had seen who it was and that they had gone to our school. He then said to me that when we go back to school on Monday, he will point him out and take care of it. My eldest brother was the strongest and most intelligent out of all of us kids. He did not take shit either and was very pissed that the boys were cursing at his father. The next morning, we arrived at school, and I pointed the guy out to my brother.

"Were you in our neighborhood this weekend?" my brother asked. He said, "Yes. What is it to you?"

My brother punched him right in the face. Everyone was just in shock after watching this boy fall to the ground. After the hard work was done, I went to the boy and told him to watch out for who he curses in the future and that if he is ever in the neighborhood again and runs his mouth at our dad, the same thing will happen again. My brother grabbed me and pulled me away. We both made our way to our classes, which was the end of that. I never saw that boy again. Years later, I told Dad of this story and laughed and said we were lucky we did not get in trouble with school. I walked out of the front of the mall and waved down a taxi, this guy was probably licking his chops, thinking he got a foreigner for a passenger. I asked him to take me to Baclaran Church and then to the Hotel. He asked me how long I was going to be in the church. I told him long enough to light a candle and say a prayer. He had already negotiated before I even got into the cab. I had asked him to use his meter, but he said there would be traffic. So, I asked him how much he would charge me, he told me maybe 500php, I told him 350 php, and he said that was the standard fare from the mall to the hotel. I said, okay, fair enough, but I will not pay you until I get to the hotel. He agreed, and we made our way to the church. There was so much foot traffic near the church that we barely moved. After all, it was Sunday afternoon. The driver also said that so many people walked around because it was market day. And the market was right next to the church. I told the driver to just go to the hotel for now. I would go to the church some other time. But I would add this to my bucket list there. The driver said he would take another route because of all the traffic. He told me we would go on some side streets to avoid the direct street traffic. I did not mind because I would be looking at other parts of Manila now. The sun was now setting on Manila Bay. If I did not mention this before, the Philippines do not recognize Daylight Savings Time, so at around five-thirty p.m. the sun will set. My whole life is in this temperature in the summer, the sun would not set until eight-thirty p.m. Just felt different to me.

As we made our way through the back streets, I could not help but notice all the utility wires up above. I know I mentioned this already, but I cannot imagine that there were so many clustered together that it could be a hazard. There were, of course, the primary power lines, but hundreds of smaller lines just laid on top of them with no rhyme or reason. What a nightmare if you had an electrical issue, I thought. You could walk across the street on these wires and avoid all the congestion. I told the driver that I had seen nothing like this, and he laughed and said welcome to the Philippines. He explained in broken English that many people tap into the power grid to get free electricity, and if they get caught, they would face a big fine. The problem was that there were so many people doing it, that it made it hard to control. I laughed and said that I understood. I saw so many bars on the streets all lined up, one next to the other. A few girls would sit at the entrance, enticing the customers to come into their place. Karaoke was a big thing here, and they called them Resto-bars.

The driver noticed me looking at them. "Sir, if you want to get a girl, I can take you to some places where you will have many options."

I told him, "No, that is okay, let's just go back to the hotel."

As we pulled up to the hotel, I asked the driver to drop me off at the corner so we would not have to go through the checkpoint again and I will just walk. He said no problem, and I paid him as we agreed. I got out of the taxi and walked across the street from the hotel entrance, where I noticed a coffee shop. I went in and grabbed a coffee and sat at the table outside. I noticed some small children talking to strangers and looked like they were asking for money. For a few minutes, I sat and watched this. I remember Uncle telling me that there was a syndicate that used children to go in the streets and beg for money. How horrible was this? A young girl of probably only ten years approached me with her hands out. She was wearing an old t-shirt, shorts and flip-flops. She was filthy with her hair, probably not brushed today. Was this the life of this young child? I could not help but feel for this young girl. I went back into the coffee shop and bought a sandwich with chips, bottled water, and some chocolate candies. I went back outside to my table and waited to see if the girl would come back. She came back as soon as she saw me take my seat.

When she came over, I handed her the bag of goodies and she said, "Salamat Po," which means thank you in English. I watched her grab a seat across the street and what I saw next just really hit me hard. She looked up and down the street to see if anyone was watching, then she said a prayer. I can see her motions with the father, son, and holy spirit crossing. Then she opened the bag and started to eat the sandwich. She was thankful for the meal and thanked God for the blessing. I felt so bad; I waited for her to finish and waved her over. She came back, and I handed her about 200 pesos in twenties. Then I told her to be careful, or "Ingat Ka" in Tagalog.

She then thanked me again, and I went back to the hotel. The staff greeted me as I went through the same security protocol. I reached my room and wanted to take a few minutes to relax. The incident with the young girl touched me as I have daughters about her age. I wondered where this little girl would sleep at night. I felt bad for her. Would she be safe in the streets at night? I had to put this behind me for now. Otherwise, I would worry about every child on the street. I am no angel by far, but I felt good about doing that little gesture for someone. I looked out onto the balcony and could see the city in the background all lit up. It was a beautiful sight. I was looking at Makati and thought maybe if I had time, I would like to go there. Makati was the financial district of Manila, where many overseas companies had made their headquarters. This was a wonderful picture I thought of the skyline. I took out my notebook and commented on the day's events. I then opened my laptop to check some emails. Even though it was still the weekend, I checked my emails. There was not anything new. I took a shower and prepared to visit the casino connected to the hotel. The bathroom was huge, with a glass shower and a bathtub to see right through to the terrace.

The room was enormous with a king-sized bed, a fully stocked refrigerator, a gigantic television, and a huge workspace. I loved the upgrade for sure.

Around seven p.m., I made my way down to the hotel lobby. I noticed a bar in the very back and got a drink before I went to the Casino. I pulled up to the bar and grabbed a seat facing the hotel entrance. The hotel was still very busy with guests checking in. I noticed many of the guests at the bar were foreigners. The bartender came and asked if I wanted a drink, and I told her to bring me a cold San Miguel Light. Within a few seconds, she was back with my beer and placed a tray of peanuts in front of me. As I took a drink of my beer, the bartender struck up a conversation. She asked me where I was from and how long I would stay in the hotel. I told her I was from the US and would only be in the hotel overnight because I was leaving for Bohol in the morning. She then asked if I was meeting a girl there, and I had to laugh because apparently, most foreigners were in for a short while at the hotel for that reason. I told her I had a business meeting there and would be back on Wednesday morning. She smiled and said that's good news. I told her I was meeting someone else here in Manila Wednesday afternoon but would stay in a different hotel. The bartenders' name was Aileen, and she spoke excellent English. Aileen continued to tell me that many Filipina girls would like me because I was good-looking. I laughed again and told her I was already 50 years old, and she said that here in the Philippines, age does not matter. I told her I believed her because I went to the mall and witnessed all the young girls walking around with older, out-of-shape foreigners. She laughed back and said yes; she sees it, even here in the hotel. She called them "Holiday Girls." Aileen explained some girls would make a date with the guy when he comes here on vacation but will have many guys throughout the year. Then she said some girls were looking for someone to take care of them. She told me to be careful out there because many girls will look at me for sure.

It was not a minute after Aileen told me this when a young lady pulled up next to me and asked if anyone was sitting next to me. I told her no that the seat was empty, and she was welcome to sit there. The young lady then asked me where I was from, how long I would stay etc....Aileen looked at me and cracked a sarcastic smile. She knew what was going on, so I played along with it. I asked the girl the same question.

Then she asked if I could buy her a drink, and I asked her, "Do you always ask strangers to buy you a drink?"

She said no, but I knew better. I said sure I would buy you what I am having. She said that she did not really like beer and asked if I could get her a mixed drink. I told her that would be fine. As soon as she received her drink, she asked me if I would like a massage. I asked her how far her shop was, and she told me she would give me a massage in my room. I could see Aileen trying to hold her laugh in while she rinsed some glasses in front of us. I then asked how much a massage was and she said it depends. I said to her, depends on what?" She said the type of massage and how long I wanted it. By now, Aileen was full-on into this and interrupted our negotiations with another beer for me. She stood there when I asked the girl how much for just one hour. The girl then said for one hour it would be 3000php.

I told her that was too much. She finished her drink and quickly left. Both Aileen and I laughed. In the half-hour that I spent at the bar, five other girls approached me, asking the same questions. The very last one was willing to negotiate. I told her that the other girls offered me 2000php. She said, "I will give you a massage for 1500php. I was shocked and told her to let me think about it. She got angry and left. Aileen said that I was a brilliant negotiator; we both laughed, and then I closed my tab. Aileen gave me directions to the casino and told me I could reach it inside the hotel. I thanked her for her hospitality, left her a nice tip, and made my way to the casino.

Casino

As I walked, I noticed many foreigners chatting with lots of Filipinas there, wondering if they were closing the deals or meeting their future mail-order brides. I arrived at the casino entrance where two tall and beautiful women stood. They greeted me as I walked in. They were dressed in long gowns and looked like they had just come from a beauty pageant. Wow, they were both so beautiful and tall. I asked if I could take a picture with them, and they said no problem at all. We had a security guard take the picture. As soon as he took the picture, he mentioned that I was not allowed to use the camera once inside. I told him that was not a problem at all. I could see the center of the casino from the entrance, where a band was on stage playing some pop music. I thought this would be a perfect place to settle down, considering I am not a gambler.

The tables were in circles all around the center stage. Some tables could hold up to ten people, while the smaller tables were for couples. I grabbed a small table, and the server immediately approached me. I asked her for a San Miguel Light. She then asked if I needed an ashtray, and I said sure. I did not notice at first, but you could smoke in this section. I sat there and glanced around the place and noticed so many girls at the bar. All the servers were tall. When my server returned, I asked her why all the servers were so tall? She told me they only would hire tall servers. I thanked her, and she was on her way. It was not five minutes before a young lady approached me. This girl was much more spirited than the others. She could hold a conversation. She asked me if she could buy me a drink, and I said sure. We had some small talk then she wondered if I went to other bars. I explained I was here for business and had not been in the city until today.

Come to find out that she was a promoter for some clubs in the

Makati area. She passed me one of her calling cards and moved on. She was a beautiful young girl with long dark hair and an impressive body, and the bodycon dress she was wearing was the exclamation point. This was a great marketing tool, considering the arena we were in. A beautiful young girl is buying you drinks!

I glanced at her calling card, and there was a picture of a beautiful woman, the name of the club, and the address. On the flip side of the card, there was a promotion that if I went there and presented the card, I would get 50 percent off my tab. I thought, I might have to check the place out later on. When I called the server, I asked for my tab. I thanked her for her hospitality and made my way out of the busy casino. It was now approaching ten p.m., and I wanted to prepare myself for tomorrow's trip.

I Became Him

Persistent Filipina

I came across the last girl that had approached me in the hotel bar. She came up to me and tried to negotiate a massage one last time. I told her that if I did not have to prepare for my trip, I would certainly entertain her by giving me a massage. So, I told her next time. She turned and walked away.

I walked past the hotel bar to the elevators and could see Aileen waving at me. I gave her a quick wave back and hopped on the elevator. When I reached my room, I opened my laptop to see if I had any emails, especially from Imelda. There was only one new email; it was from the client I was meeting in the morning. He told me we will meet at the airport around eleven instead of seven a.m. He had asked for my personal information so that he could purchase the airline tickets. I gave him all the information I thought he would need, including my passport number. He returned an email saying thank you, and he would see me tomorrow.

I made some more notes in my notebook and thought about the massage. Since I did not have to get up so early, I thought I might get the last girl to give me a massage. I put all my belongings into the closet and locked my valuables in the safe. I made my way down to the lobby and looked for this girl. There were so many girls that they all looked the same.

Out of all the girls who had approached me, she was the prettiest and had the best shape. As I made my way through, I had many more women approach me. I could not find her and thought that I might just grab anyone of them. I went out to the smoking deck of the hotel to grab a quick smoke. I walked over to the edge of the deck to look at the golf course, but it was too dark to see anything. It was on the same side as my room, but too low to see the Makati skyline. I heard a girl's voice talking on her cell phone and turned to see a young woman sitting in the deck's corner. It was her; she had been here the whole time.

I walked up to her, but she was still on her phone. She asked me to wait a minute as she finished her call. I nodded to her. There was no one else on the deck.

She finished her call and again asked if I wanted a massage, and this time I said yes. She smiled as if I made her day. As we walked over to the elevators, I asked her what her name was. She told me it was Maylene. So, I introduced myself properly to her. She told me she had had no clients tonight, and that I was her first. We reached my room, and she asked if she could use the comfort room or CR, as they all called it. I told her to go ahead, no problem. I told her the bathroom was see-through and that I should drop the curtain first. She laughed and said, please do so.

I turned on the television and looked for HBO. A war movie was playing, and I kept watching it. Maylene soon came out of the CR. She had changed her clothes into what looked like a bikini.

I was thinking, What did I get myself into? I asked her why she changed, and she told me so that she could be more comfortable while giving the massage. She told me to undress and laid a towel down on the bed. I took my shirt and shorts off and had nothing on but my boxers. She told me to lie down on my stomach facing the TV. When I laid down, Maylene took my boxers off and explained to me she did not want to get the massage oil on it. Maylene then straddled me and started working on my shoulders. Little by little she added oil in and asked if I wanted soft, medium, or hard. I told her hard, like deep tissue. The hard massage felt so good on my lower back that I asked Maylene for ninety minutes instead of an hour.

I woke up around six-thirty the following day and went downstairs to the hotel restaurant for breakfast. I grabbed a seat in the bustling café and the server came with a cup of coffee and asked if I wanted the buffet. I wanted to check the buffet first and said yes, please check our buffet first. I walked around and could not believe how much food had been prepared for this buffet. This was way too much for me so I asked the server if I could order a la cart. She said no problem. I ordered the traditional breakfast, tapsilog. Tapsilog comprises beef tapa, garlic fried rice, and a fried egg. The name is a combination of all three ingredients: beef jerky or Tapa, Sinangag (fried rice) and Itlog (egg). This became my favorite breakfast.

I finished my breakfast and went back to the room to shower and shave. I packed my things and looked at some emails one last time. It was now about eight a.m., and I was to meet my client, Fred, outside of terminal one. I never met him, so I hope we can find each other. The client was actually an electrical contractor who had worked with our company a few years back. He had more projects of the same construction in the pipeline and wanted to get in front of his clients. He told me it is a big deal if the manufacturer comes and visits their offices because it never happens. This will show the client that we respect and appreciate his business. My client, Fred, was probably more excited than I was. We would fly to Cebu and then take a ferry over to Bohol.

Mesmerizing Bohol

This is my first trip to the Philippines, exciting enough for me. I got to see more places than I expected. I went downstairs to check out, and since I was a member of status, I just dropped my card key off in the box and left. The doorman asked me if I wanted a taxi, and I said yes, please. I told him I needed to go to Terminal 1. He made a call on the radio and asked me to wait over in a line. A few other people were waiting on taxis as well. I was number three in line. I noticed a taxi pull up and a Chinese man that came from inside the hotel walked straight up into the taxi and took off. I got so pissed and told the doorman that he had to wait like everyone else. By then, the taxi had sped off.

I could hear the doorman tell his coworkers that I was so pissed. He came to me and apologized that most Chinese are rude here and do not obey the rules here. I told him that I was not pissed at him but at the Chinese man who cut in line. My taxi soon pulled up, and the doorman, who I would come to find out was from Cavite also, waved me over and wished me a safe flight. I thanked him and gave him a tip. The traffic was so bad, and I was glad we did not have to go so far. I still could not get over how people drove here. It was just crazy; the drivers basically did whatever they wanted. When my taxi driver had to make a left into oncoming traffic, he inched his way out; other cars followed and shut down the oncoming traffic. I laughed at this. It reminded me of a pick in basketball; once one car got in, others would follow.

To break this, the oncoming traffic would have to inch their way forward until all the turning cars would submit and not hit the oncoming vehicles. Taxi drivers were the experts at cutting off traffic. We arrived at the terminal and paid my fare and asked the driver for a receipt. He printed it off. The trip was 175 php. It was like a three-dollar ride. Wow, I thought. I gave him a 50 php tip, and he was delighted.

I got out of the taxi and was now in front of Terminal 1, but so were about a hundred other people. I heard a man's voice calling my name. I turned to see who it was. He walked up to me and asked if I was Kris; I said yes, you must be Fred. We shook hands and made our way into the terminal. Fred was very excited that I was here in the Philippines. Since our flight was at eleven a.m., we had some time to check-in and get familiar with each other. Fred had made all the arrangements, including the hotel there in Bohol. All I needed to show at the airport was my passport and printed out my ticket. Once we had our documents, we went through security and found a place to sit and grab a cup of coffee. Fred asked if I was here on vacation. I told him yes. He then asked out of all the places, why the Philippines? I told him I wanted to take the same footsteps as my father once took. He asked if my father was a soldier here and I told him he had been in the Navy and was born here in the Philippines. At first, he could not understand, so I explained my father was Filipino. He looked at me and said he would have never guessed that I was half. I told him that my mother's French, Irish blood was thicker. We both laughed and continued our conversation. He then asked if I still had family here and where they were. I explained that my father's siblings were here and in the US. This made him more excited to meet his clients because he could now use the Filipino bloodline to secure the business. I told him of my adventures in the first couple of weeks in Cavite, where the family name was born. Fred had asked where my father was and did he take the trip with me. I told him. Unfortunately, Dad had died. He apologized and gave his condolences. We then got down to business and talked about our first project together. I mentioned to Fred that I was the original contact he had from the states on the first project and that I tried to reach out to him afterward. He gave me details about the upcoming projects there in Bohol, and the reason we were going there.

Bohol was one of the islands located in the Central Visayas region of the Philippines. It is the tenth largest island of the Philippines and comprises seventy-five smaller islands. Most of the power to the grid came from a power plant there, and the island power was generated by diesel generators that were regulated daily. A big inconvenience for the people and businesses that lived on the smaller islands. The concept was simple, to bring power from the grid to the islands. The difficulty was how to do this in very shallow channels. Since the Philippines comprised so many islands and volcanos, the channels were not deep enough for the large submarine cable laying vessels to navigate through. So, Fred developed an installation plan and designed a line for these projects. This is what we were going to pitch to the Electrical Co-ops there.

We boarded our flight on Philippine Airlines destined for Cebu Mactan airport. It was about an hour's flight. I took the window seat to see the Philippines during the day for the first time as it. was at night when I flew in and could see nothing.

This would be a treat, I thought. I noticed all the flight attendants were young, beautiful, and tall. Just like in the casino, I thought. It was becoming a common theme here in the Philippines, with so many beautiful women. I wondered why Dad never married a Filipina. Dad was the only sibling that married a foreigner.

Mom and Dad had been married for over forty years before she passed. I was told that Dad was very good-looking when he was younger and courted many women, but he never settled down with any of them. I could see the earliest pictures of Dad when he had just joined the Navy, but those pictures were so old and in black and white only.

I remember going through his picture collection when my siblings and I cleaned out his apartment after his passing. Dad had one particular album of just his family in the Philippines. This is where I saw all the pictures in black and white. Then there were pictures of special occasions like weddings, birthdays, christenings, etc. We never really knew how big the family was in the Philippines during our childhood. I remember sending letters to our cousins. But they were few and far between. So, neither of my siblings nor I had any idea. We would just go off with what Dad told us now and again. None of us realized how big our family was here.

As we took off, I could see the many houses surrounding the airport with different color roofs. As we got higher, it looked like puzzle pieces. It was such a fantastic view. We took off to the north and circled the city until we made our way south. There were hundreds of skyscrapers and so many cranes. I could see the Taal Volcano from where I was sitting. That is when I saw all the mountains and islands. Such a beautiful view on a clear day. I think this is where I fell in love with the Philippines. There were large islands and tiny islands. It was something that would stick in my memory. This is the first time I have seen anything like this in my life. I thought that I would like to see as many of the islands as I could. I would spend my vacations here exploring the many islands and traditions of the Philippines. I took so many pictures of those islands; I was just amazed.

Cebu consisted of 150 to 167 islands, depending on who you asked and if it was low tide or not. A running joke in the Philippines. They say that Cebu City was the first capitol and the oldest city in the Philippines. Some of the architecture remained in this ancient city from the Spanish colonization.

While in the air, I read an article in a magazine that mentioned that Cebu City was the second-largest metropolitan area in the Philippines after Manila. It is the principal shipping port for the Philippines.

The flight was shorter than the one hour they told us; it was like forty minutes. As we approached Cebu, I saw more islands on the horizon.

I saw the same things I noticed while taking off in Manila, puzzle pieces all over the place. There were not as many skyscrapers as in Manila, but many mountains close by. The airport was a lot smaller as well. When we deplaned, I followed Fred to the exit, and we made our way straight for the taxi stand. We had to take a ferry from here to Bohol. Fred told the driver to hurry because we had the ferry ride in an hour. The terminal was only a few miles away, but the traffic going over the bridge from the airport to Cebu city was heavy. Once we got over the bridge, the traffic seemed to die down and we were at the ferry terminal in no time. I had never ridden on a ferry of this size, only the small one when we went to Corregidor Island, so this would be another first experience for me. They called them fast ferries and the company's name was Super Cat. The ride would last about 2.5 hours. We made our way to the dock. There were a few different carriers there, all going to different ports. So, we had to make sure we got to the right dock. We would enter Bohol through Tagbilaran City. This was the capital of the province of Bohol. As mentioned before, Bohol comprised seventy-five minor surrounding islands. The views from the port of Cebu were all beautiful except the ports themselves. This was a very industrious area with many ships berthed, waiting on containers. Fred had told me that the people here in the Visayas region spoke a different dialect than in Manila. The language they spoke is called Cebuano, or Bisaya. We boarded the ferry as soon as we arrived. I can remember seeing all the soldiers around the port in full gear. I thought that these guys had to be burning up in their uniforms. It was so hot still outside and the sun had been beating down on us. Some so many people had a small towel to wipe their faces. I could see the mothers wiping down the children as well. Once inside the Super Cat ferry, one could feel the air conditioner blowing. This felt so good. The main deck, which was covered, could probably hold up to 100 passengers. They had a big screen TV with a food and beverage bar. I thought this was so cool. Fred took us over to our seats, and I asked if I could have the window seat. He said no problem. As I sat down, I looked out of the window and could not see much as there was a larger ferry berthed right next to us. This ferry had been loading large trucks. Fred said that many international trading companies were located here in Cebu and Manila because of the large ports. Most of the containers would be broken down in these two cities and loaded onto trucks for transport via ferries to other provinces. He mentioned that if we landed the projects in Bohol that he would also load his trucks and equipment into the larger ferries. They were slower and took three times as long to offload than the more miniature Super Cat. As ferry stewards closed the cabin doors, you could feel the pilot switch gears.

We would coast out of the port until we reached the harbor. Immediately, you could feel the pilot switch into high gear and the nose of the ferry went up about twenty degrees before the pilot settled the ferry into cruising speed. You could feel every wave that we hit. I glanced out of the window only to see the spray of the hull hitting the surface of the water at high speeds. The Super Cats had a top speed of fifty knots.

I could not believe it, but I actually fell asleep for a bit while watching an old Filipino detective movie. Everything was in Tagalog, without captions, so it was hard to understand. When the Super Cat slowed down, the nose of the craft became level with the water. I could see out of the windows again. I stared at all the palm trees that lined the shore. It was so beautiful to see. The water was crystal blue, and the beaches were mixed with rock and white sand. We docked at a concrete pier full of passengers awaiting the ferry. The sun set as we made our way off the ferry. Fred had a driver waiting for him as we got out of the port. Fred told me we would meet a client for dinner and go to the hotel to freshen up first. We were staying in a city called Panglao Island. This was actually a resort with beautiful beaches. I read a flyer that spoke of some attractions in Bohol. The Chocolate Hills were the major tourist attraction here. It was a group of approximately 1300 hills that turned brown during the dry season, thus the name. People from all over the world traveled to Bohol to see the Chocolate Hills. They were located pretty much in the center of the Island. Its highest point was only about 120 meters, but the natural formation was pleasing to the eyes. I would have loved to see them, but we certainly would not have the time during this trip. I added this to my bucket list of the Philippines.

The driver was speedy; we arrived at our destination in only a few minutes. Fred asked him to be there at seven-thirty a.m. sharp tomorrow. Panglao Island was very different from the big cities I saw in the Philippines. It was like going from Manhattan to the eastern shore of Virginia, to put it into perspective.

We crossed over a small bridge that led into Panglao Island, and the view from the bridge was so beautiful. Palm trees lined the beaches, and the water was so blue. I would have to come back here and tour this beautiful island. We soon arrived at the hotel. The rooms were cottages. Fred told me to freshen up and meet him at the restaurant in thirty minutes for dinner. The restaurant was on the beach deck, just a short distance from the front desk. I was starving by now. I went up to my cottage and read a sign out front that talked about animals' natural habitat in the area and not to disturb them. The one that popped into my mind was the python snake. I thought, This will be great, dodging pythons while walking to the restaurant. It freaked me out a bit.

The cottages were very nice and cool inside. The hotel had the air conditioning running before our check in. The rooms were small but efficient. They even had Wi-Fi there. I quickly took a shower and turned the TV on while I prepared. I noticed that there was HBO, the Asian version. I took out my notebook and quickly made some notes about the day's travel so I would not forget. I grabbed my wallet and phone, then made my way to the restaurant. The sun had set, and I thought this would be a great time to see a python. I carefully walked down the lighted path to the restaurant on the beach. It was a lovely setting. I met Fred there, and we grabbed a seat on the deck overlooking the Bohol Sea. I could not wait to see this view in the day. As a tourist, I took a few quick pictures. Our guest soon arrived, and Fred wasted no time introducing me to him. He was a middle-aged man, maybe right at 40 years of age and very dark-skinned. His name was John, but everyone called him JP. JP started business right away. I gave him my verbal resume, and he seemed pleased that I had made my way to the Philippines to pitch our project to him. JP explained to us that there has never been a salesperson visiting them in the past. Fred was pleased to hear this and thought this would solidify the business. JP asked for my business card, and I was happy to give him one. He took notice of my last name right away. He asked me if I was a Latino and I told him no; I was half Filipino. He smiled and said really, but you do not look Filipino. We all laughed. I said that my mother's mixed blood was more potent than my fathers. JP continued to ask about my father, where he was from, how he ended up in the US, and where he was now. I answered him as best as I could. JP was happy to hear that I was of a Filipino blood line that could help them with their project. I could see that Fred was pleased as well. Fred had put the order in without asking us what we wanted. This was customary there. Fred interrupted the meeting to ask us what we wanted to drink. JP had asked for a San Miguel Lite, so I ordered one as well. This was going to be a perfect night. JP jumped right into the projects that they had been engineering. There were seven in all that would be bid as soon as Fred could put the package together. Fed broke out his laptop and started his presentation. It was a brief presentation and very well put together. He then had my presentation attached when he was done, and I took over from there. Soon the server came back with our food. It was perfect timing as we were into our second round of drinks.

Our server was as beautiful as all the women I had seen on the island. Long dark hair, dark skin and a dazzling smile. Her name was Jennelynn, according to her name tag. How she bounced around told me she was full of life. I could hear her singing as she walked around the deck. And the one thing I noticed about her was she did not wear make-up and was still beautiful. Made me quickly think of Imelda.

By the time we had finished our dinner and drinks, the deal was practically closed. Fred was a happy camper. We would meet up with JP in the morning at his office and go to the sites.

Including the very first site that Fred and I worked on together. JP thanked us for the time and dinner. Fred and I stayed and chatted longer. He asked me if I could put a pricing profile together tonight so he could present this to them in the morning. I told him no problem at all.

I asked Jennelynn for the check, but she told me that Fred had already paid for it. I told Fred he should let me pay for it since he had already paid for this entire trip. Fred explained I was doing him a huge favor by traveling with him to visit his clients because no outside salesperson ever visited the Philippines, let alone a VP of sales with a Filipino blood line. This was a tremendous bonus, and he was grateful. Fred told me we are going to get these projects. He was very confident. This was a multimillion-dollar project for my company, and we only would supply the sub-sea cables. Fred would profit from a project this large. There was so much more outside of the wires that were involved.

I took a quick shower and made notes of the day's events and how beautiful Bohol was. I was excited to tour the island in the morning. I put together the offer that Fred had asked me to. I shot off a few emails to my boss about today's meetings. And checked my email to see if there was anything from Imelda. There was an email from her. She was excited about our date in a few days. I emailed her back and told her I was just as excited as she was and that I had been looking forward to this day since we met on the plane.

There was a knock at my door. I could not imagine who it could be. I opened the door, and a young lady walked in and said hello. I told her that maybe she had the wrong room or something because she had just walked in. She said, "Sir Kris, right?"

I answered, "Yes."

She told me she was in the right place and that Sir Fred had paid for a one-hour massage.

She told me to get more comfortable and lay on the bed.

I woke up at six a.m. to the roosters squawking. I jumped in the shower and prepared for the day's travel. I ran out to the restaurant to see if I could get a cup of coffee. They were already open, so I took a seat on the deck. What a beautiful sight, I had to take some pictures of the beaches and water. I really could not see it that well coming in. I would make this one of my vacation spots in the future. Fred made his way over to my table.

The driver would be here in thirty minutes. I told Fred that I was already packed up and wanted just to have some coffee. He said that breakfast was included with the room if I wanted to eat. I just settled for the coffee. The driver showed up right on time. The trip would take maybe thirty minutes to pick up JP at his office.

We made our way over the bridge to the Bohol mainland. As we got away from Panglao Island, I could see the real rural areas of the Philippines. This is what I wanted to see. This is what all Filipinos refer to as the province. It was such beautiful, extensive fields with mountains in the background. There were tiny houses far apart. I thought that this is how Dad grew up in Cavite back in the day. Was this how it was back in his heyday? Old concrete houses that were not painted with colored roofs. Tiny streets, not so many cars on the road, no skyscrapers. Anyone coming from an area like this and going into Manila for the first time had to be shocked at what they saw. I noticed a lot of tarps on the road with rice, so I asked Fred what this was. He said that it was harvest season for rice and that what I was seeing was the rice being dried. This is a must-do for approximately twenty-four hours. The rice contains moisture after harvesting, so this is the best method to store the rice before selling. They were everywhere and could see bodies in the rice fields harvesting the rice. Just like you saw in movies these people wore the traditional paddy hats and long sleeves while working the rice paddies.

Bohol is Visayas' top rice producer, year after year. One would never realize the manual labor that goes into this process. The views from the road were just amazing. Palm trees, banana trees and coconut trees all mixed but seemed like in a pattern. I was just in awe of what I saw, thanking God for giving me this opportunity to see his work.

We arrived at JP's office a few minutes early. JP met us in the lobby and wanted to introduce us to his boss and the other department heads. I looked at Fred and he smiled and gave me a wink. He knew this was a good thing to be introduced to officers of the electrical co-op there. As we made our way through the office, everyone stood and greeted as if we were the president or something. The driver waited in the car along with our bags.

When we met the chairman, they wanted a picture of us. So, I put on my best smile and went for it. We then took off to one of the job sites. JP told us it was about twenty minutes away.

The drive was just as beautiful as when we were coming in. Many banana trees lined the highway. Every now and again, I would see a caribou tied up to a tree right on the side of the road in the middle of nowhere. We pulled off the main road onto a mixed dirt and gravel road. There were a few houses located a hundred yards off of the road. Goats and chickens were all over the place. I could see the road open up to the sea in front of us. We parked in front of a couple of houses near the shore. The sight was so breathtaking. I could imagine waking up every day next to the sea. There was an island about a half of a mile out. We took a walk over to the high voltage sign and Fred mentioned this was the sight of the first job. I told him it must have been challenging to work here because of how close the houses were. I asked why not a few hundred feet away from here? He told me they had to preserve the mangroves on both sides of the shores.

It is mandatory not to disturb them. Since they would be burying the cables on both shores, I understood.

We walked down the water's edge, and the first thing that came to my mind was that I could live right here. It was just so beautiful. Fred pointed out the laying of the cable's direction next to a high voltage sign. We all loaded up onto a Banca to follow the line's path to the opposite shore. The water was so clear, you could actually see exotic fish swimming below. It was not long before we reached the other shore. We didn't leave the boat because we had to go see another project site. I took many photos of the shore and the mangroves. Looked like a picture from a movie.

I wondered if Dad saw all of this beauty in his home country. I hope he was happy seeing me here for the first time. I was able to take some of the same footsteps as he did. My siblings would be so jealous of this. I would definitely put a slide show together for them.

We landed back at the same port where we boarded the boat. The driver pulled the car up and, just like that, we were on our way to the next project site. It was on the other side of the island, so it would be a longer ride. I got to see so many rural areas here in Bohol, not like in the city. There were not as many cars on the road here; things were more spread out than in the city as well. True province living here. The mountains seemed like they were so close, but you would look in the rice fields and realize that they were miles away. It reminded me of some old Vietnam war movies. The landscape was just breathtaking.

We arrived at the job site we were bidding on now. This project would take place right away. This was at the northern tip of Bohol. The town of Bien Unido was known for its abundance of seaweed. The mainland city was the delivery point for the Jao Island. This would be a large project and take several months to complete. On the shores, we discussed the lead times for the cables. When JP realized the lead-time, he practically gave us the order confirmation right there. My boss back in the US would be pleased to hear this. The project would be done ahead of the allotted time frame. The water was so clear here I could see out into the bay. Jao Island looked so far away but was only a little over a mile from where we stood. A quick boat ride, and you were there. The people of Bohol turned this island into a resort area. Because of its natural white beaches and plenty of diving attractions, this would soon be a popular vacation spot. So, the Bohol local government wanted to get power to the island right away.

There will be many more projects throughout the Philippines in the coming year. I looked forward to writing a report and presentation when I got back to work. We drove to Tubigon Port, as that is where we would take the ferry back to Mactan airport in Cebu. Fred wanted to find a hotel near there as it was getting late in the day and our scheduled ferry ride was early in the morning. The ride would take almost two hours, but we would soon stop for a late lunch. We pulled into a small restaurant where they were serving barbeque. It smelled so good and by this time I was hungry. I ate some rice and chicken, and it hit the spot. We were back on the road with about an hour left. I had asked Fred why we did not leave tonight, and he said that he did not know how long we would be here, plus the ferries could not get us to Cebu fast enough to make the flights. Fred had this well planned out. We arrived at the hotel around three p.m. It had been a long day of traveling around the island. The hotel was small but served its purpose. There was no air conditioner in my room, only a fan. I thought it was going to be hot as hell. I went to the front desk to ask the young lady if they had a room with air-con and she said no, only the lobby and restaurant. This would be a first for me. She continued to say that the breeze off the water at night keeps it cool. No problem, I said. I asked if they had a bar in here and she told me I can just grab a seat anywhere in the lobby and someone will serve me. I said OK. I went to my room, opened the fan to medium, and let it run. I grabbed my laptop and went back into the restaurant/lobby. As soon as I sat down, the same girl at the front desk came to wait on me. She laughed and said, "Yes, I am the server as well."

I ordered a San Miguel Light. She mentioned that since the hotel was small compared to other hotels in the area, she could handle doing everything. I noticed she spoke English very well. She always had a smile on her face and loved to sing. I thought I had Déjà vu. She reminded me so much of the server we had at Panglao Island. Long dark hair, dark skin, no make-up and naturally beautiful.

I opened my laptop and started working on my presentation right away. I would ask Fred later for more information about the scope of the projects, the TIV, total investment, and a number of meters if he had them. I downloaded some photos from my camera to use during the presentation. The server came and sat next to me. She had seen what I was working on and was interested. Her name was Annabelle. Anabelle seems so full of life. Immediately, she started firing off some questions about what I was doing. I asked Annabelle why she was so interested, and she mentioned she was in her last year of college. I then asked Annabelle about her studies, and she said that she had been studying geology.

That was odd. Why geology?

Annabelle answered that mining is one of the largest industries in the Philippines behind OFC workers and call centers. I was very interested in speaking with her more. I immediately added this to my presentation. Come to find out, Annabelle was on point with everything she told me about mining. I asked her if I could buy her a drink, and she was not allowed during working hours. She said there was a bar about ten minutes away and asked if I wanted to meet her there later. I told her I could not because I had another early wake-up tomorrow but thanked her for the invite. She must have seen my cigarettes on the table because she got up and brought me an ash tray. She said we may smoke in the lobby but not in the rooms. Annabelle left me her number and email address and told me to call her if I was ever in Bohol again. I told Annabelle that I would be happy to meet with her on my next trip here.

After a few hours, Fred joined me for a quick dinner, as he had to meet one of his colleagues at the power plant nearby. Fred mentioned that there was a problem there, and he, being an electrical engineer, would look at the situation. Fred asked me if I wanted to go, and I told him I had some work to do here and that I would pass. After I finished up my dinner, I sat and had one more beer before I went to my room. I made a few extra notes about how beautiful Bohol is and how I wanted to visit here again in the future. Since Fred was in a hurry, I could finally pay the tab. He shared some more information on the upcoming projects, and I could load this into my presentation.

As I was packing my things up, Annabelle stopped by and said I could not leave yet. I asked her why and she said that I had one more beer. I told her I did not order another one, and she knew she bought it for me. Since she was not busy, she grabbed a seat and started telling me about the places here in Bohol. She was a very proud Filipina; I could see it in her eyes and smile as she continued to say to me. I finished my beer, thanked Annabelle for her hospitality, and gave her a nice tip. It had been a long day, and I was so looking toward taking that well-deserved cold shower. I opened the door to my room, and surprisingly enough, the room was cool. I showered and laid down on the bed, and just like that, I was out cold.

I could not stop thinking about dad living here in the Philippines when he was younger. I could only imagine that in his time, how difficult it must have been. Being from a huge family and growing up, not only during the end of the depression but during the Japanese invasion. This was all happening during the first ten years of his life. He and his family had survived these hard times. My siblings and I have no idea how to live through what Dad lived as a kid. I started to appreciate and understand his culture and why he was so hard on me growing up. When you think about all the modern conveniences that we live with these days, it is hard to imagine living without the simplest of things, such as air conditioning, running water, and cell phones. When we were still kids, we grew up as we were raised in the Philippines.

Both mom and dad taught us always to turn the lights out or power down things we were not using. Our parents got so angry if they found the faucet's water dripping. Even if we left the hose on outside, someone would have to pay for that mistake. It seemed like I was the guilty one most of the time. Growing up, my siblings and I had this rule; if you touched it last, you were responsible for putting it away. This caused many arguments, a good example of this as in the mornings when we would sit down for breakfast, someone would get out the cereal and milk. And if you were just reading the back of the cereal box and not touching it, you were guilty of touching it last. I laugh now at some things we argued about.

I woke up around six a.m. and quickly showered and packed my bags. I went out to the lobby to grab some coffee. Fred was already there and said that the driver would be here at seven. I said, perfect; then I have time for coffee. The room came with a breakfast package as well. So, I grabbed a bite to eat. I had the Filipino breakfast, garlic rice, fried eggs and beef tapa. It was delicious. This would be something I would miss when I got back stateside.

Fred told me he did not get back until three-thirty a.m. last night and he was exhausted. The issue at the power plant was traced back to a faulty recloser. A recloser or ACR (automatic circuit recloser) is a class of switch gear. Fred had spent all night replacing the faulty recloser with the staff. This would certainly go a long way with the electrical co-op.

We arrived at the port and boarded the ferry back to Cebu. Both Fred and I fell asleep on the ferry right away. It felt like only a few minutes before we arrived in Cebu. We grabbed a taxi to the airport from the ports in Cebu. While we were on the plane, I noticed a beautiful mountain to the left of us. I was going to ask Fred for the mountain's name, but he was fast asleep again. I later learned that what I had been looking at the Mayon Volcano. The Mayon volcano was a perfect cone, rising some 8000 plus feet into the sky. It was a beautiful sight as clouds circled the tip of the volcano. The Mayon was located in Bicol, a large province in Southern Luzon. There is a lot to see around this area and I would certainly put this on my bucket list for future trips.

We landed around two p.m., and Fred was exhausted. He thanked me for attending the meetings with him and we said our goodbyes. I took a taxi to the hotel on Manila Bay. As soon as I arrived outside the airport, many vendors asked to take their taxi. I was not comfortable doing this, but my phone battery was very low, and I could not get a grab taxi. I walked over to the airport's official taxi stand and asked them for a taxi to the hotel. When I mentioned the hotel's name, they told me that there was a shuttle service for the hotel located inside. I said okay and made my way to the shuttle counter. I found the hotel and asked the young lady if a shuttle was available. She said no, but they have private cars to and from the airport. I asked how much she asked if I was checking in, and I told her yes. She took my passport and confirmed my stay. Then she said there was no charge because I was staying in an executive suite. I told her that was perfect and where was this car at? She sent a porter to me right away, and he grabbed my bags, and I followed him out to the car. The car was a nice Toyota brand, one that we did not have in the states. I did not see many cars in the states that are here, even the US brand of cars are different. Ford and Chevrolet are all over the Philippines, but they are tiny cars and totally different models.

After about thirty minutes, we arrived at the hotel. What a beautiful setting. As the car pulled up to the gate, there was another security check with bomb-sniffing dogs and armed guards. The security around here was no joke. Once we were cleared, we made our way to the front of the hotel. Right away, porters were grabbing the luggage out of the trunk. I did not see my luggage until I reached my room.

I went through another scanner and finally entered the hotel. Two beautiful girls dressed in long gowns greeted me and walked me over to check in. Wow, this was very professional. There was a line at check-in, but the girls noticed I got out of the hotel car and told me I was going to a distinct line. I was received right away, and all I had to do was show my passport and credit card, and the room key was in my hand.

Less than five minutes was all it took to check-in. Doing these things online is worth it. The room was in pesos, so I never thought about the expense; my company would eventually pay for it. The young lady then came from behind the counter and walked me over to the elevators. She told me I needed the room key to start the elevator to my floor and showed me how. I reached my executive suite in minutes. I found my room and entered to find my luggage already there. How impressive was that? I went to the balcony and had a beautiful view of Manila Bay and the pool area. I really liked this place.

Manila Bay

I opened my laptop to send Imelda a message that I was back in Manila and where I was staying. I could not wait to see her this evening. This place was just beautiful. I quickly changed into my bathing trunks because I wanted to see the pool area. I took a tour of the hotel lobby area before making my way out to the pool. This hotel was probably the most excellent place I ever stayed in during all my travels. I have stayed in some really nice hotels in Vegas, but this topped it. There was a massive spiral staircase leading to one of the largest buffets, and the area was just as elegant as the lobby. The place was immense. I would suggest to Imelda to have dinner here with me. I made my way to the pool area, and the attendant asked for my room number and key.

They then gave me bracelet; I asked what they were for, and the attendant explained it shows if you are just a pool guest or an actual guest of the hotel. Then there were different colors to determine if you were staying in a standard room or a special room. I said wow, that is pretty cool, but why would I need this? She said it was for the staff working in the area, so they know to take care of the hotel guests with priority. And the color determined the status of your stay. Jokingly, I asked her what my color represented, and she said that I had the highest priority. Wow, I thought, I love this place.

As soon as I found a spot next to the pool, I took my belongings, placed them under my towel, and jumped right into the water. The pool water felt so good. I went to my lounge chair and dried off. I wanted to get some sun while I still had a few hours to prepare for Imelda. As I sat down, a young gentleman came up to me to take my order. I asked for just a bottle of water and if I could see a menu. I wanted to grab a sandwich. The setting in the pool area was very nice. From where I was sitting, I could see Manila Bay. I could not wait to see the sunset here. The lady at the front desk told me it was beautiful. The young attendant came back with my bottled water and a menu. I asked him if there was anything that was light on the menu because I did not want a full meal. He told me he could put an order in for just a sandwich if I wanted. I told him it would be perfect if he did that. He came back a few minutes later and said that he could do it. I asked for just a club sandwich. Then I asked his name; he told me his name was Nick. Nick turned out to be a pretty cool guy. He told me some history of the hotel and on a clear day, you could see Bataan and Corregidor Island. I asked him how long he had been working here, and Nick told me about three years now. He spoke excellent English and was friendly.

I could not understand that they had to wear these long white shirts as if they were working inside. They had to be hot. Nick went on his way, and I sunbathed for a few minutes. About fifteen minutes later, Nick was back with the sandwich. I thanked him and ate my sandwich like there was no tomorrow. As soon as I was finished, Nick was back, picking up the dishes as if he had been watching.

What great service this place had! I realized that the people of the Philippines were very hospitable; I wanted to say courteous, but I remembered the traffic and how nobody gave a shit.

I went back to my room to ensure the time that Imelda was to meet with me and where. I opened my laptop and looked for the message from Imelda, and to my surprise, there was a new one. Imelda said she would be available after six p.m., and we could meet in the Starbucks at the Mall of Asia. I messaged her back and said that was fine. I had a few hours to rest. I sent a couple of emails back to the office and the purchase order from Fred. My boss was going to be a happy camper. I took a quick shower and then went to smoke out on the balcony. My view was just amazing. I thought about the time that from the time that I landed and until now. There was not a moment or place where I tried to picture Dad. This was his native land. I walked in the same footsteps, saw some of the same things, and more importantly, I got to spend time with his siblings and my cousins. What a bountiful trip. I was happy. I hoped he was looking down at me right now and was proud of me for trying to understand him more. All the emotions of the trip hit me at once. I cried, thinking of how Dad had suffered. I laughed about some of the crazy things he did. Most of all, I felt empty because he was gone.

It was now around 4:45 p.m., I would prepare for the evening's events with Imelda. I remember telling her that I would just be in shorts, so I made sure to wear my nicest shorts. I also put on a nice polo shirt to match. I figured it would only take maybe fifteen minutes to get to MOA from my hotel, so I had some time. For a while, I would just relax. After all, it had been a long day traveling from Bohol, then Cebu to here. Since I did not have a picture, I hoped I would recognize Imelda when I saw her. I remember she had her hair up, which might throw me off a bit. And she had a little makeup on. Wow, now I doubted myself and really tried to think about what she looked like.

Because I have seen so many beautiful women there already, I will have difficulty remembering her looks. I had to think if there were any distinguishing marks. She had dimples, okay now it is coming back to me. I went back out to the balcony to watch the sunset. There were many people watching this from the pool area. The lights were on there and it looked like a band was setting up. The ambiance of this place was perfect for a night out with a young lady. I would ask Imelda if she wanted to come back to this area for sure.

Meet-Up with Imelda

I grabbed a taxi from the hotel and went to the Starbucks in MOA. I was about fifteen minutes early, and I decided not to order anything. I waited for Imelda to show. I watched the door open each time only to see one beautiful girl after another enter. I remembered asking Dad one time if he wanted anything from Starbucks and he freaked out. He told me just to go straight to his place and not go to Starbucks. He said his coffee was better anyway. I laughed as Dad always would make an excuse not to go somewhere as he got older. Especially if it were a dish, he could make better. Dad turned out to be an exceptional cook. All of my siblings would look forward to Dad's infamous roast beef during the holidays. It was a gigantic piece of meat that literally came apart in your mouth. We would bring containers to take some home. I tried to replicate it after he was gone, but it was not the same, and I am optimistic that Dad did not spend seventy-five dollars on a piece of meat.

Right then the door opened, and a naturally beautiful dark- skinned woman with long hair walked in and looked around. She saw me and smiled; I recognized the dimples. It was Imelda, and she looked magnificent. I went to her and hugged her. It seemed as if everyone noticed her walk in. She was wearing a floral sun dress that fit her to a tee. The colors really accented her skin tone. What a beautiful girl, I thought.

We sat down for a minute and exchanged greetings. She was as happy to see me as I was to see her. She immediately agreed to grab a bite after I asked if she was hungry. I told her I was staying at the hotel on Manila Bay that had this amazing restaurant and she said I should have told her to meet me there. I explained to her I did not want to invite her to my hotel because she may have gotten the wrong impression about me. We laughed and walked out of the Starbucks. I flagged down a cab, and we made our way to the hotel. Imelda told me on the way there that she had been to the hotel a couple of times because she had attended a few weddings there. The hotel had a great wedding package because of its location. We talked about my time there and she was pleased that I could travel to other places and see how beautiful the Philippines is. I told her I could see all the islands while on the plane and that I fell in love with the place right away. I told Imelda that on the way back from Cebu, I could see this high volcano. It was an almost perfect point. She was so excited to tell me that what I was looking at was the Mayon volcano. She told me so much about the place, and I asked her how she knew about that area. Imelda told me that Albay in the Province of Bicol is her home province. I was so surprised to hear this. Jokingly, I told her we should go there for the weekend. She immediately agreed, and I laughed and asked if she was serious. She told me she took off all of next week, knowing that I still had a little over a week there in the Philippines. I guess Imelda was more interested in me than I thought. I told her we should discuss this over dinner.

We reached the hotel and went through all the security and Xray machines. The one porter I met earlier looked at me, smiled, and gave me a thumbs up. I waved back at him and smiled. I was with one of the most beautiful women I have ever been with, and everyone saw it. I was proud to be walking by her side.

We made our way to the restaurant, and the hostesses were dressed in long gowns and the waitstaff were all wearing shirts and ties. This was the evening wear. The restaurant was crowded, but we were seated immediately. We were sitting next to a pond that circled the spiral staircase I mentioned earlier. Such a beautiful setting. The server came by and asked for our drink order. We both ordered the San Miguel Lite. He mentioned to us if we wanted to look at the buffet just to go when we were ready. I asked Imelda to come with me.

I grabbed her hand and held onto it as we gazed through the huge buffet. I saw prime rib, crab legs, Filipino, Italian and American foods. This was a grand buffet. I told Imelda, this is what I am having. She agreed, and we went back to our table. As soon as we sat down, I asked her if she was serious about going to Bicol and she said she certainly was. So, we started planning our trip for Friday morning and returning Sunday evening. She mentioned all the really close places we could see. She was so happy and was very excited as she spoke of her hometown. When the server returned, I told him we would both be having the buffet. He said that whenever we were ready, we could just go.

We sat for a few more minutes talking about the trip and then went to feed our empty stomachs. After we finished our second plate, the server told us to visit the dessert section. I laughed and said I would pass, but Imelda wanted to see it, at least. We walked over, hand in hand again, to the dessert section and found there were so many choices it was like walking into a bakery. I would have certainly enjoyed some dessert if I were not so stuffed. Imelda grabbed a piece of chocolate cake; come to find out she is a chocolate fan. I asked her where it all went because she was in great shape. If I forgot to mention Imelda had an impressive body! After we finished, we would take a walk outside. I ran into Nick again; he greeted me again and then said to Imelda, "Good evening, Ma'am. Is there anything I can get you?" He continued to tell her, "You are with a great guy."

She laughed and asked how much I was paying Nick to say those things. We both ordered another beer, and I thought, This is great that Imelda likes beer as well.

We took our place right in front of Manila Bay. The hotel had prepared seating for guests just for the evenings because I did not see them here during the day. We sat in one of the open seats and continued our conversation. We traded stories of our childhood and our families.

A small band included a violinist, a sax, and a trumpet. They started playing, and it sounded so romantic. Imelda mentioned it was the perfect evening. I told her that the evening was still early and that if there was anything else that she wanted to do, just let me know. She wanted to stay there a little longer and talk. I told her I would make the arrangements for the upcoming travel. She smiled and kissed me on the cheek. I would have to contact Uncle Ren and let him know I will not be there on Friday but to expect me late Sunday. For sure, he would be worried if I did not tell him. But I had so much respect for them I would send a message first thing in the morning, giving him enough notice.

The seat that we had was as big as a couch and reclined. Imelda wanted to recline it so that she could be more comfortable. As soon as we reclined the seat, she laid her head on my shoulders and turned her body into me. She then whispered, "Thanks for a wonderful and perfect evening." I wanted to react, but I wanted to be a gentleman since this was our first real meeting. So, I kissed her on the forehead and leaned more into her. She asked more about my parents and how they became to be family. I explained my father had joined the Navy here and met my mother in Washington, DC. I told her it must have been love at first sight because my parents got married as soon as they met. Mom and Dad got married on June third of 1960. I also mentioned to Imelda that I was their anniversary present because my birthday was also June 3rd. We exchanged more stories, and Nick returned with drinks on the house. We asked Nick if he would not mind if he took a few pictures of us, and he said of course. We must have stayed out there for hours because when we were ready to go, I looked behind us in the pool area and it was almost empty.

I looked at my watch and was approaching ten at night. I asked Imelda if there was anything else that she wanted. She replied no, so I asked Nick for the check and gave him a large tip. We walked back into the bar section of the restaurant and heard a piano playing. Upstairs, there was a young lady playing the piano and singing. She was very good with a magnificent voice. I told Imelda that I would go to the restroom, and she would wait literally outside the door. I thought at first that was weird, but I guess she did not want me to bump into any other women there. She asked me if I would also wait for her as she needed to go to the restroom as well. So, I waited outside for her. When Imelda came out, she grabbed my hand and wanted to go see the pianist upstairs. I was like, okay. I asked her if she had work tomorrow, and she said she did not have to go back to work until a week from now. And that she wanted to spend as much time with me as she could. This led me to the question of how far she had to travel to get here from her home. She said about an hour because of traffic on Edsa. I asked her what Edsa is? She said it was the main highway in Manila. She told me it was always busy except on Sundays. I told Imelda that she did not have to go home this evening if she did not want to. I made a lame excuse of it being late, and it was not safe for her. I told her I had plenty of room and that I even had a couch in my room so that she would be comfortable in the bed. It was almost like she was waiting for me to ask her this, because she immediately agreed to stay. I was a lucky man for sure. We got into the elevator, hand in hand with another couple. They got off on one of the lower floors and as soon as the elevators closed, Imelda grabbed me and I could feel her body pressed up against mine. We kissed for the very first time, for a long time. We reached my floor and made our way to my room. Imelda wanted to see the site from the balcony that I mentioned earlier. We went to the balcony and kissed again.

I woke up to Imelda staring at me. We both kissed again. She was smiling and told me how happy she was that we had met. I told her I was just as happy. I asked her if she wanted breakfast because I was starving. It was only seven a.m. We showered together and to my surprise, Imelda had a change of clothes in her purse.

After I dressed, Imelda came to me, looked at my hands, and said she would give me a manicure later.

I agreed. Because of her beauty and gracefulness, Imelda commanded respect. It was so natural to see this. I would never forget this about her. She never had to ask for respect from me.

We went downstairs to the restaurant to eat some breakfast, and as expected, there was a huge breakfast buffet. It was a beautiful morning, so we sat outside and enjoyed the fresh air. I ordered some coffee. I asked Imelda if she wanted the buffet, but it was too much for her, so we ordered à la carte. I got some toast and fresh fruits. Imelda ordered coffee as well, with a Filipino breakfast. We talked more about our trip, and it seemed like it would be a good time. Imelda was excited. She would have some errands to run this morning. I told her I would take care of everything and email her the itineraries. She asked if it was okay if she came back to the hotel this evening, and I said sure no problem. She said she would be back around seven, and I said no problem. I told her she should just pack her bags for the trip because we would leave the following morning. She agreed and said that she would.

After breakfast, I walked Imelda out front to catch a taxi. She had the Grab ap on her phone, so it was easy for her to get a ride. I asked her how much the fare was because I wanted to pay for it, and she told me not to worry about it. The same porter walked over to us and asked if we wanted a taxi, and I replied no, we have a grab car coming. He smiled at me and said okay.

As the Grab car drove up, Imelda and I said our goodbyes. She looked as gorgeous as she did the evening before. Everywhere we went while we were together, it seemed like all eyes were on us. And why not? Because I was with a gorgeous young lady. I could not wait to spend more time with her this evening. Immediately after she left, the porter came over to me and said that I was lucky because the girl looked like a movie star there. I thanked him and told him yes; I am lucky.

I made my way back to my room to check on some emails. My boss sent me an email asking how the trip went. I told him it was fine, and that I had already sent him the purchase order. Since he questioned it, I thought it would be best to call him since it was only about eight p.m. back home. I called his cell phone and waited a few minutes to connect. I explained I had already sent him a purchase order, but he never received it. I asked him to wait, and I will check. I did not see it in my sent box, but I noticed there was a saved draft. I opened up the draft and there it was. I never sent it. I told my boss that I have found it and never actually sent it. He laughed and said I was getting old. He was impressed with the size of the order, and I told him I had a presentation to give him when I got back. I told him that this was just the tip of the ice burg. He seemed happy and told me to enjoy the rest of my stay there. After I hung up with my boss, I made some more notes of last night's events so I would not forget.

I wondered if Dad had ever been to this hotel. There was so much I missed growing up that I never got to ask him. I only remember Dad speaking to me when I was in trouble, or he was giving me directions. Now that I think about it, this went on until I was a teenager. Growing up, we definitely had some distance between us, but I could not understand this until I was older. When all of us were together, it was more of a group conversation, not really one-on-one. I lived like this for a long time but was always busy doing something, so it never really crossed my mind as a kid. We grew up in this environment and I believed all families were like this. I figured Dad was raised in the same manner. A product of his environment.

I checked to see if I had enough clothes to go to Bicol because I had left my big bag at Uncle Ren's house. I think I had enough. I would have to find a laundry mat somewhere close. I called the front desk, and they told me they had a laundry service in the hotel and that the price list was in the information booklet. I looked at the booklet; I am finding a laundry mat. The prices were for an individual item, and it was expensive. I got online and found one near MOA and since I was already familiar with the place; I did not mind going there. I gathered my things and went downstairs to grab a taxi. I asked the driver to take me to the laundry mat first, then into MOA. He agreed. It was a quick ride, and the laundry mat was basically across the street from MOA, so I told the driver just to go. I gave him a nice tip. I entered the laundry mat and asked the young lady when my clothes would be ready; she said tomorrow.

I told her it was too late because I was flying out tomorrow. She told me they have express service, and I asked how much. She weighed my clothes and then told me 350 pesos. I did not argue and agreed. She told me to come back by two pm, and the clothes would be ready. I started walking over to the mall. It was still early, maybe ten a.m. so I had a lot of time to burn. I decided to get coffee at Starbucks and sit outside, and people watch. I had a habit of doing this when I was traveling and was stuck at the airports. I always enjoyed doing simple things like that. I watched a girl walk down the terminal and see how many guys would look at her. Or watch children sneak away from their parents and the parents not even notice. Or watch people eat and see if they would leave their trash in the seat. I enjoyed watching all the people from different walks of life to see how they react in the crowds. In the Philippines, it was very different as most of the people were Filipino and you could easily see everyone else was foreigners. So, I sat at the table outside while sipping on my Grande Pike. I watched so many people going through the scanner machine and then get patted down to get inside the mall. From old to young, there were so many. I imagine getting out of the heat. Every day in the Philippines was summer, unlike in the US, where we had our seasons. The Philippines had a rainy season and a dry season. No fall or winter. The mornings were delightful here, especially if you were in the shade. There was a breeze, so it was really nice outside. As I was sitting there, I saw a familiar face going into the mall; it was my cousin. I called out to her, and she looked and said, OMG, what am I doing here? I told her I was staying in a hotel down the street and just waiting for my laundry to be finished.

 She asked me if I was still coming tomorrow, and I told her I will probably come late Sunday instead. She was there with some of her co-workers working in one of the booths in the middle of the mall. She worked for a bank and was promoting some savings and money market accounts. I told her I would come see her in a few. I had only burned an hour, so I went back to the hotel and worked on my computer. I stopped by to see my cousin first and say goodbye. I grabbed a taxi outside and went on my way. When I reached the hotel, I grabbed my laptop and went outside to the pool bar to have a bite to eat. I sat at one of the covered tables and started working on emails. I remembered we had clients here in the Philippines from way back, so I tried to search for them and send messages. I received emails back to my surprise, forgetting it is still a weekday here. I would reach out to them and let them know I was working in the region, and I could possibly visit their offices shortly.

They all agreed, so this was ammunition, along with my presentation, for my next trip. Nick came up to me and thanked me for the generous tip, and I told him no problem because the service was great. I asked him if he could order the sandwich for me again and bottled water. He said no problem at all. I went back to checking my emails. I tried to answer as many as I could before my lunch arrived.

When I leave for vacation for work, I never turn on my "Out of Office" in Outlook. I want my clients to know that I am always available. A trait I got from Dad. My siblings and I always talked about how Dad would never miss work. He would miss birthdays, christenings, and family gatherings because he felt his work was his life. I could never understand this about Dad until my visit here, hearing the stories from my uncles and aunties.

I also learned from talking with other people here in the Philippines that work is scarce. Because the Philippines was so densely populated; jobs were scarce. So many Filipinos held onto what they had. And knowing Dad, if he was ever a dishwasher, then he was the best damn dishwasher there ever was. Dad was very dedicated to his work. This I saw always. We used to make fun of Dad when we were older in how he thought his work would not operate properly if he were not there. When Dad gave me instructions to do something, I did it exactly as he told me to do. Even if there was a better or easier way, Dad made sure we did it the way he told us to. As I got older, he would tell me that the reason he told me that was to know and understand hard work and appreciate things more. This is where I got my work ethic from. No matter what was going on, we could go nowhere if we did not get our chores done. And you did nothing half-ass because Mom and Dad would check up behind you.

When Nick brought me my sandwich, he commented on Imelda and how beautiful she was. He asked how and where we met. I told him we met on the plane on my way here and she was my flight attendant. He said that was good, and she seemed happy to be with me. I thanked him again and ate my sandwich. I had about thirty minutes before I had to pick up my clothes. While I ate, I continued to answer emails. I waited to confirm my next trip until my boss approved my presentation. I also included a list of potential clients to spice things up.

I finished my lunch, gave my regards to Nick, went to my room to drop off my laptop, and made my way back to the lobby. I wanted to get back to the room and make the arrangements for our trip. I told the porter I needed a cab to the laundry mat near MOA, and he got on his radio. Right away, a taxi pulled up. I got in and told him where to go. As we got closer to the mall, I told him instead of going to MOA to make a left instead of a right because I wanted to pick up my laundry. We pulled up, and I asked him to wait for me, and I would give him a good tip, and he agreed. When they presented my laundry to me, it looked like it had been in a vacuumed-packed plastic bag. I asked if they were sure this was all of my clothes because it seemed so small compared to when I dropped it off. She assured me that everything was there. I got back into the taxi and asked him to take me back to the hotel. When we arrived, I asked the driver what the amount on the meter was and he said 200; I gave him 500 and thanked him for waiting. He was pleased and thanked me. When I got to my room, I opened the bag, the smell of the clothes was so fresh. I loved the smell. Everything was there. They had folded them perfectly. They impressed me.

The Holiday Girl

I started immediately working on the trip. The flight would take about an hour, so I tried to get the earliest flight available so we could spend the rest of the time sightseeing. You could drive from Manila to Legazpi, but the ride would be around twelve hours. I found our flight and booked two seats. I then started looking for hotels. I found one hotel that looked straight out over the Mayon Volcano. It was maybe between eight to ten miles from the Volcano. I booked the room for two nights right away. I was excited to see the area since I saw it from the sky back from Bohol.

I still had about four hours to burn before Imelda would show up, so I went back down to the pool area to get some sun. I grabbed a lounge chair next to a foreigner and his Filipina girlfriend. They greeted me and I noticed the guy had an American accent. I asked him where he was from, and he said Wisconsin. I told him I was from Virginia. He was a retired Navy sailor, so he knew the area I was from, having been stationed there for a few years. He looked a few years older than me, and the girl was younger. She was attractive and one of those girls who knew she was. I asked them how they met, and they told me they had met on a dating site. I laughed and said, really are you serious? They told me that there was a dating site that catered to men worldwide looking for a Filipina girl. I apologized for laughing, but I told them I never heard of that. So, I asked the guy, named Ben, how did he hear about the site? He told me that his friend back home in Wisconsin was married to a Filipina and that was how he found out about it. I was like, wow, really. I asked him if he ever been to the Philippines; he told me this was his first time. At that moment, Nick showed up to take my order. I ordered my usual beer and asked the couple if they wanted anything. So, I bought the first round of drinks. Ben asked what I was doing here, and I explained to him I had some work in the area and also that my family was from here. The girl, Carmen, looked surprised and asked if I had a Filipina mom. I told her that my father was from here. They both said I did not look like a Filipino. I laughed and said everyone that meets me says the same thing. I told them that my mother had mixed blood, Irish and French. I asked Carmen where she was from originally, and she told me Bicol. I told her I was going there tomorrow.

She then looked at Ben and said, "See, he is going there, so there will be nothing to be afraid of."

Since Ben was in this foreign land, he was very cautious and did not want to travel outside of Manila. He had flown Carmen up from Bicol a few days ago. Ben seemed like a nice guy, but a little gullible at times. I imagine he never had such a beautiful woman as was Carmen in his life. He excused himself to the restroom, and Carmen and I continued to talk.

She started to really drill me about things. How long I will be here? Was I married? Did I have a girlfriend? And many more things in such a short period. She asked if she could give me her number so we could get together the next time I come to the Philippines.

I asked her, "Are you and Ben a couple? Did he spend a lot of money traveling here and visiting with you?" I could not believe what I was hearing.

When Ben returned, I did not mention the conversation Carmen and I just had. She looked at me and winked. Ben jumped into the pool and waved to Carmen to join him.

She got up and walked by me and said, "I think you are handsome and would rather spend time with you than Ben."

Then she blew a kiss to me. She had an impressive body and was attractive but had a little too much personality for me.

I laughed and thought, This poor guy has no idea. I got up and walked over to the bar to have a smoke and ordered another drink. I asked Nick if he knew the girl there with the foreigner. He said no, has never seen her before. I laughed and explained to him what had just happened. He knew what kind of girl she was because he had seen this happen many times. He called her a "Holiday girl," or someone that would meet a different man every month. I asked him if she were an escort, and he told me it was almost the same thing, that the type of woman would drain the foreigners for everything they had. Nick told me not to worry because Imelda was a much classier woman than this, and he could tell she was not the type. I went back to my lounge chair and Ben suggested we meet for dinner, so I told him I was actually waiting for someone and that she would not be here until around seven this evening. He was very persistent about this. So, I agreed to hope that Imelda would not have a problem with this. I can only imagine what was going on in Carmen's mind. Certainly, she would be curious to see what kind of woman I was associating with. I could not wait to show her off. Ben wanted to have dinner at the buffet, but I told him we would probably just meet for some drinks. I said my goodbyes and made my way back to my room. I could hear someone call my name as soon as I got back into the hotel. I turned around to see Carmen waving me down. I waited for her. She told me she never gave me her number, and I told her I thought she should focus on Ben.

She handed me a napkin with her number on it. Then she said goodbye and kissed me on the cheek. I was like, what in the hell is wrong with this girl? She is probably not used to being rejected. I sent Imelda a quick message just to see if she was on schedule and if she wanted to have a late dinner. There was no immediate answer, so I would let the evening play out. I went to work out for a bit. The hotel's gym was really nice and not crowded at all. I put in a good hour and achieved a pretty good sweat. I went outside to have a smoke and some water. Yes, I know, I just finished a good workout and then went for a smoke. It was a habit of mine, one that I tried many times to quit but just never got close. Imelda did not seem to mind, either.

My own siblings and children always mentioned this to me, but it was my only vice. I know that smoking was a huge contributor to my parents' passing. It crosses my mind a lot, and I have plans to quit someday, eventually. The funny thing about it is that I hate second-hand smoke.

First Encounter

When I finished, I went back to my room and took a quick shower to rinse off and went back downstairs to the bar area. I sat facing the entrance so that I could watch people again. It was around five p.m. now and I wanted to have a drink.

The bartender asked me what I wanted, so I ordered a Jack and Coke. This was one drink I knew I could sip for a while. I noticed out of the corner of my eye someone approaching the bar.

She asked if anyone was sitting next to me. I answered no. She sat down next to me and ordered a drink as well. I cannot remember the drink she ordered, nor did I ever turn to look at her. I thought this was the same thing happening in the other hotel bar a few nights ago. The bartender brought her what looked like a margarita. She then asked how I was doing, and I told her I was fine and just wanted to relax and drink. She had an odd voice when she spoke. So, I had to turn and look at her. It shocked me to see my first lady boy up close. I asked her or him if that was her real hair, and she said, yes, that she had let it grow out. She had long eyelashes, obviously not real. And she had a boob job.

When I looked her up and down, I think she knew I knew she was a lady boy. She then asked me if I had ever been with a lady boy and I told her no offense, but I like a woman. She then told me they were better lovers than a real woman because they knew what men like. I told her I respect all people, genders, and races and that I prefer actual females. I hope this does not offend you.

She understood and thanked me for my time. I said goodbye and the bartender laughed. When the lady boy got up and walked away, she looked like a real girl from behind.

I laughed and shook my head and continued to follow her around the bar to see where she would end up. The bartender came to me and jokingly asked why you did not go with her and said that she was beautiful. I laughed and told her I prefer a real woman. The lady boy pulled up next to what looked like a middle easterner. She was not there five minutes before she walked out of the bar arm in arm with this guy. I hope he knew what he was getting himself into. The bartender and I both looked at each other and laughed. What a crazy afternoon this has been thus far. I was making some notes on this.

The Reunion

Imelda showed up an hour early, which was fine with me. I told her I had met a couple at the pool this afternoon and they wanted to have dinner tonight. She said that would be fine but wanted to rest early. I gave her all the flight and hotel information, and she was excited to go back to her hometown.

Imelda put on this pretty white sundress with white sandals, so I had to make sure that I looked as good as her. I put on some khaki shorts with a white, long-sleeved button-down and just rolled the sleeves up. I had to stop and just look at her because she was gorgeous, wearing no makeup at all; she looked like a beauty contestant. We made our way down to the restaurant, and as soon as the elevator doors opened, all eyes were on Imelda. I felt as if I was walking with a movie star. She grabbed my hand, and we proceeded through the lobby. We reached the staircase, and I could see Ben and Carmen waiting to enter the restaurant. I waved, and they both acknowledged and waved back. He had put in for a table of four, so we did not have to wait at all. We joined them at the entrance, and I introduced Imelda to them. I immediately saw Carmen look Imelda up and down.

I thought, Really, Carmen, you already showed your true colors.

I never told Imelda about my conversation with Carmen, as I did not want to stir things up during dinner. We were seated in just a few minutes. Imelda did not want the buffet, so we would order à la carte. We ordered a bottle of wine also. Carmen asked Imelda where she was from and came to find out they were both from the same province but different towns, miles apart. Right away, Imelda could see what I saw in Carmen. While they spoke, I could feel Imelda tap me with her leg. It was so funny. For sure, I would tell Imelda everything when we were alone.

I heard Carmen tell Imelda that she was so lucky to have me, then heard Imelda's reply to Carmen, "We are both lucky that we bumped into each other. Our meeting was very random and without purpose."

I wanted to jump up and kiss her and rub it into Carmen's face, but I acted mature and simply smiled at Imelda, grabbed her hand, and squeezed it.

Carmen's reaction was so expected. She immediately started bragging about how she and Ben met and why they were together now. I was thinking about how much shit she was full of the whole time.

The icing on the cake was when Imelda told them we would go to Bicol in the morning and soon have to leave.

Carmen's attitude changing; it was like she competed with Imelda. Carmen told us they were talking about going to Boracay, a huge tourist spot in the Philippines.

Ben chimed in and said, "I thought we had talked about this already before I came to the Philippines. I do not want to travel anywhere while I'm here. That's the reason I flew you up from Bicol." After Ben squashed that conversation, we asked if they would take a picture of Imelda and me together.

Ben agreed to take the picture, and I could see the disappointment in Carmen's eyes. We said our goodbyes and wished them both good luck and that things worked out between them. We got up and left and went for a quick walk outside. There was a pleasant breeze blowing out on the pool area and Imelda and I walked hand in hand once again.

I saw Nick at the bar; he waved and gave a thumbs up. We walked back to the room. Imelda seemed eager to go into her hometown. We lay on the bed and talked about the hotel. She said she knew exactly where the hotel was and mentioned that we could see the Mayon Volcano. I told her that is why I booked that hotel.

Imelda was very excited. When I met Carmen and Ben earlier, I mentioned to her that Carmen tried to hit on me while Ben went to the bathroom. She told me she knew the type and said the same thing Nick had said about her, that she was a holiday girl. I laughed and kissed her. Then she got serious about me and wanted to know more about Dad. I had briefed her on the plane a bit about Dad's passing. I kindly told her I was not ready to talk about it with her because I knew I would become emotional, and I did not want to spoil the mood. She accepted and asked me to lie on my stomach so she could massage me. I would not argue with her about that, so I immediately rolled over and took my clothes off.

Journey to Bicol

We woke up around six a.m., and I went downstairs to get us some coffee. Imelda waited for me to get back because she wanted us to shower together again. After our shower, we dressed, packed our remaining things, and left for the lobby. I had to check out still, so it would be a few minutes before we left. Imelda grabbed a seat while I waited for someone to go to the room and check out the minibar to make sure everything was there. It was the policy during check out. This way, they could release my deposit. Everything checked out and we were on our way to the airport. We grabbed a taxi, and we were on our way. Imelda mentioned we will have a car waiting for us when we arrived in Bicol. I asked her what she meant, and she told me she had hired her nephew to drive us around the entire weekend. I was happy about that. Seems like we had everything we needed. We arrived at the airport early and checked in. We grabbed something to eat before going to our gate. There was a coffee shop nearby that had some pastries, so we grabbed a few of them and sat down and had our coffee.

Imelda told me about some things we would see besides the Mayon Volcano. There had been an eruption many years ago, and a church was half buried in the ground from all the lava and volcanic ash. The name of the place was Cagsawa Ruins National Park. I thought this would be pretty cool to see. Also, there was a site with the fourteen stations of the cross that Imelda wanted to take me to. I am all about learning the cultures of a place that I have never visited before, so this will be interesting. She thanked me for making this trip with her and was excited to see some of her family.

I asked Imelda if they knew we were coming, and she said yes, that she had told them we would be there by lunchtime. I can see how happy she was and proud of her hometown when she spoke of it. We made our way to the gate after we finished the pastries. Imelda wanted to bring some Otap. It's a kind of pastry, as a gift. We went looking for some at the local pasalubong or gift store. We found a big box of them and bought them and some chocolate mangos. The chocolate mangos looked good, and I was so excited to try some. I bought a smaller bag just for us.

We grabbed our things and went to the gate. We were just in time for boarding. These planes were smaller, and we took a bus from the gate to the plane. We then walked from the bus to the plane. There was a cart for everyone to drop their luggage off that would later be loaded onto the plane. We climbed the ramp to the plane and grabbed our seats. As soon as we sat down and got comfortable. Imelda started taking some more pictures of us. I did not mind at all. Then she rested her head on my shoulder, and I leaned into her and kissed her on the head. As the plane took off, we both looked out of the window. It still amazed me by the number of islands, mountains, and beaches seen from the sky. I told Imelda that I fell in love with the Philippines when I first saw this on my way to Bohol. She said, "It's More Fun in the Philippines." Then she said this was a slogan meant for tourism here. I mentioned to her I saw this while we were taking off on the runway fence. She smiled and yes, that she had seen it as well. We chatted about life and how fair and unfair things are in the world. Imelda was brilliant. She had gone to college there and received her MBA. But she mentioned she loved traveling and made more money as a flight attendant than she would working for a corporation. I asked her what she did with her daughter, and she told me that her mother was watching her. Come to find out, she lived with her mother. Imelda was looking at me weirdly for a minute. She told me she needed to trim my eyebrows later.

I was thinking, where was this coming from? I told her okay, if she wished to, it will not be a problem. Then she turned my head and looked into my ear. Then the other one. I asked what she was doing. I laughed when she said she had to pluck some hairs out of my ears.

Bicol

We landed early, and the flight was a little under an hour, just like the Bohol flight. We grabbed our things and deplaned. I did not notice when we landed; I guess because Imelda and I had been busy talking, but the damn Mayon Volcano was right there as soon as we got off. We could see its beauty. The airport was tiny, and we actually walked from the plane to the terminal in just minutes. I pulled out my camera and took pictures of the volcano and some of Imelda with the volcano in the background. Of course, I took a few selfies as well. We grabbed our luggage, and I followed Imelda to the exits. As we walked through the exit, she could see her nephew. He quickly grabbed our bags and asked us to follow him to his car. It was a minivan. Imelda introduced him as Bon.

I said that is his real name, and she told me that is his nickname because his first name is too difficult to pronounce. I laughed and said, "Bon it is."

As soon as we sat in the van, Imelda pulled out a small hand towel and wiped my face and neck down. I asked her what she was doing.

She said, "Wiping the sweat off."

In the Philippines that many people wore a hand towel around their neck or tucked into the back of the collar. This was to, of course, wipe sweat away. But that Imelda was doing this showed me a different side of her. She was showing ownership. A couple of other things I noticed about Imelda was that she was always looking at me, at my hair, in my nose, in my ears, at my eyebrows. This is because she said she always wanted to me look good. So, she would pluck and trim my eyebrows or pull a hair out of my ear and even cut my nose hairs. She said she always wanted to take care of me like that.

The ride out of the airport was just gorgeous. Bicol was just as laid back as Bohol. There was no traffic, houses were spread out, it was like a totally different world there in Bicol. It seemed like there was a view of the Mayon everywhere we turned. We would go sightseeing early in the morning. We asked Bon to take us to the hotel so that we could freshen up first before meeting her family. It was funny because of how Imelda and I interacted. One would think that we have been together for years, not just a few days. I felt as if Imelda was making her claim, showing the rest of the world that I was hers. I liked that about her. It was also different from how women treated or reacted to you in the states.

As we made our way to the hotel, I was trying to take in the land's beauty here. The Philippines reminded me of a huge resort. I saw some young kids playing in the street with some sticks. Everything I looked at made me think of Dad. I would never find out if Dad ever traveled the rest of his country, as I had been doing. He never talked about other places. If Dad was anything like Uncle Ren, if there was no purpose in going anywhere, he did not. Funny how I went all of my life not knowing certain things about Dad. The only thing that I remember Dad telling me about when he was a kid was that they would catch a beetle and tie a string to it like a kite and let it fly as long as the line would let them. Crazy, I thought. I always wondered if my siblings felt the same way. I would certainly bring it up when I got back stateside.

Imelda wanted to grab something to eat before we went to the hotel, so Bon took us to the mall, where there was a food court. If I did not mention it before, but the Philippines had all the larger fast-food chains like McDonald's, Burger King, KFC, and Subway, to name a few, as we did in the states. We went to Burger King; I had missed their double bacon cheeseburger. We grabbed a burger and some fries and continued our trip to the hotel. We had to drive up a winding road to get there. Once we arrived, the view was spectacular. We could see the whole town of Legazpi. The airport, the mall and the Mayon volcano. I was in awe of the view. We could check in early, that was a plus. Imelda wanted to freshen up. She also took a damp hand towel and wiped the back of my neck and face while I was setting up my laptop. I knew Imelda wanted to see her auntie and cousins, so I asked her if she wanted to go there first, and she said that we were going to have dinner there, so for now, we could go to the Cagsawa Ruin Park. I happily agreed and said let's go.

Cagsawa church was initially built back in 1587 and was burned down by Dutch pirates in 1636 and rebuilt in 1724, only to be destroyed again by the Mayon's eruption in 1814. According to the history of Cagsawa, the town had been buried from the explosion and thousands of people had died, and the grounds were sacred. Cagsawa would become a national park of the Philippines.

We arrived in the early afternoon. The church steeple was still there and leaning to the right. I read a few of the placards placed at a few of the sights and was very surprised to learn about the dates they built this church. We think in the US that a building constructed in the 1800s was old; we have no idea.

There were a few vendors selling bracelets and things out of a bag. There was also a photographer that would place you in a certain position to make you look like you were pushing the steeple back into place, or that you looked like you were holding the Mayon volcano in the palm of your hand. He would ask for a few pesos to do this.

I had no problem throwing a few bucks his way. We sat on an old stone fence and just looked at the park, the old steeple with the Mayon in the background. I thought, This is such a beautiful site. I thanked the good Lord for allowing me to see some of his creations on the other side of the world. I was so in deep thought that I did not hear Imelda talking to me. She was asking me what I thought of this place. I explained to her exactly what I was thinking. We took a few pictures together as we sat on the fence. Imelda was seated next to me. She grabbed my hand and laid her head on my shoulders. She told me when she was a kid; they would come here and visit and say prayers for all the people that died here. She pointed out that it seemed like there was always a cloud at the tip of Mayon, so one could not see the perfect cone at the top. From a distance, it looked like this as manufactured, was too perfect, just incredible, I told her.

She then took out the hand towel and wiped my face and the back of my neck again.

I thought this would be the right time to ask her about her daughter. "You told me you were a single mom. That you had a ten-year-old daughter."

She laughed so loud and said she had forgotten about that.

I looked at her strangely. "What do you mean you forgot about it? How do you forget your child?"

She said, "No, that's what I tell every foreigner on the plane so they will shy away from me."

I told her I even asked you about your daughter and you said your mother would care for her while you are away. I believe she gets hit on almost everywhere she goes. I laughed at her and said, really?

She said yes because many foreigners would ask her out, and this was her way of saying no gently.

So, I asked, "You don't have a child?"

She replied, "No."

"Why did I receive special attention?"

She told me she had never spent as much time talking with a passenger before, and all the other flight attendants were joking with her because of the time she spent with me.

This brings me to the time when I was leaving the plane, and another flight attendant said to me as I walked by her, "Good Luck." Now I know why she said that.

My Fishing Credentials

I told Imelda about my family and siblings and how we were brought up more in the traditional Filipino way than in America. She said that even though Dad left the Philippines, he never forgot his roots and culture. I explained to Imelda that Dad had many friends who were Filipino when he was in the Navy. He had many of his friends over for dinner or cooking out with their families when we were growing up. It seemed like most of his friends were married to an American as well. We all went fishing together and actually spent the night on the beach. It was fun back in those days.

One thing Dad took care of was his fishing gear. He was always proud to show off his new gadgets to his friends. We would fish from the time we got there in the morning until the next afternoon. Mom never came because she did not want to sleep in the car, and my sisters usually stayed with her. We caught all kinds of fish from spot, croaker, bluefish, and stripers. There would always be shit fish also, like sting rays or blow fish. We would use bloodworms for the smaller fish and once we caught a small spot or croaker, dad would use it as cut bait to catch bigger fish. I can remember Dad being so happy fishing. It was about five in the morning, and the bluefish made a run. You could hear them chopping the smaller bait fish. This is the time of the trips I liked the most. Dad would have maybe four surf cast poles in the water. Each with its holder that was secured in the sand. He used to put bells on the very tip so you could hear the bell when the fish were on at night. We even had three poles ringing all at once. Dad told me to grab one and start reeling it in. My brothers had reeled their poles in this one time with only one small fish. They were telling me to hurry before the fish was gone and I told them the line seemed very heavy and that I was struggling to get the fish in. Dad came and asked what was going on and I told him I think it was a big fish. He told me to take my time and tire the fish out so that they did not break the line. As a kid, this was one time Dad was coaching me, and he was excited as I was. I will never forget it. It took me a while to bring the fish to the shore, but once I did, everyone came to see how big the fish was. I had a crowd of people watching now, and the sun was not even up yet. As I pulled the fish closer to the shore, some of Dads friends went in the water to make sure I did not lose the fish. When the fish finally showed themselves, I would never forget how loud the beach got. I had landed not one but two big ass bluefish. I could hear Dad talking to his friends in Tagalog.

They were much larger than the fish my brothers had pulled in. My arms hurt so badly from this, but I was happy because Dad seemed proud of me when it was the one time. He came and hugged me and said marvelous job. My brothers were also happy. It was a glorious morning on the beach.

All this came crashing to an end years later when we were all on a fishing pier. Dad had taken us to a pier one night, and we were all excited to be there. My brothers were showing off how far they could cast their lines. Dad got irritated and said we needed to leave the lines in the water until we got a bite. Well, I thought I had a bite, but missed the fish. I reeled the line in, and I can remember my brothers teasing me because I could not cast as far as they could. I told myself that I will show those bastards this time. I put fresh cut bait on my hooks and gripped the pole; I then leaned way back to get some extra torque out of my cast. I launched forward and gave a massive swing.

I felt the entire rod and reel leave my hands. I immediately regretted this. I had just thrown my fishing pole off the pier. My brothers were cracking up and then I saw the look on Dad's face. He was steaming; he came over to me and told me to sit there and watch everyone fish for the rest of the night. Glad I was not at home because I would surely get my ass whipped, but because we were on the pier with many people, Dad just gave me that look. I had disgusted him. All my great fishing credentials meant nothing now. My brothers were teasing me all the time. I went from being the family fishing king to a worthless goat. I was mad that I had let them put me in this position. I sat there for maybe an hour before Dad came and gave me another fishing pole. He handed it to me and told me I had better not lose this one. I almost did not want to use it. I would eventually buy Dad a new pole from my paper route earnings. When I gave it to him, he told me just to keep it and take care of it. Then I got the lecture that money does not grow on trees, and if I took better care of our things, they would not have to be replaced. This would stick in my brain forever.

Imelda's Family

We arrived back at the hotel to rest before dinner. We had about an hour to rest, and the ride was maybe thirty minutes from the hotel to her auntie's house. Imelda told me we were having a Bicolano dinner. Bicol had a few specialty dishes well known throughout the Philippines, and she had asked her aunt and cousins to prepare for us. I asked Imelda what it was, and she said it would be a surprise. I forgot to tell her I did not care for fish, so I hope it was not fish. Then she told me that if I did not like it, they were barbequing chicken and there would, of course, be some rice. I told her that would be excellent. We would stop somewhere and pick up some water, soda, and a beer. Sounded like a fun night. Imelda asked me not to forget the pastries we had bought at the airport as we prepared. We made our way down the winding hill from the hotel onto the main road through town. We stopped at a small store to pick up some drinks. Like everywhere else I had been in the Philippines, all eyes were on me. I had to laugh and told Imelda that it was like this wherever I went. I did not know if there were any children there, so I picked up some chocolate just in case. Imelda asked if that was for her because she loved some chocolate, and I told her, of course!

We got back into the car and pulled off the main road onto an unlit street. It would seem like we were driving through a rice patty because we could not see anything but rice fields. It was getting dark, so we relied on Bon to get us there safely. He told us he was so used to driving back and forth that he could make this drive in his sleep. We stayed on the unlit road for about ten more minutes before seeing any lights. We came to a corner that had a very dim streetlight and had not seen a car since we left the store. We finally arrived at her auntie's house; many large trees surrounded that. Imelda told me they have so many fruit trees here that they never have to buy any. It reminded me of my family's place back in Alfonso. I could smell the food. Perfect timing, as I was getting hungry. Another one of her cousins greeted us. She guided us to the dinner table outside on the lawn.

There we met her aunt. Two small children belonged to her cousin. I asked where the father was and the cousin, Anne, told me he had been working abroad for the last two years. Many Filipinos worked abroad to provide for their families when work was unavailable. They would sacrifice a few years of being separated just to make ends meet.

Anne asked us to take a seat as she introduced us to her mother. Her mother spoke excellent English. It surprised me because she was older. I told her that, and she laughed and said that she had been a schoolteacher for many years and English was one subject she would teach the children. When Imelda told her I was half Filipino, she was surprised and said that I did not look like a Filipino. Yes, my mother's blood was mixed and stronger as I told everyone else. We all laughed, and Anne told everyone to eat when they were ready. I already had my eye on the chicken because it smelled so good. Imelda named some dishes in front of us. Bicol Express was one of them. It was a very spicy pork dish sauteed with vegetables. Then there was Pinangat, another spicy dish that was more of a vegetarian dish that had some coconut taste to it. All the dishes smelled great, and I would try everything. Imelda told me we would eat in the traditional Filipino style, with no utensils. We would just grab what we wanted from the main dish and put the food on our own plate and eat it with our hands.

My father has done this many times. I grabbed a bit of everything, including rice. I remembered watching Dad, holding some meat and rice together, then down the shoot. When Imelda saw me do this, she thought I was a natural and asked if I had done this before. A couple of weeks ago when I was in Alfonso, I told her we had a boodle fight, and that is when I first tried it. Even though my cousin gave me utensils to use. But I wanted to be traditional, so I have had some practice. During dinner, Imelda's aunt asked how we met, and I told her we actually met on the plane during my trip here. She laughed and said that I worked fast. I explained I was not looking for anyone but had the purpose of the trip on my mind. Imelda just made an impression on me. I was not expecting to meet anyone here with whom I would have a relationship. Then she asked me what my intentions were with Imelda. I quickly answered that we will see how things move. We wanted to take our time, and it is very early to be talking about that right now.

Her auntie was very protective of her because her other daughter was single with children. I did not want to open that can of worms, so I did not ask what happened. Her cousin was younger and lived with her mother here in Bicol. I thanked Auntie for the delicious meal, and Imelda wanted to show me the area. I told her it was dark and maybe we should come back in the morning. I thought for sure there would be some snakes or lizards around here. Imelda told me to stop being a baby and come on. We walked around her property to the actual house she grew up in. I asked her why her mother was not living here because it was a beautiful area. Many residents travel to Manila because of the lack of work in their province. They keep the house for their vacation home. Imelda first left the area when she could land a job with the airline. She needed to be closer to the airport. I asked her if she had been in a relationship before and she explained that her family came first. Her father had gotten sick, and the family could not really pay for all the medical expenses. It is a shame to just let a life deteriorate, but it is the brutal life cycle we all live in. She has one sister that works abroad in Dubai as a nurse. Imelda and her sister did their best to support the family. When their father died, they did not return to Bicol, only for vacation. When Imelda bought a condo in Manila and asked her mother to come and live with her. Her mother was a teacher as well. Her mother would take care of the place when Imelda traveled for work. So, this was her reason for never getting into a serious relationship. Family first! Her Auntie is the one that takes care of the family's property since she only lives next door. I would learn that Auntie's husband had died at an early age from cancer. But these women from the province were powerful and passionate about the family. Imelda then wiped me down once again. I thought Imelda was the model woman from the province.

I tried to take in all that Imelda had just told me and was ready to explain my dad's passing to her if she asked. I would wait for her to ask. I knew she wanted to hear my story about how we grew up with a Filipino father. After all, I gave her a little of it when we were on the plane.

We made our way back to the table, and Bon had built a small campfire. We grabbed a seat and opened up a couple of beers. The night was very peaceful. The stars were so bright here compared to back home. Auntie asked how long we would be here, and I told her we had a flight back to

Manila on Sunday morning. I told them I would spend the remaining two days with my family in Cavite. Auntie was very smart and picked up really fast that this was a culture shock to any foreigner visiting, but I explained to her I had adjusted very well to the culture and the humidity. I said that my upbringing was near to the way things were here. I had to ask them about all the skin whitening advertisements that I saw on billboards and the TV. Imelda chimed in and said that this is an extensive business here. It was a status thing from what she explained. If you were light-skinned, it meant that you were wealthy and living a good life. If you were darker, it was supposed to mean that you were struggling, and that you were a maid or nanny or worked in the rice fields. Imelda was dark and gorgeous. I told her she was living proof that the myth was only a myth. She was successful and never changed her color. We talked for about an hour more and then said our goodbyes. It was getting late, and we had another busy day of sightseeing tomorrow. I thanked Auntie and her family for their hospitality and told them that the dinner had been delicious.

We jumped into the car and made our way back to the hotel. Along the way, Imelda grabbed my hand and held onto it. She would lean her head on my shoulder and fall asleep quickly. We soon arrived back at the hotel, and Bon told us he would be there around 9:00 a.m. We quickly showered, and I knew Imelda was exhausted. I told her I would just check some emails and join her. I made some more notes of the day's events and joined Imelda. She quickly came to me and curled her body around me. She was fast asleep.

We both woke up around six-thirty a.m. and went downstairs to have some breakfast. I just wanted something light, so I ate fruit and had coffee. I told her that last night was fun and an excellent experience. We talked about what we were doing today. We would see the Mayon today and then stop by the religious site. It was then she asked if I was ready to talk about Dad. I started by telling her that Dad was the typical stubborn Filipino. Dad imposed his will on all of us at a very young age, making sure we grew up understanding he was the boss. He would never go to the hospital to get checked up. I explained that I often asked him to get a checkup and if he was scared, I would accompany him, but Dad let pride stand in his way. I told her the entire story and that I would never forgive myself for not being there during his surgery. I knew he was scared, and I left him. That was why I stayed with him every minute when I got back. Imelda noticed it was hard for me, so she told me it was okay and that my father had forgiven me. I did not want to become emotional, but it slowly slipped out of my control. I got up, grabbed a cigarette and went out onto the terrace. Imelda gave me a few minutes before she came outside.

All I can see right now is the look on Dad's face the night he passed. He had that exhausted look; he had given up. He could not die on his terms. He was in a place that he had dreaded all of his life and felt that we would not help him leave. He felt trapped and probably did not understand why we would not help him. This I felt deep in my heart. Not understanding his reasoning at the time, we all thought that the doctors were right about him staying in the hospital. But as I spent my time here and understood his culture more and more, I knew he wanted to die on his terms and not anyone else's. I finally understood this after it was too late. Something that I would regret for the rest of my life, I thought.

I remember sitting in the mausoleum with Uncle Ren and him asking me if my siblings or I visited my parent's grave site. I could not answer for my siblings. I told Uncle Ren, but I would go as much as possible. When the flowers faded, I would clean the area and give new flowers. This, I told Uncle Ren, I owed it to Dad for not being there. Uncle Ren would say the same thing that Imelda would say, "He is watching you right now and is very proud that you have walked the path he once had, taking the same footsteps as he once did and, most of all, came to learn who he was."

I broke down thinking about this. Imelda saw and came to my side.

Mayon Volcano

Imelda and I prepared for today's events. She looked me over every morning now, and I would laugh about it. It became a routine inspection, ears, check, nose, eyebrows, fingernails, etc. Then she would finish with a wipe down off my face. It was so cute. We finally arrived at the Mayon Volcano Park. You could drive about ¼ of the way up before the road stopped. Then you would have to hike the rest. The Mayon Skyline Deck was the name of the park and the closest spot you get to the top. It was so beautiful. There was a cloud that hovered over the tip of the Mayon, hiding the perfect cone shape. I marveled at the sight and its base. You could see for miles out to the shores. I loved the most about the Philippines because you could almost look in any direction and see more mountains.

They would always make a perfect backdrop for any picture.

On a clear day, I remember driving into Manila with my cousin and seeing the mountains in the background. I had not noticed this before, but it was so amazing to see a metropolis with these vast mountains in the background. Almost looked like Vegas.

We visited the Stations of the Cross near to the Mayon. This was on a hill, and you had to climb the stairs to each station. While we made our way up, Imelda grabbed her towel and continued to wipe me down. I thought this was the cutest thing. She was always looking after me. This was actually an excellent workout. We talked about religion during the hike and come to find out; we were both confirmed Catholics. I know that the people here in the Philippines take faith to the next level. I told Imelda I have attended a mass here with my auntie and uncle. It was my first mass in Tagalog. But I understood because Catholic mass was the same in any language. So, it was effortless to follow. The climb was exhausting. We both agreed a dip in the pool at the hotel was a great idea. We still had a few hours of sunshine remaining, so we told Bon to take us back to the hotel as soon as he could.

The pool area overlooked the city, and we could see the Mayon from there. It made for an impressive picture. Imelda was gorgeous and always knew how to accent her skin tone when dressing. She had the entire pool area watching her. Not only did she have beautiful long dark hair, but her brown skin was outfitted with a yellow bikini that almost reflected beauty. Even the guys with a girl at the poolside were watching her. I felt, that I was beneath her because of her beauty. She was all natural. The way she carried herself without trying to impress anyone was impressive. There was nothing clumsy about Imelda.

We both jumped into the pool, and I swam over to her and kissed her. I thanked her for bringing me to her hometown. Imelda was a superb swimmer as well. When she said she would do a few laps, I thought, okay, have at it. But as I watched her, I found her to be very efficient, with no wasted motion. I asked her how she learned to swim so well, and she told me that her grandmother used to own a resort, and when she was little, she would spend so much time in the water. She could do just about every stroke there was. I asked her if she ever competed, and her reply was no. We stayed at the poolside and sunbathed for about another hour before going in. By this time, we were both hungry. I asked Imelda what she wanted to do for dinner, and she said anything I wanted. I suggested we go into the city and see some nightlife as this was out last night. Imelda wanted a quiet evening and to just spend it alone together. I thought that was a great idea. We would just eat at the hotel restaurant and spend time in the room. We grabbed a quick shower and went downstairs for dinner. The restaurant was not crowded at all, and we were quickly seated. We both ordered something lite. Back in the room, we opened the curtains to see the city lights and enjoyed the view over a couple of beers. We talked more about my work here and then the question I tried to avoid came up. Imelda had asked where we were going with this situation. I told her I knew this would come up. But I also understood that this would be our last night together. I explained to Imelda that I would love to keep this going but I was not used to having a long-distance relationship.

I assured her that there is no one else back home in the states and that I would love to have her in my life. Then she asked, "So we are a couple now?"

"Of course, we are." I told her we would continue to communicate when I got back. She smiled and gave me a very seductive kiss. I pulled her out of her chair and took her to the bed.

Back To Cavite

While we were at the airport, I picked up some Bicol paraphernalia for gifts to give my family when I got back home. I would also pick up some of the Otap for my family back in Cavite. As we sat on the plane, Imelda would not let me go. She knew our time was short now and I could feel her sadness showing. Imelda asked me when my flight was back to the states on Wednesday, and I told her it was at eight a.m. She told me she would not be back in time to see me off at the airport. So that meant that our official goodbye would be when we landed. She would head back to Quezon City, and I would go back to Cavite. Imelda held me tight during the flight. She was teary-eyed, and I tried to calm her by saying that I would come back to be with her. She spoke of how hard it would be for her, but I simply reminded her it would be a sacrifice that had to be made right now. I promised her she was the only one for me and she felt a little more comfortable after that. She asked me if I would download this app on my phone so that she could communicate with me freely. I agreed and reminded her we were twelve hours apart.

Imelda understood and thanked me for the trip that we had just taken. I asked her to share some of her photos, and I would do the same. We landed and walked hand in hand to the baggage claim. We picked up our bags and made our way to the exit.

Again, all eyes were on us as we walked through the crowds. All the guys for sure thought what a lucky guy I was, and the girls were thinking the same of Imelda. When we reached the passenger pickup area, we made bookings with Grab and waited for the cars. Hers pulled up first. I gave her a big hug and kiss, told her I would miss her very much, and thanked her for accompanying me to her hometown. She thanked me as well and got into the car. She never looked back. My car soon showed up, and I was on my way back to Kawit. I had messaged my uncle that I would be there in about an hour. He acknowledged. The driver asked if this was my first time in the Philippines, and I told him it was my last few days, and that I had been here for a little over three weeks. He was a very proud Filipino and wished for me to come back and see more of what the Philippines offers. I told him I would be back and looked forward to seeing more of the sights here. I explained to him how I fell in love with everything here. He said, yes, many foreigners who come here for the first time are very surprised by everything. He then asked me, "Sir, why are you going to the Aguinaldo straight from the airport? There is no hotel close to there."

I explained to him I did not have my uncle's address and that he lived next door to the shrine. He asked me if my uncle is American, and I said no, he is Filipino. I could see some confusion in his expression, so I explained to him I was half and that my uncle was my dad's younger brother. Like everyone else in the Philippines, he said I do not look Filipino.

I laughed. "I know, right?"

When we were close to the shrine, I gave him directions to the house. When we pulled up, he said to me it looked like your family has big money.

I said back to him, yes; they are very comfortable here. I gave the driver a tip that was the same amount as the ride and thanked him for getting me there in a timely fashion. He was grateful and thanked me over and over. I told him that if he was in the area early on Wednesday, he could take me to the airport. Come to find out, he lived in the neighboring town of Imus and said yes, that would be great if he could give me a ride. I asked him to be here at five-thirty in the morning. And message me to confirm. As we spoke, I could hear the gate opening and Uncle coming out to greet me. He asked me if everything was okay, and I explained to him I just hired the driver to take me early on Wednesday morning. I then saw Uncle Ren point his finger at the driver in a serious tone. The driver answered Uncle Ren with respect, "Opo, Walang Problema Po."

The driver left his number with me and took off. I asked Uncle what he said to the guy, and he explained to him it was important to be here on time because I had an international flight. I laughed and told my uncle that I thought he was arguing with the driver. He just wanted the driver to know the importance of being on time here. I thanked him for that, and we went inside.

It was early afternoon, and I sat on the terrace to make more notes of my trip to Bicol. Uncle soon joined me, and we talked about my trip to Bohol. He was delighted that we had landed that project. I mentioned that when I came back from Bohol; I met with the flight attendant, and we were together over the weekend. Then I told him we went to Bicol for the weekend because that is her hometown. It shocked him I did that and said I needed to be more careful when traveling around the Philippines. Many factious groups would love to get their hands on an American and take them for hostage. He told me the one story of a missionary group that was captured in Palawan by a factious group from Mindanao. I told him I remembered that because there was a movie about that. I told him I would be more careful in the future if ever I came back. He then asked me about the girl and her hometown.

It pleased uncle that I was able to spend time here in the Philippines and meet the family. He seemed like he was more excited than I was. I thanked him for his hospitality and asked him if I came back, could I stay here again? He told me I would always be welcome and that the room is mine. He then asked me if I wanted to do anything on my last night here, and I said it's okay. I have two more days and I would just relax here tonight. He then looked surprised and said that I better check my flight because when I changed my flight back, I told him I would leave on a Monday, not a Wednesday. I immediately checked my flight, and Uncle was correct; my flight was for eight a.m. tomorrow. What the hell had I been thinking? Then I thought that my original flight may have been on a Wednesday.

I said shit; I had better pack my things. I then called Jhonnie, the driver, to make sure he knew to come tomorrow instead of Wednesday. Jhonnie answered and said that would not be a problem at all.

Uncle then spoke to him in Tagalog to make sure he understood it was tomorrow and not Wednesday. Uncle Ren also reminded me to tip the maids, and I said, of course. They were inside watching TV while ironing and folding clothes. I gave them each 5000 pesos. Uncle Ren freaked out and said I am ruining the economy because that is almost their monthly salary. I laughed and said that it was okay. He said since it was my first time, he understood, but 1000 pesos would have been good enough. I apologized to him because I thought he was joking. He said next time I come to remember.

I had to message Imelda and tell her that my flight was tomorrow morning and not Wednesday. I went upstairs to check on my things, and basically, everything had been packed. I would have to rearrange all the gifts I had bought, but that was about it. Pretty simple.

I checked into my flight on my mobile app to not have to wait in the lines and would just have to drop my luggage off. I double- checked everything and was ready. I went back downstairs to join Uncle Ren on the terrace.

Uncle Ren then told me that Auntie Wen and Uncle Met were also coming over for dinner and say their goodbyes. I told Uncle I was so happy that I came here. I would push for my siblings to do the same. I thought about all the adventures I had had in a short period. Then I thanked Uncle Ren for showing me around and for taking me to places where my dad had been. I saw where Dad went to school as a kid, the house he grew up in, where he hid from the Japanese, and where he left the Philippines for the first time. There were so many things in between that I would discuss with my siblings. I did not know the number of relatives that were still here. It had been a fantastic experience for me. From work to my personal travel here, I have seen more of the Philippines than most Filipinos living there. This is the reason I wanted to make notes.

My phone was vibrating, and I could see I received a message. It was from Imelda. She had received my message and was replying. She would not have to be at the airport until later but asked me if she could come earlier to meet me. I told her, of course, you can meet me. I would like that. I hate goodbyes. I would miss Imelda for sure. In the short period that we had together, she really became close to me. Imelda made her claim on me; I was hers now. She really knew how to treat her man. I was not used to this back in the states. Some of my most inner thoughts that I never shared with anyone I would share with her. This was going to be hard.

Dinner was excellent. My cousin made her fried chicken again and there were lots of other dishes. I joked with my relatives about how much I ate since I was here. I told them I would get so big so fast if I lived here. We all laughed about it, then Auntie Wen thanked me for coming. She said, "I know you will be back because I talked with your uncle." Then she laughed, so I asked about what? She said that I have more business here, and I agreed. Then she said, "Not proper business, but monkey business." Everyone laughed, and I told them I had become fond of one young lady I met on the plane. Then Auntie Wen chimed in again, "See,

I told you that these girls will try to get you." So, I had been the butt of the joke. Then she got serious and wanted to know when I would return with my siblings.

I told everyone that I planned on being back as soon as they approved me to come back and as far as my siblings, I would try to sell them on visiting the Philippines with all the pictures I took and the notes that I made. They all gave me hugs before they left and said their goodbyes. Since I had to get up early, I tried to sleep a little earlier tonight. So, I said goodbyes to my cousins and auntie because they probably will not be up that early. I double-checked to see if I had any clothes at the maid's station, and there were none. I went upstairs to pack the remaining things, shower, and then rest. I was not as excited to leave as I was coming here.

I woke up at four-thirty a.m. and took a quick shower and dressed. I brought my bags downstairs and was surprised to see my uncle up waiting on me. He wanted to thank me one last time and tell me how special this trip was to him and his family. I told him it was just as unique for me and thanked him again for taking me all around the place. He told me that the car was here already, so he grabbed one bag and carried it out to the car. We embraced one last time. I felt like I was saying goodbye to Dad. I promised I would be back and would let him know. He instructed the driver for the last time to be careful and make sure I got there on time.

The driver answered, "Opo."

There was hardly any traffic, and I had been staring out the window the whole way, not even realizing that we were at the airport already.

"Thirty minutes, sir," the driver was proud of his time in getting me there. He asked me to please let my uncle know. I told him I would and gave him a big tip on top of the fare. He was happy and told me to please contact him if I ever returned and needed his services. I agreed and grabbed my bags. I turned to the airport entrance to see my beautiful Imelda waiting for me. She had just gotten there a few minutes before me. I told her I would check my bags first to go have some coffee. She walked with me hand in hand all the way. I forgot she worked for the airline and had the credentials to go just about anywhere she wanted in the airport. Imelda was only wearing half of her uniform and said she would just change after I left because her flight was not long after mine. When we arrived at the airline counter, there was a long line, but having preferred status, I could get to the preferred counter where there was no one. Took me less than five minutes to check my bags. We grabbed a seat at a Starbucks and had some coffee. She told me she would not go through security when I did, so this would be the last time that we would see each other until I came back. She really wanted us to be a couple, and I told her she does not have to worry about anything because I wanted her in my life. We took a few more pictures and talked about our plans for my next visit here. She mentioned Boracay, one of the tourist hot spots here, and I agreed we should go together soon. After our coffee, I made my way over to customs, where there was a line already. She said that I better get in line now to have a few minutes to get to my gate. I gave Imelda a big hug and kiss; only she did not let go when I did. Finally, Imelda let go and stepped back. There were tears in her eyes. I promised her I would be back and not to worry. I turned and walked over to the customs entrance and showed the security my ticket and passport and they waved me through. One last time, I turned to wave. My goodness, this girl was so beautiful! She waved back, and we went our separate ways. As I was waiting in line at customs, I received a message from Imelda. I looked down to read my message. It was simple.

Imelda said, "I love you and will miss you."

I turned around to see if I could still see her and there she was, almost waiting for an answer. I gave her a nod and blew a kiss to her. The agent asked me to step up. I handed him my passport but continued to stare at Imelda in the distance.

The agent laughed. "Sir, are you sure you want to leave?"

I laughed back at him and told him I wished I did not have to leave. He stamped my passport, and I paid the exit fee of 800php and went on to security from there.

Imelda was gone, out of sight. I would miss her dearly.

I Became Him

I sat at my gate, opened my laptop, and downloaded all my pictures from my phone and camera for my siblings to see when I got back. This would make for a great presentation. I just had to remember names and dates at this point. I remembered I booked the same seats on my flights back, not to be disturbed. As we boarded, I looked around for the flight attendants to see if they were familiar to me, but I really could not remember them, only Imelda.

I took my seat again and stared out of the window at the very back again. I remembered Imelda told me when we first met that I would not want to leave. She was right; she was perfect for me. I was not used to having this in a relationship before. This trip made me think about a lot of similarities that I had with Dad. The time that my uncles were here for my dad's birthday and he kept me around as his driver or gopher, keeping the Philippine tradition. I received notes from my uncles thanking me for my hospitality and patience. Dad was proud of this. As far as the upbringing and how I was like him, I never was big on buying brand names versus purpose. I always tried to fix things as a last resort before throwing them out and replacing them. I always worked hard and kept my nose to the ground. I did not mingle in everybody's business or express my feelings openly. I tried not to waste things and put a price tag on everything. I rarely went to the hospital if something was not broken. I realized I became him more and more. I adopted his ways of living and never knew that we had become the same. I became defined by who I was and where I had come from. The how, the when, and the what have been answered by living his way. After all these years, I finally understood him. And he was gone. I found some peace after all this time.

I messaged Imelda at each connection to let her know I had made it safely. When I landed, I messaged her.

I had never had a long-distance relationship before and knew this would be a struggle, but I promised her I was hers.

United States

I finally landed back home some twenty-four hours later. I was utterly exhausted. I sent the message to my siblings that I was home and wanted all of us to get together as soon as possible to hear about the amazing trip I had just taken. We all agreed to do it over the weekend, the following Sunday, and we would each bring a dish for dinner. When we finally got together, I passed out all the gifts I had purchased for them. I was eager to get into the presentation. I had plugged my laptop into my TV to be seen on the big screen. I had my notes to make sure that I did not forget names or places. After about two hours, I was finally finished, and throughout the viewing, there were many tears and some laughter. I broke down after everyone had thanked me for doing this. I could not help my emotions. It was over. All the things I held in since Dad's death, the things I had to deal with while cleaning his apartment and storage, the entire trip, and this presentation. I told my siblings, "I became him."

Afterward, I explained to them how we were raised in a different culture compared to most American families, the culture that surrounded us daily. I would also mention that the Philippine people were strong and proud people. They never waited for their government to help them in a crisis; they would always come together as a community and help each other out; whether it was the lack of food or a natural disaster, they took care of things. People looked at the Philippines as a third world country, and the many foreigners that visited there did not really respect the culture. Think about what the Philippines brings to the table Miss Universe many times championship boxing, cage fighting, and billiards. There is also something to be said about their singing and performing. Just about every island is a resort. The Philippines will soon be one of the top resort countries on the Pacific rim. The economy is booming and there is construction everywhere. I told my siblings they needed to visit this fantastic place Dad called home. It was amazingly beautiful. I will never forget the feeling that I had and the understanding of Dad and his mentoring now that I have walked on the same soil as he once lived on. His quietly instilled values in all of us gave me a new perspective on life. I came back to the states and see it differently now. I would crave to learn more about the people and languages in the Philippines. I would see him in me now that I have experienced his culture. I would definitely visit there as often as I could. I fell in love with the way of life there, the beautiful weather and the beautiful islands. I fell in love with the Philippines and its way of life.

A month later, my sister was dropping me off at the airport. They were so used to doing this, they thought it was just another business trip. My sister asked, "By the way, where are you going this time?"

I turned and smiled at her. "Back to the Philippines."

Reflection

During the long flight back home, I reflected on the last three and a half weeks and how I could gain so much information about my father's past, the reason he was the way he was, and how similar we both were. Dad growing up in the Philippines and me growing up in a different culture would not make so much sense on paper, but because he affected our lives early on and never really changed his ways, I adapted to many of his habits and traits. I think about the little things such as running around the house to check to see if all the lights are out to make sure the faucets are not dripping. I think about how Dad never went to the hospital and in a way; I am like that, only I get annual check-ups. I have his complex work ethic and am not afraid to get dirty. Even in the most tedious of chores, I never took shortcuts. He taught me not to waste things and appreciate what we have. I also thought about how he held his feelings inside and did not express his emotions most of the time. Dad was very thrifty and never threw things away. I'm like that; I have clothes and shoes in my closet that are older than my children.

Having put feet on the ground where Dad grew up gave me a feeling of closeness to him. To live in his culture gave me a proper understanding of who he was and how he came to be the man we all knew. Having the family back home even mention that I resemble him made me closer to him. I would never hear this until I went there. Obviously, Dad spoke of how proud he was of his children to all of his siblings because of the conversations I would have with everyone back home. Something he never expressed with me, but I could feel this as I traveled throughout the Philippines.

It was a sad moment when I left the Philippines, not only because of Imelda, but because I felt I was leaving him. I had fallen in love with the way of life there, adapting to the climate and the culture. It seemed like it was very easy for me, and I know the family had a lot to do with it. They made me feel as if I was home, a part of him. The trip really brought me closer to Dad.

About the Author

Kenny was born in 1963 to Cecilio and Kathleen in Bethesda, Maryland. As a military dependent, he traveled coast to coast with his family and finally settled in the Hampton Roads area of Virginia where his father retired. Kenny went to work right out of high school in the electrical industry, allowing him to travel the world.

In his spare time, he enjoys all outdoor activities including fishing, camping, free diving, basketball, and golf.

www.ingramcontent.com/pod-product-compliance
Lightning Source LLC
Chambersburg PA
CBHW050334010526
44119CB00004B/138